Bloody Words

BLOODY WORDS

hate and free speech

by
David Matas

Bain & Cox, Publishers
Winnipeg • Niagara Falls

First published 2000 by Bain & Cox, Publishers
an imprint of Blizzard Publishing Inc.
73 Furby Street, Winnipeg, Canada R3C 2A2.

Distributed in the United States by General Distribution Services,
4500 Witmer Industrial Estates, Niagara Falls, NY 14305–1386.

Cover art by Robert Durocher. Cover design by Otium.
Printed for Bain & Cox in Canada.

5   4   3   2   1

Bain & Cox, Publishers gratefully acknowledge the support of the
Manitoba Arts Council, the Canada Council for the Arts, and the
Government of Canada through the Book Publishing Industry
Development Program for our publishing program.

Cataloguing in Publication Data

Matas, David.
  Bloody words
  ISBN 1-55331-0004
1. Freedom of speech—Canada. 2. Hate speech—Canada. I. Title.
KE8952.M37 2000   342.71'0853   C00-911268-5
KF9345.M37 2000

"Sticks and stones will break my bones.
Names will never hurt me."

"Auschwitz was not built with stones.
It was built with words."

Contents

Introduction

I WAS BORN IN WINNIPEG during the Holocaust. It did not take me long to realize that I was lucky to be alive.

Four messengers come to Job, one to tell of the loss of his oxen and asses with their attendants; the next to tell of the death of his sheep and shepherds; the third to tell of the slaying of all of his camels with the servants; and the fourth to tell of the death of all his sons and daughters. Each messenger says: "I only am escaped alone to tell thee." So does Ishmael, in Herman Melville's novel *Moby Dick*, at the end of his tragic tale of Captain Ahab and the ship Pequod.

Strictly speaking, I am not a survivor of the Holocaust, since all four of my grandparents came to Canada before World War I. Yet, in a very real sense, I and every Jewish person are survivors of the Holocaust. Six million Jews were killed. All Jews were targeted. It is only the fortunes of war that gave an Allied rather than an Axis victory in World War II. If the Axis powers had won, not I, not one Jewish person would be alive today.

I have escaped to tell. If we can give any meaning at all to the meaningless slaughter of so many millions of innocents, we must learn the lessons of the Holocaust. To say "Never again" is easy. To make it happen is not so easy. The reality is that since World War II genocide has happened again and again, not to Jews, but to Cambodians, to Hutus, to Tutsis, to Bosnians, to Somalis, and one could go on.

The lessons I have drawn from the Holocaust are the need to prosecute, convict, and punish mass murderers; to ban hate speech; to protect refugees; and never to accept in silence gross violations of human rights, wherever they occur. The Holocaust would not have happened if at the time there had been an effective universal system in place to bring mass murderers to justice; if refugees fleeing persecution had been offered protection; if laws had worked effectively to ban the propagation of hatred; and if people everywhere had protested gross violations of human rights anywhere as soon as they occurred.

I have engaged in human rights work to act on these lessons, to join the human rights struggle on four connected fronts. In my fight, I have had to combat four different enemies that prowl throughout the human rights battlefield. These four horsemen of our very own human-made apocalypse are indifference, hypocrisy, helplessness, and absolutism.

Indifference has been the main foe in bringing Nazi war criminals to justice. Canadians got all worked up about prosecuting Paul Bernardo or Clifford Olson or extraditing Charles Ng to the United States. However, when it comes to bringing to justice those who have committed Nazi crimes every bit as evil as what Bernardo or Olson or Ng, have done and on an even greater scale, many Canadians are indifferent. One of my books, *Justice Delayed: Nazi War Criminals in Canada*,[1] written with Susan Charendoff, argues in detail about why that indifference was misplaced.

The second horseman of our twentieth-century apocalypse has been hypocrisy. Human rights values are accepted everywhere. Human rights vocabulary has become universally accepted. Human rights has become the secular global religion of our time. The worst perpetrators are often those who mouth the human rights vocabulary most vociferously. Instead of human rights rejection, what we see instead is acceptance in principle and violation in practice. In Canada, that hypocrisy is well demonstrated in the refugee field.

In *Closing the Doors: The Failure of Refugee Protection*,[2] co-authored with Ilana Simon, I detailed that hypocrisy and the forms it takes. Canada accepts refugee protection in principle. Yet, a narrow application of the refugee definition, a denial of fairness in refugee determination procedures, harsh treatment of those awaiting determination of their refugee claims, exaggerated scepticism that leads decision makers to disbelieve claimants even when they are telling the truth, insistence on obtaining evidence that is impossible to get, and interdiction procedures preventing claimants from coming to a country where they can be protected all mean that, in Canada and elsewhere, a commitment to refugee protection in principle has often been coupled with denial of refugee protection in practice.

The third human rights nemesis is helplessness, the sense that human rights violations are so massive, and so far away, that nothing can be done about them. It is to this nemesis I turned in a third book, *No More: The Battle against Human Rights Violations*.[3] It is my view not only that individuals in countries like Canada far away from gross and flagrant violations can have a positive impact on respect for human rights. It is the voice of individuals around the world speaking through non-governmental organizations which is most likely to lead to respect for human rights. There is a tendency to turn to governments or to the United Nations to promote respect for human rights. Yet, human rights belong to individuals. Unless individuals promote respect for rights, these rights are bound to wither.

My struggles to have effective hate speech laws have led me to battle with a fourth horseman, absolutism, the belief that one human right, the right to freedom of expression, trumps all others. Of all of the lessons to be learned from the Holocaust, there is none more important than the need to ban hate speech, because the banning of hate speech, if effective, prevents atrocities from occurring. Punishing mass murderers, protecting refugees, protesting massive violations, all come too late for many victims. Effective banning of hate speech means that there will be no victims.

Yet, of all the lessons to be learned from the Holocaust, the need to ban hate speech is the hardest to learn. The opposition to the banning of hate speech does not come just from racists or xenophobes. It comes from within the human rights community itself, from free speech absolutist, civil libertarians. This book, *Bloody Words: Hate and Free Speech*, the last in a human rights quartet, is an argument against that free speech absolutism.

For people to decide themselves where the boundary between free speech and banning hate speech should be drawn, they need to know the arguments for both sides. The arguments for one side, freedom of speech, are hallowed, well known. The arguments in John Milton's "Areopagitica" written in 1789 and John Stuart Mill's "On Liberty" written in 1859 are part of public consciousness, the foundation of constitutional revolutions, the source of modern democratic values. Many, if not most, people who follow public affairs can recite the arguments in favour of freedom of expression. The right to freedom of expression is ingrained, received wisdom.

The arguments in favour of the right to freedom from incitement to hatred, on the contrary, are not well known. The right arouses puzzlement even amongst those hesitant to accept free speech absolutist dogma. Though many have an intuitive sense of the value of the right to freedom from incitement to hatred, it has been my experience that few can defend that right against the arguments of free speech absolutists. There is not a widespread general appreciation of the arguments on the other side.

The aim of this book is to attempt to redress the balance. This book marshals the arguments in favour of banning hate speech. It is not directed primarily to free speech fundamentalists—who are unlikely to be persuaded—but rather to the open-minded reader, who senses that there may be something to the right to freedom from incitement to hatred, but is not quite sure what to make of it.

If I had my way, the book would persuade every reader. At least, I hope it serves to present the arguments in favour of the right to freedom from incitement to hatred so that each reader can make up his or her own mind on the weight to be given to this right. My working method is rebuttal of the arguments in favour of free speech absolutism. My aim is to enable the reader to internalize the free speech–hate speech debate.

I have been on many public platforms arguing in favour of banning hate propaganda. People often approach me after these debates to say that they had agreed with me even before I started, but appreciated nonetheless what I said, because it gave them the arguments to defend their views. This book is also directed to these colleagues, people who assert the need to ban hate speech but are not quite sure how to answer the many criticisms they hear of that view, as well as people who hesitate to say what they believe, that hate speech should be banned, because they do not have the vocabulary to defend their position. My hope is that this book will increase the pool of people who can speak publicly in support of the banning of hate speech.

Because anti-hate laws are interspersed throughout the legal system in Canada and elsewhere, there is a whole host of people responsible for the administration of these laws. One theme of this book is that these laws do not work now all that well. One reason, perhaps the main reason, for the failure of these laws is a failure, even amongst those responsible for them, to appreciate the need for them. My aim, through this book, is to inform workers in the anti-hate field why what they are doing is important, indeed, essential.

The book draws many examples from the Canadian experience. Canada is rich in legislation and litigation about the banning of hate speech. However, the arguments presented here are applicable internationally, in every rights-respecting state.

The first chapter looks at the harm of hate speech. Hate speech leads to hate crimes and violence. Waiting until that violence happens before the state reacts is waiting far too long.

Despite widespread condemnation of hate crimes, there is little concern expressed over the hate speech that leads to those crimes. Chapter two attempts to explain the myopia and inaction in response to hate speech.

The third chapter situates the right to be free from incitement to hatred in the context of the debate between individual and collective rights. Is the debate between hate speech and free speech a debate, in another form, of the debate between individual rights and collective rights?

The fourth chapter attempts to set out the boundaries of hate speech. There are six different ways to explain what hate speech is: by definition and counter definition, by example and counter example, by context, and by impact.

The fifth chapter examines a particular definitional issue, Holocaust denial as hate speech. What does the conclusion that Holocaust denial is hate speech mean for an overall definition of hate speech?

The sixth chapter examines the case of Ernst Zundel. That case has been used by civil libertarians as an argument against any prosecution of hate speech. Is that the proper lesson to be drawn from the *Zundel* prosecution?

The seventh chapter examines hate laws in the German Weimar Republic. The argument is sometimes made that the Weimar Republic had hate speech laws, but those laws did not stop Hitler and the Nazis from coming to power in Germany. The validity of this argument is assessed.

The eighth chapter examines the particular issue of how academic freedom and respect for the right to be free from incitement to hatred fit together. Does prohibition of hate speech help or thwart the realization of the idea of a university?

The ninth chapter looks at libraries. Libraries have an understandable affinity with freedom of speech values. Should libraries allow their meeting rooms to be used by promoters of hatred?

School teachers, obviously, should not teach hate in the school room. However, what if they promote hate off duty, in their spare time? Should the school system be concerned with that? The tenth chapter examines these questions by considering the case of Malcolm Ross.

The eleventh chapter looks at the issue from the other side of the looking glass, in particular, at South Africa. In South Africa, laws restricting freedom of speech go too far, rather than not far enough.

The twelfth chapter examines hate speech on the internet. Does the rise of the internet make all attempts to regulate hate speech futile?

The thirteenth chapter examines the various legal remedies available in Canada today for violations of the right to protection from incitement to hatred. In particular, civil remedies are compared with criminal remedies.

The fourteenth chapter deals with truth as a defence to the offence of propagating hatred. Should truth be an answer to a charge of promoting hatred?

What is required to make laws against hate speech effective? More than dealing with the defence of truth is necessary. Chapter fifteen examines other elements that are needed to make anti-hate laws work.

The concluding chapter argues that the right to be free from incitement to hatred is as much a human right as any other of the basic rights found in international instruments; that for overall human dignity and worth to be respected, the right to be free from incitement to hatred needs to be respected and valued as much as any other right.

Parts of this book have appeared in a different form elsewhere. I acknowledge "Lessons from Rwanda" in *International Social Welfare in a Changing World* edited by Jacqueline Ismael (Calgary, AB: Detselig, 1996, pp. 125–136); "The Extreme Right in the United Kingdom and France" in *The Extreme Right: Freedom and Security at Risk* edited by Aurel Braun and Stephen Scheinberg (Boulder, CO: Westview, 1997, pp. 84–106); "Countering Hate on the Internet: Recommendations for Action" in *The Holocaust's Ghost: Writings on Art, Politics Law and Education* edited by F. C. Decoste and Bernard Schwartz (Edmonton: U of Alberta, 2000, pp. 483–495); and "The Universal Declaration of Human Rights: Fifty Years Later" in *Peace, Justice and Freedom: Human Rights Challenges for the New Millenium* edited by Gurcharan S. Bhatia, J. S. O'Neil, Gerald L. Gall, and Patrick D. Bendin (U of Alberta, 2000, pp. 83–94).

I thank my publisher, Bain and Cox, for their commitment to my work as well as their careful editing; Betina Kuzmarov, for her research; Irwin Cotler, for his inspiration and reinforcement; Marvin Kurz, for his insight, knowledge and steady work in combatting hate speech; Wendy Harris, for her suggestion of the title and her efforts to make this book happen; and Karen Mock, Frank Dimant and the whole B'nai Brith family, for their institutional support. Although he may not appreciate this thanks, I would also like to thank Alan Borovoy with whom I have argued the hate speech–free speech debate throughout Canada and who has served as a foil for many of the arguments I raise in this book.

Notes

1. Summerhill Press, Toronto, 1987.
2. Summerhill Press, Toronto, 1989.
3. Dundurn Press, Toronto, 1994.

Chapter One

Hate Speech and Hate Crimes

ARE FREEDOM OF EXPRESSION and prohibition of hate propaganda compatible? My answer to that question is yes. Indeed the very question, put this way, is superficially puzzling. The right to freedom of expression is in the International Covenant on Civil and Political Rights.[1] The obligation to prohibit hate propaganda is also in the Covenant, in the immediately following article.[2] The Covenant was approved by the United Nations General Assembly in 1966. It had 143 states as signatory parties as of August 2000, including Canada, and four of the five permanent members of the Security Council, the United Kingdom, France, the United States, and Russia. China has signed the Covenant but not ratified it.

It is hard to believe that the nations of the world would place two obligations in the same instrument, and right next to each other, if they were incompatible. Surely the nations of the world would have noticed if the two obligation were incompatible and objected.

The summary records for the Covenant show a vigorous discussion how, if at all, the obligation to prohibit hate propaganda would inhibit freedom of expression. The view that prevailed was that prohibition was imperative if all communities were to live in peace and in harmonious relationship.[3]

The proliferation of human rights instruments after World War II, starting from the Universal Declaration of Human Rights, have their origin in revulsion to the Holocaust. Human rights have been placed front and centre on the agenda of the international community because of the Holocaust and it is no coincidence that the international human rights instruments generated after the World War II contained the obligation to prohibit hate propaganda. The drafters of these instruments saw a direct link between hate speech and the Holocaust. If the need to respect human rights is the general legacy the Holocaust has left us, the need to prohibit racist speech is part of that legacy, one very particular and important component.

Today, that legacy is foresaken. There is a direct connection between the horrors in the Balkans and Rwanda and that foresaken legacy.

After World War II, in the days when the Iron Curtain still divided Europe, the West came to the table to raise human rights concerns, and the East came for the legitimacy those discussions gave to their governments and the sovereignty of their territories. The East came, but did not listen. The human rights dialogue between East and West during the Cold War was a dialogue of the deaf. From the USSR, when the West asked for respect for human rights, the answer was "nyet."

Now the Iron Curtain has lifted. The totalitarian repressive Communist states are gone. However, human rights violations remain. Everything in the newly democratized states, including repression, has been privatized. Big brother has been replaced by little brother. The state's protective apparatus has disintegrated. Order without law has been replaced by an absence of both law and order.

The old ideology of communism has been replaced by a new ideology of ethnic hatred of minorities. Most dramatic in the old Communist states is the situation of the former Yugoslavia where ethnic hatred has lead to ethnic cleansing and genocide. The armed conflicts in Bosnia, Serbia, Croatia, and Kosovo have been accompanied by atrocities against innocent unarmed civilians not seen in Europe since World War II. People outside the Balkans reacted with incomprehension as much as dismay. Yet, anyone who was following the media outpourings of hate in the region would have understood all too well what was happening.

It seems every national grouping in the Balkans refuses to admit the existence of its neighbouring nationalities and demeans anyone who claims to identify with those nationalities. Croatian nationalists consider all Southern Slavs as Croats. Serbian nationalists deny the existence of separate Croat and Slovene identities. Croats, Serbs, and Greeks challenge the existence of a distinct Bulgarian nation. Serbian nationalists consider Albanians "lost Serbs," who have become "savages." Serbian nationalists attribute Albania nationalism to Austrian and Italian intrigue. Greek nationalists contest the existence of a separate, non-Greek Albanian nation. Croat and Serbian nationalists have no room for the Bosnians, demeaned as "Asians, unstable, perverted" Serbs. Bulgarians and Greeks have never come to terms with the presence of culturally distinct Macedonians. The Macedonians have been considered as "Southern Serbs" by the Serbs, "Western Bulgarians" by the Bulgarians, and "Slavophone Greeks" by the Greeks, who have regularly called the Republic of Macedonia with the demeaning name "a Skopjan statelet," and its inhabitants "Gypsy-Skopjans," "Balkan Gypsies," "Skopjan Viahs."

Panayote Elias Dimitras, in the introduction to *Hate Speech in the Balkans* (1998),[4] writes:

> Only when the wars in former Yugoslavia reached their height did many people discover that . . . systematic deprecation of the (potential) enemy had been in the workings of the mass media of the—still supposedly coexisting—Croatian and Serbian federal republics. . . . The problem has not been confined only to these two countries. Throughout the Balkan region, the media are producing such "hate speech," that the public are being conditioned to support any new conflict that may arise. Public opinion polls, in fact, indicate that there is hardly any people in the area which has widespread positive feelings for any of its neighbours, as they almost all have for example, for many West European peoples.

This denial of the existence of the other is accompanied by a dehumanization of those who are incontestably different. Throughout the region outside of Croatia, Croats are described as Ustashas, the name of the supporters of the Nazi puppet regime. The media in Serbia presented Croats as brutal and ruthless people, who try to destroy everything pertaining to Serbs.

Outside of the Muslim area of Bosnia, Bosnian Muslims are called terrorists. Muslims are presented as people who burn Serb villages and fire at the people who remain behind. Serbian media refer to all non-Serbian former Yugoslavs as bloodthirsty.

Outside of Serbia, Serbians are called "beasts" and Chetniks, the name of a vicious militia operating during World War II. The former Croatian president has said that Serbs are a cancer destroying the Croatian national being.[5]

The Romanian media accuse its Hungarian minority of attempting to crucify Romania. The Macedonian media refer to Greeks, Albanians, and Bulgarians as liars and dishonest merchants. The Albanian media refers to Greeks as sly. The Greek media in turn refers to Albanians as barbarians.

Nafsika Panikolatos says this: "what we have [in the region] are deprecatory descriptions in order to minimize or even to debase and humilate [foreign Balkan peoples] to such a degree so that the non-recognition of their respective rights and their treatment as non-beings is justified."[6] It is little wonder that these descriptions have preceded and accompanied the non-recognition of rights and the treatment in the Balkans of foreign Balkan peoples as non-beings.

The story is repeated in Rwanda. The case of Leon Mugesera provides a blood curdling example. Leon Mugesera, on November 22, 1992, in a speech at a public political meeting in Kabaya subprefecture and attended by the President, urged the Hutu majority to rise up and decimate sympathizers of the Tutsi-led Rwandan Patriotic Front. Mugesera was at the time vice-president of the ruling party, the MRND (Mouvement républicain national pour la démocratie et le développement) for the prefecture of Gisenye and an adviser to the then President Habyarimana. Between December 1991 and April 1992, he had been General Director of Information. The speech was delivered in the Kinyarwanda language and was recorded at the time.

In 1959 there had been a mass exodus of Tutsis from Rwanda, after the Tutsi monarchy was overthrown by a Hutu-led elite.[7] In 1990 the Tutsi-led Rwandan Patriotic Front launched an invasion of Rwanda from Uganda. The MRND viewed the Tutsi families who remained in Rwanda as potential recruits for the Rwandan Patriotic Front. Mugesera said: "the fatal error we made in '59 when I was still a child was that we let them leave."[8] "What are we waiting for to decimate these families and the people who recruit them?" "Are you sincerely going to wait for them to come and decimate you?" "We cannot have peace if we do not unearth the battle axe." "Be warned that he whose life you save will not save yours."

The MRND had been propagating a racist, anti-Tutsi ideology, referring to Tutsis as foreigners, who had immigrated generations ago from Ethiopia. The Nyabarongo river flows through Rwanda. Many of those killed in the Rwanda genocide of 1994 were dumped into the Nyabarongo river. Mugesera called on Hutus to kill Tutsis and dump them in this river. In his speech he recounted a conversation he had with a Rwandan Patriotic Front sympathizer. "I continued by explaining to him," he said, "that his home was in Ethiopia but that we would find a shortcut, that is, the Nyabarongo river." "I want to emphasize this point." "We must definitely react."

After the 1990 invasion, a confluence of international and national pressures led President Habyarimana and the ruling MRND to share power in a coalition with three opposition parties.[9] This coalition government was in power at the time Mugesera spoke. Mugesera called for the former opposition members of the coalition government to be tried for treason and executed. He said: "The punishment for irresponsible authorities who allow the enemy to do what he wants in our home is foreseen." "The law is unequivocal on this. Anyone guilty of committing acts aimed at weakening the morale of the armed forces will be punished with capital punishment. What are we waiting for to execute it?"

The Prime Minister of the coalition government was Dismas Nsengiyaremye, from one of the former opposition parties. Mugesera called for his arrest. He said: "The court has only to condemn him to capital punishment as the law stipulates. Do not tremble at the idea that he is prime minister." Mugesera said much the same about other opposition politicians.

Hundreds of Tutsis were killed in the days following the speech.[10] The speech was given almost two years before the full blown genocide took place. In the years prior to the genocide, Rwanda was flooded with speeches and radio broadcasts like this made by government officials and sympathizers. I have quoted the Mugesera speech in detail because the entire text of the speech has survived in recorded form, because it was particularly virulent, and because Mugesera was a high-ranking person in the MRND, the leading partner in the government coalition. But as hate propaganda and incitement to genocide, the speech was far from unique.

Mugesera came to Canada as a landed immigrant through the visa office in Spain. He has since been ordered deported on the basis that he has committed crimes that if committed in Canada would constitute indictable offences. The offences were advocating hatred and genocide. In November 1998, he lost an appeal from that deportation order.[11]

Outpourings of hate speech have not been confined to the Balkans and Rwanda, where the most dramatic crimes against civilians have occurred in recent years. Racially motivated crimes spurred on by untrammelled hate speech are almost everywhere in Eastern Europe and Africa and states do virtually nothing. The disintegration of state protection in Eastern Europe and Africa has shown that the state can do too little as well as too much.

Take, for instance, the Ukraine. Hate propaganda against Jews is everywhere; it is virulent; it advocates ethnic cleansing of Jews and it is unchecked. Antisemitic graffiti and literature, rumours about pogroms, verbal and physical harassment of Jews create a pervasive negative atmosphere against Ukrainian Jews.[12]

The initiative for this antisemitic wave comes not from the government but rather from extremist Ukrainian nationalist groups.[13] One such group is the UNA/UNSO. UNA/UNSO views the presence of Jews in the Ukraine as the most dangerous threat facing Ukrainian society and its economic and religious development. Since its founding, the organization has collected information about the Jewish population, is active in all the major cities of the Ukraine, and it engages in constant propaganda against Jews and other minorities.

The government does nothing to stop the UNA/UNSO. The organization has not been controlled by prosecutors.[14] Ukraine has a statute in the criminal code against incitement of hatred, but the attorney general does not apply it, citing freedom of the press. Local authorities have done little to oppose antisemitism.[15]

Complaints of antisemitism at the local level are downplayed by the local police as mere acts of hooliganism. As a result, it is difficult to get a statistical sense of the breadth of the problem of racially motivated violence, except from anecdotal evidence. The anecdotal evidence, however, is substantial and indicates a widespread, serious problem.[16]

The American Association of Russian Jews reported that an elderly Jew was brutally beaten in the street in January 1991 in L'vov.[17] In another incident, hooligans broke into the home of an elderly Jewish couple in L'vov. The man was murdered. The wife died of wounds from the beating six days later. No investigation ensued.

A bomb was placed in the Kiev synagogue. Two demonstrations of Kiev Jews in December 1991 requesting an investigation of the bomb attempt were dispersed by the police. The first time they were fined and the second time they were arrested for hooliganism.[18]

Numerous Jewish graves in three Odessa cemeteries were desecrated on March 29, 1992.[19] A Jewish dentist was the victim of a car bomb on April 20, 1992 in Donetsk, Ukraine. In November 1992, Jewish gravestones, and the Babi Yar monument (commemorating Jews killed in the Ukraine during the Holocaust) were desecrated with red paint.[20] In Bolograd, Ukraine, on October 9, 1992, a Jewish man was beaten by two Russians who said "You are a Jew—we beat you."

The National Council of Soviet Jewry reported that, in March 1997, the Israeli Cultural Centre in Kharkov was firebombed two weeks after it had opened. According to the source, although an investigation revealed that two bottles of explosives caused the fire, the culprits were not found and no Ukrainian newspaper reported the incident.

According to Antisemitism World Report 1997, gravestones in the Jewish cemetery of Berdichov were vandalized in April and May 1997. In July 1997, a Jewish cemetery in the western city of Khost (Hust) was desecrated; 58 gravestones were overturned and 18 destroyed.[21]

The United Council of Soviet Jewry and Antisemitism World Report 1997 reported a break-in at the United Jewish Community of Crimea building on September 20, 1997.[22] The organization reported a fire in a synagogue in the town of Drohovich, just before the March 1998 election. This synagogue had been vandalized on four earlier occasions, including two instances in 1997.

A number of panels of the Canadian Immigration and Refugee Board have found that Jews in Ukraine have a well founded fear of persecution because they are Jewish. The Federal Court of Canada on several occasions has either upheld Immigration and Refugee Board decisions or overturned negative decisions on that basis.

A paper put out by the Canadian Immigration and Refugee Board in 1999 states:

> The enforcement of laws protecting minorities in Ukraine is a problem due to the lack of an effective legal system. . . . Two sources stated Jews could have no recourse for protection from antisemitic actions because of the weak application of laws regarding the protection of minorities and inconsistent government efforts to control antisemitic activities at the local level.[23]

In Western Europe and North America, hate speech does not indicate or threaten state disintegration. Yet it still works its deadly poison. The linkage between racist speech and violations of individual civil liberties is as topical as newspaper headlines.

Even in Canada or the United Kingdom where the general level of crime is less than in the U.S. and the control of hate propaganda is a good deal stronger, there have been threats, conspiracies, vandalism, harassment, and hate-motivated violent crimes. Marcellus Francois of Montreal was an innocent young black man killed by the Montreal Urban Community police on July 3, 1991. A coroner, Harry Yarosky, in his report, found a "totally unacceptable" level of racism within the Montreal police force.

The Government of Quebec in 1991 refused to press hate charges against the Ku Klux Klan for distributing hate literature. The Klan were prosecuted and convicted in April 1992 for violating customs regulations by smuggling their literature into Canada, but the plea-bargained fine was derisory. It is hard to disassociate the 1991 killing of Marcellus Francois from the reluctance to prosecute the Klan at the time for disseminating anti-black hate propaganda.

Judge William Stewart of the British Columbia provincial court in November 1999 sentenced five skinheads to between 12 and 15 years in jail for the killing of Nirmal Singh Gill, an elderly caretaker of a Sikh temple. The skinheads were linked to the group White Power. Racist compact discs as well as Nazi and Aryan Nations paraphernalia were found among their belongings.[24] Judge William Stewart, in sentencing the skinheads, said: "Nirmal Singh Gill died simply because he was Indo-Canadian."

In the United Kingdom, Stephen Lawrence was an eighteen-year-old student killed in April 1993 at a London bus stop in an unprovoked knife attack. The only reason for the murder was that Stephen was black.

Tragedies like these show that, because we have to be concerned about hate-motivated crimes, we have to be concerned about hate propaganda. Marcellus Francois, Stephen Lawrence, and Nirmal Singh Gill would all be alive today if it were not for racist attitudes. Given the high number of minorities killed by police or street gangs throughout the West, of how many other victims can that also be said?

Hate speech, whether gross or subtle in form, is nothing less than the incitement of violence against minorities. Waiting until that violence happens before the state reacts is waiting far too long.

Hate propaganda laws, if they work, prevent the occurrence of discrimination, hostility, or violence. Discrimination, hostility, or violence are violations of individual human rights. With effective hate propaganda laws these violations are less likely to occur. They are nipped in the bud. Hate propaganda laws work by attacking the root causes of individual human rights violations.

France provides an insight into both the dangers of hate speech and the effectiveness of hate speech laws. In France there is a whole range of remedies available against incitement to hatred without much debate about whether they should exist.[25] Statutes prohibit racial defamation and racist slurs.[26] Non-governmental, anti-racist associations are permitted to join as civil parties in prosecutions against those who commit racially-motivated crimes.[27] As well, these anti-racist groups can join as civil parties in prosecutions for incitement to racial hatred, group defamation, or racial slurs. When these non-governmental groups join in a prosecution, and the person is convicted, the court decides on civil liability at the same time.

The government has the power to dissolve any organization that incites racial hatred.[28] The French legislature, in July 1990, made it an offence to contest the existence of crimes against humanity as defined in the London Charter of August 8, 1945, on the basis of which Nazi leaders were tried and convicted by the International Military Tribunal at Nuremberg in 1945–1946.[29] Because of that law, Holocaust denial is an offence.

In each region of France the police have organized advisory public committees to assist in the fight against racism. Representatives of anti-racist organizations participate in these committees. The committees examine racist incidents and literature and advise on what steps the police should take, whether to prosecute an individual, seek a ban of a publication, or close a book store.

Despite the general acceptance of anti-hate laws in France, there is a large extreme right-wing movement, the National Front. Does the existence and widespread support of the National Front throw into question the value of French anti-hate laws?

In answering this question, one has to keep in mind that throughout the last century, antisemitism and the extreme right have had significant minority support in France. The history of this support, going back to the Dreyfus affair, casts a spotlight on this question.

Alfred Dreyfus, a Jewish officer of the French general staff, was convicted in 1894 by court martial of communicating military secrets to a German military attaché named Schwartzkoppen and sentenced to life imprisonment. The true author of the communication was Major Walsin-Esterhazy who had forged the communication in the handwriting of Dreyfus on orders of his superior Colonel Sandherr.

Esterhazy fled to England and revealed his forgery there. The Court of Cassation in July 1906 annulled the sentence of Dreyfus and acquitted him.[30]

The Dreyfus case was more, however, than a miscarriage of justice. Throughout the reviews and appeals, and even after his sentence was annulled, the case became a rallying point for the extreme right in France. Anti-Dreyfusards used the polemics around the case to promote their agenda of antisemitism and anti-republicanism. The army general staff, amongst whom was Marshal Pétain, future head of the Vichy regime, was solidly anti-Dreyfus.

Despite all the polemics and the considerable antisemitic mob violence it generated, the anti-Dreyfusard movement never amounted to much politically. At its peak, the antisemitic, anti-Dreyfusard movement elected nineteen members to the French parliament.[31] The right-wing extremist group with the largest membership between World Wars I and II, le Parti Populaire Français, founded by Jacques Doriot in 1936, had at most 250,000 members.[32] Tolerance in France was sufficiently widespread before World War II to allow the election of a Jewish prime minister, Léon Blum, who was Prime Minister of France from June 1936 to June 1937 and from March to April 1938.

When Germany defeated France in June 1940, Germany occupied the northern part of France. A collaborationist regime was installed, on July 2, 1940, in the southern part of France, headed by Marshal Henri Philippe Pétain, with its capital in Vichy.[33] The Prime Minister under Pétain was Pierre Laval.

Wherever the Nazis went, they relied heavily on local police, local administrative personnel, and home grown fascists organized into militias to round up Jews for the death camps. In France, the police and administration, both in the north and the south, participated on a massive scale. Jacques Doriot's Parti Populaire Français assisted in the roundups.[34]

With the German occupation of northern France, many Jews fled to Vichy France. The Germans demanded that the Vichy regime hand over for deportation the Jews in its jurisdiction. The Vichy government distinguished between French- and foreign-born Jews, rounding up the foreign-born Jews for the Germans, but refusing to hand over the French-born. In November 1942, the Germans occupied all of France and proceeded to round up the French-born Jews whom the Vichy regime had refused to hand over.

While the Vichy regime dragged its heels on the deportation of French-born Jews, otherwise it was enthusiastically and autonomously antisemitic. The Vichy regime had its own anti-Jewish campaign, not in response to German demands, but as a result of long term priorities of the politicians who made up the regime.[35] All Jews in Vichy France, including French-born Jews, were prohibited by Vichy legislation from holding public office; they were banned from the judiciary, teaching, the military, banking, real estate, and the media; their presence in the professions was limited; their property was expropriated and their organizations dissolved.

Before the War, there was an estimated 350,000 Jews in France. Of the 350,000 Jewish pre-war French population approximately 90,000 were deported, executed or perished in internment camps.[36] Of that 90,000, 76,000 were in deportation convoys that left France for concentration and extermination camps in Eastern Europe. Of the 76,000, only 2,500 survived.[37]

The French history shows that a large danger lurks in a small number of fringe hate advocates. The seeming political insignificance of the promoters of hate in pre-War France was misleading. Even a small group dedicated to hate can become the engine of the machinery of death when political misfortune puts it into power.

There is a direct historical line from the anti-Dreyfusards to the Vichy regime and the Parti Populaire Français, and to the National Front. The Front National was founded in 1972 but took off electorally in 1983.[38] Prior to its electoral success, it was a splinter right-wing group, indistinguishable from the others, with a membership in the neighbourhood of 500. It did not grow slowly, but jumped out of nowhere to 15% of the polls. Given the history of extreme right-wing support in France, it may be more accurate to say that rather than having jumped out of nowhere, the extreme right jumped out of its grave.

The National Front eventually fractured. A breakaway faction, in January 1999, chose Bruno Megret as its president at a special congress. By March of 1999, the original National Front was left with just nine of its twelve Members of the European Parliament, 28 of its 44 politburo members, and one mayor out of four elected from major cities.

This split had many causes, but one of them was the workings of European anti-hate laws. From the beginning those laws prompted Jean-Marie Le Pen, the original leader of the National Front, to moderate his discourse in an attempt to skirt the law.

Holocaust denial is a crime in France. Rather than denying the Holocaust, in 1987 Le Pen called it a detail of history. Even that circumlocution led to a conviction in 1990 under French law. He was sentenced to a fine of 1.2 million francs plus costs.

Le Pen repeated this remark ten years later in 1997 on a visit to Munich, Germany. The Munich public prosecutor laid a charge against Le Pen under German law for denying the Holocaust. In October 1998, the European Parliament lifted Le Pen's parliamentary immunity so that the Munich prosecutor could proceed against him. The vote against Le Pen was 420 votes to 20. The breakaway at the National Front congress followed less than three months after the European Parliamentary vote.

When Jean-Marie Le Chevallier, mayor of Toulon, resigned from the National Front in March 1999, he said: "This resignation follows a number of acts of Jean-Marie Le Pen harmful to our movement." Many National Front members saw Le Pen's run-ins with Europe's anti-hate laws as hampering the Front's prospects for electoral success. Polls showed that, while up to 30% of voters agreed with the nationalist themes of the National Front, only 4% of voters agreed with Le Pen's antisemitism.

The lesson to be learned from the mass crimes of the twentieth century is the need to protest and prohibit hate speech in any country long before actual killings. Every country must have functioning anti-hate speech laws. Any country where hate speech is circulating without hindrance must be the subject of international concern. The obligation to prohibit hate speech in international treaties imposes a duty on the international community to promote compliance with that duty.

This lesson is an old lesson, recognizing the historical connection between hate speech and genocide. This lesson, is, in another sense, a completely new lesson, one that still has to be learned.

Notes

1. Article 19.
2. Article 20.
3. M. J. Bossuyt. "Guide to the *travaux preparatoires* of the International Covenant on Civil and Political Rights," Martinus Nijhoff, 1987, at page 407.
4. Edited by Mariana Lenkova, published by the International Helsinki Federation for Human Rights, Vienna, Austria, p. 8.
5. At pages 39 and 98.
6. "Hate Speech in the Balkans," p. 12.
7. Paul LaRose-Edwards. "The Rwandan Crisis of April 1994: The Lessons Learned," for the Department of Foreign Affairs and International Trade, Government of Canada, November 30, 1994, p. 60.
8. Alexander Norris. "Deport Rwandan who urge genocide, Ottawa told," *Montreal Gazette*, June 10, 1994, p. A1.
9. "Rwanda: Mass murder by government supporters and troops in April and May 1994" Amnesty International, May, 1994, AI Index: AFR 47/11/94, p. 3.
10. Luc Reydams. "Universal Jurisdiction over Atrocities in Rwanda," *European Journal of Crime, Criminal Law and Criminal Justice* (1996), p. 37.
11. IAD M96–10465, November 6, 1998, reported in Immigration and Refugee Board, RefLex105, December 23, 1998.
12. "Inside the Newly Independent States of the Former Soviet Union," National Conference on Soviet Jewry, *Spring 1994 Country Reports* (May 1994), Vol. 2, no. 2.
13. Daniel Sneider. "Jews Find Complex Ties with the New Ukraine," *Christian Science Monitor*, April 20, 1994.

14. Immigration and Refugee Board response to Information Request UKR32483.E, 11 August 1999.

15. Martin A. Wernick, Executive Vice-President of the Hebrew Immigrant Aid Society, testimony to the U. S. House of Representative Judiciary Committee subcommittee on International Law, Immigration and Refugee, July 30, 1992, at page 10.

16. Immigration and Refugee Board response to Information Request UKR20184.E.

17. "Anti-Semitism in the Former USSR, Chronicle of Violence, 1991," American Association of Russian Jews, *Ukraine*.

18. "Anti-Semitism in the Former USSR, Chronicle of Violence, 1991," American Association of Russian Jews, *Ukraine*.

19. "Jewish Graves in Odessa Desecrated," *News from the Union of Councils for Soviet Jews*, March 31, 1992.

20. *Monitor*, Vol. III, No. 4.

21. NCSJ, 9 February 1998; UCSJ, July 1998; Forward 29 August 1997.

22. "Antisemitism World Report 1997"; UCSJ July 1998.

23. "Ukraine: The Situation of the Jews," paper issued by the Immigration and Refugee Board, January 1999, reissued February 1999, p. 13.

24. Dene Moore. "Skinheads jailed in death of Sikh," *Toronto Star*, November 17, 1999.

25. See David Matas "The Extreme Right in the United Kingdom and France" in *The Extreme Right: Freedom and Security at Risk* edited by Aurel Braun and Stephen Scheinberg. Boulder, CO: Westview Press, 1997.

26. Law of 29–7–1881 amended by the law of 1972.

27. Article 2.1 of the code of criminal procedure, amended by statutes of 3.1.85 and 3.7.87.

28. Article 1 statute of 10.1.36 amended by statute 1972.

29. Law of 13 July 1990, the "Gayssot Act," amending the law on the Freedom of the Press of 1881 by adding an article 24 bis.

30. Hannah Arendt. *The Origins of Totalitarianism*. Harcourt Brace Janovich, 1951, chapter four.

31. Arendt. *The Origins of Totalitarianism*, p. 46.

32. R. J. Soucy. "The Nature of Fascism in France," in W. Laqueur and G. L. Mosse (eds.) *International Fascism 1920–1945*. New York: Harper, 1966, p. 30.

33. Marcel Ruby. *Le Livre de la Deportation*. Paris: Robert Laffont, 1995, pp. 39 and 40.

34. Michael R. Marrus. *The Holocaust in History*. New York: Meridian, 1987, p. 71.

35. Michael R. Marrus and Robert O. Paxton. *Vichy France and the Jews*. New York: Stanford University, 1981.

36. Lucy S. Dawidowicz. *The War Against the Jews 1933–1945*. Bantam, 1976, pp. 488–491.
37. Serge Klarsfeld. *Le Mémorial de la déportation des Juifs de France*. Paris, 1978.
38. See Guy Birnbaum, *Le Front National en Politique*. Paris: Balland, 1992; Nonna Mayer, "Le Front national" in *La vie politique en France* edited by Dominique Chagnollaud. Paris: Seuil, 1993, p. 329; Christopher T. Husbands, "The support for the *Front National*: analyses and findings," *Ethnic and Racial Studies* (1991), Vol. 14, no. 3, p. 382.

Chapter Two

Myopia and Inaction

IT IS COMMON FOR GOVERNMENTS, non-governmental organizations, and inter-governmental agencies to protest killings of innocents. The genocides in Rwanda and Cambodia, the ethnic cleansings in Bosnia and Kosovo, generated an outpouring of condemnation from the global community, governments, inter-governmental agencies, and non-governmental organizations alike.

Yet, it is rare for any government, any international agency, any non-governmental organization to protest the incitement that led to the killings. Although there is a clear link between the genocides, the mass crimes of the last century and the hate propaganda that preceded them, the international community has expressed concern only about the violence itself and not the hate speech that preceded and generated the violence. This glaring reticence exists in spite of the obvious complicity of the governments in hate speech and the duty at international law to stop it.

The international community has historically ignored the obligation to prohibit hate speech. It remained a theoretical obligation without a practical follow through. There have been no compliance mechanisms, no compliance assessment of this obligation either through governments, inter-governmental agencies, or non-governmental organizations.

Right now, for instance, "Article 19" is a non-governmental organization devoted to promoting the right to free expression set out in Article 19 of the Universal Declaration of Human Rights and of the International Covenant on Civil and Political Rights. However, there exists no "Article 20," no non-governmental organization devoted to promoting the duty to prohibit hate propaganda in Article 20 of the International Covenant on Civil and Political Rights.

One reason for the absence of effective international enforcement is the absence of effective anti-hate speech laws. Canada, for example, has a hate propaganda law on the books, but it does not have an effective law. James Keegstra, an Alberta teacher who taught antisemitism in his classroom and examined his students on it, was prosecuted for promoting hatred. After twelve years of litigation, he received a fine of only $3000. Canadian federal civil remedies for hate speech are fragmented and piecemeal. There is no offence of Holocaust denial. The Supreme Court of Canada in 1992 struck down the offence under which Holocaust denier Ernst Zundel was prosecuted for spreading false news likely to cause public mischief as being unconstitutionally overbroad. Canada would place itself in an awkward position if it urged other countries to institute an effective system for banning hate speech. The Canadian situation is far from unique. Laws against murder exist everywhere. Any government can tell another government not to tolerate killing without appearing hypocritical. However, there is no country that has a completely satisfactory, functioning, effective hate speech law.

Intellectual snobbery is also at play. Because the West has won the Cold War, there is a prevailing sentiment that ideology no longer matters, that the Western democratic ideal of free enterprise has won the ideological battles of history, and that ideological history has come to an end.[1] The ideologies of hatred and genocide that now stalk the world, whether in Rwanda, Bosnia, or elsewhere, do not speak to the planet. They are localized in language, in history, and in appeal. Ignoring these ideologies, pretending they do not exist, is intellectual isolationism, chauvinism, myopia.

It may be tempting to say that this blindness, this isolationism, is economic, not intellectual. We pay little attention to countries like Rwanda because Rwanda, in financial terms, means little to us in the West.

While perhaps valid for Rwanda, that explanation, is not valid elsewhere. The Iraqi invasion of Kuwait mobilized Western economic interests and Western military activity. There has been a voluminous and detailed criticism of human rights violations in Iraq, by governments, inter-governmental agencies, and non-governmental organizations alike. An outpouring of hate speech in Iraq has lead to human rights violations of the first order.[2] Iraq has ratified both the International Covenant on Civil and Political Rights and the Convention on the Elimination of All Forms of Racial Discrimination, both of which obligate Iraq to prohibit hate speech. Yet, in spite of all this, the world was as silent about the proliferation of hate speech in Iraq as it was about the proliferation of hate speech in Rwanda.

Non-governmental organizations do not face this problem. But they face another, the need to decipher discourse. Mass killings are immediately comprehensible to everyone. Understanding hate speech requires language skills, and an understanding of the context in which the speech is uttered. Hate speech often involves veiled or coded references. Understanding is a work of decoding.

For instance, the speech that Leon Mugesera gave in Rwanda, and for which he was ordered deported from Canada, a speech that advocated hatred and genocide, was in the Kinyarwanda language, not a commonly spoken world language, and not a language of work of any of the main international human rights organizations. Understanding what he was saying required some awareness of both the history and geography of Rwanda. A listener who knew neither might have found the speech more mystifying than appalling.

Even for human rights advocates, there is a blindness to the ravages of hate speech which stems partly from the absolutist free speech tradition. There is a hesitancy to criticize any speech at all as something that should not be said.

Intellectuals value ideas. The notion of ideology as pathology, ideology as a set of problems rather than a set of options meriting serious consideration goes against the liberal intellectual tradition. Analyzing hate speech is essentially a philosophical exercise. "Philosophy," from its Greek root, means "love of knowledge." To accuse *ideologies* of being the root causes of human rights violations appears anti-intellectual. The very exercise of analyzing ideology as hate speech puts the liberal intellectual tradition at war with itself. It is a lot easier to say that ideological history has ended than to say that it continues and is killing millions.

There is also an attitude within the human rights community that though violations of the duty to prohibit hate speech may be wrong, they are not important, not as important as other violations. While in theory human rights are indivisible, in practice a division is made between them. Some human rights, such the right to freedom of expression, benefit from energetic advocacy. Other human rights, and most notably the right to be free from the intimidation of hate speech, are friendless.

This downplaying of violations of the duty to prohibit hate speech and the disassociation between hate speech and genocide are causally linked. Because human rights advocates themselves do not see the connection between hate speech and genocide, even in retrospect, they do not become concerned about the violation of the duty to prohibit hate propaganda. The mass crimes of the last century, and, indeed, the last few years, by making the connection so clear and obvious, should teach the human rights community that they ignore this connection at their folly.

While the obligation to ban hate speech can be found in several international human rights instruments and, in principle, is one of the obligations states must respect, just as attempts in the bad old days to have the states of Eastern Europe respect human rights, current efforts to have states ban hate speech meets with a big fat "no." This time the "no" comes from the United States of America. Because the international community works by consensus and places special stress on the concurrence of the permanent members of the Security Council, and because the United States is the one remaining superpower, the U.S. has ended up with a veto over international efforts to ban hate speech.

The 1997 meeting of the United Nations Commission on Human Rights in Geneva, which I attended as a non-governmental delegate, illustrated this veto. There was a draft resolution on racial intolerance put out by Turkey which had strong language prohibiting racial hatred. The U.S. was opposed to this language, wanting nothing to do with the notion of prohibiting hate speech. The resolution on racial intolerance was mired in a debate about whether anti-semitism would or would not be mentioned. Raising other issues complicated this debate. Making sure anti-semitism continued to be mentioned had a higher priority than doing something about hate speech. So, the language on prohibition of hate speech was dropped.

The U.S. veto over international language prohibiting hate speech comes from a culturally based view of human rights. The American human rights culture is one of free speech absolutism. The United States has as the first amendment to its constitution a provision guaranteeing freedom of speech. For Americans, first in time means pride of place.

The U.S. constitution asserts freedom of expression before all other rights, because to the framers of the constitution, the denial of freedom of expression was the greatest of all wrongs. Americans of the eighteenth century identified British oppression of its American colonies with British repression of fundamental freedoms and especially speech. Irving Brant wrote:

> The spectacle of freedom of opinion suppressed in England was always in sight, and the sight of it not only stirred sympathy, but carried a warning that linked freedom of speech, press and assembly with the rights whose infringement was carrying the people of the colonies to-

ward independence. The actual evils in England were potential American evils that merged with the revolutionary grievances of America and built unwritten bills of rights in the minds of the people.[3]

Four cases that were prominent in the American consciousness at the time of the First Amendment were those of John Wilkes, Alexander MacDougall, Junius, and William Shipley. John Wilkes, a member of the opposition in the British House of Commons, was stripped of his parliamentary seat and sent to jail for calling a 1763 government speech "the most abandoned instance of ministerial effrontery ever attempted to be imposed on mankind." The publication in which his comment was published was ordered to be burned. His constituency re-elected Wilkes, but the House of Commons expelled Wilkes again. This election and expulsion went on six times, until finally, the House of Commons placed his opponent, whom he had defeated by a vote of four to one, in his seat. An American society called "Society of Supporters of the Bill of Rights" conducted an active campaign on Wilkes' behalf.[4]

Alexander MacDougall was prosecuted and sent to jail in 1770 in the New York colony for criticizing the colony's support of British soldiers. MacDougall had denounced what he claimed was a collusive agreement made by the New York Colonial Assembly with British troops. The collusion was to furnish supplies to the troops in exchange for the British Governor's signature on an Assembly bill authorizing the printing of money. The fact that MacDougall was sent to jail for, in effect, criticising British colonial rule, inflamed the supporters of the American Revolution and rallied people to his cause.[5]

Junius was the pseudonym of an anonymous writer in England who wrote that the policies of George III were driving the American colonies to rebellion. In 1769 he addressed a letter to the king which said: "Come forward to your people . . . Tell them you have been fatally deceived." Since Junius himself was unknown, he could not be prosecuted. Instead, the publishers of two magazines who printed his letter, as well as a bookseller who sold one of the magazines, were prosecuted. Of the three accused, two were never convicted, and the third received only a small fine. Nonetheless, the very fact of their prosecution raised a storm of protest both in England and America.[6] A quote from Junius adorns to this day the mast head of the *Globe and Mail*: "The subject who is truly loyal to the Chief Magistrate will neither advise nor submit to arbitrary measures."

William Shipley was prosecuted for publishing a pamphlet in 1783 arguing for apportionment of the House of Commons according to population. A jury returned a guilty verdict which was overturned on appeal only because of a defect in the indictment. Americans and British alike were appalled that British law put anyone at risk of going to prison for doing no more than voicing ordinary political sentiments.[7]

Globally, the notion of human rights has evolved, in part, in response to the evolving nature of wrongs. Much of the current human rights regime, including the duty to ban hate speech, is a response to the Holocaust, an attempt to learn its lessons and to prevent a repetition of what should never have happened in the first place. For U.S. constitutional jurisprudence, it as if the Holocaust never happened. The Bill of Rights in the U.S. constitution is an eighteenth-century document, but for U.S. courts, human rights are what is in the Bill of Rights and nothing more.

American jurisprudence would be far different if the duty to ban hate speech had the same status as the right to free expression. As it is, the right to free expression is in the U.S. constitution and the duty to ban hate speech is not. As a result, in U.S. courts the right to free expression sits in judgment on the right to be protected from hate speech, and that judgment is harsh.

U.S. constitutional jurisprudence about free speech is not just a technical legal doctrine. It articulates the way Americans approach free speech issues, at home and abroad. The banning of hate speech, to Americans, is plainly and simply wrong. Any international document or resolution that requires consensus to succeed will run up against American objections, if it incorporates the duty to ban hate speech.

In many countries, the situation is not what American free speech absolutists fear, a slippery slope leading to ever greater restrictions on speech, but the slippery slope assumed not to exist, one leading to ever more allowance of bold and direct hate speech directed against minorities. A theoretical fear of undue restriction of speech has meant turning a blind eye to real, acute, injurious incitement.

Kathleen Mahoney in the *University of Illinois Law Review* summarizes the issue well:

> The argument that a commitment to the democratic system of government requires an unqualified and preeminent commitment to free speech is simply false. It sets up an "either-or" dichotomy which is not relevant in modern, Western democracies. It relies on the proposition

that governments are a constant threat to the freedom of the citizens; that they are perpetually hostile and aggressive towards individuals and society; and that once in possession of power, they will revert back to the autocratic powers of their eighteenth-century predecessors. In the context of Western democracies in the twentieth century, this argument is overplayed. It is defensive and rigid to the extent that any attempt to limit or make exceptions to the free speech principles is almost subversive. By its dichotomous nature, it is a conversation stopper.

The reality is that speech issues raised by hate propaganda today are entirely different from speech issues that faced fledgling democracies in the seventeenth and eighteenth centuries. To equate discussion of public issues and free elections of that era to the hate speech of today conceals the social functions of speech, minimizes the harms and abuses hate speech causes, and ignores the responsibility of government to maintain a civilized society.[8]

Notes

1. See Francis Fukuyama, "The End of History?" *The National Interest,* Summer 1989.
2. Samir al-Khalil. *Republic of Rear: The Inside Story of Saddam's Iraq.* New York: Pantheon, 1990.
3. Irving Brant. *The Bill of Rights: Its Origin and Meaning.* Indianapolis: Bobbs-Merrill, 1965, p. 193.
4. Brant, pp. 189–192.
5. Brant, p. 194.
6. Brant, pp. 195–199.
7. Brant, pp. 203–207.
8. "Hate Speech: Affirmation or Contradiction of Freedom of Expression" *University of Illinois Law Review* (1996), pp. 789—797.

Chapter Three

Individual and Collective Rights

THE DEBATE BETWEEN freedom of expression and prohibition of hate propaganda is, in substance, a question whether individual and collective rights are compatible. Freedom of expression is an individual right. The right of a member of a group to be protected from hate propaganda is a group or community right. Can the two live together? My answer, as I stated at the outset, is yes.

People live in community. Rights are exercised in community. For freedom of expression to be respected there has to be a functioning society. The flourishing of hate propaganda corrodes and disintegrates the society that is needed for free speech to flourish. The 1965 Report of the Special Committee on Hate Propaganda in Canada, chaired by Maxwell Cohen, put it this way: "if we do not maintain a society that is tolerant of vagaries and differences we shall not maintain individual freedom of expression and action."[1]

Individual and collective rights are not in conflict, but rather different facets of human rights. Human rights are grounded in the individual human being. What assists and protects the individual in his or her self-worth, dignity, and self-realization is the ultimate touchstone for human rights. However, this does not mean individual human rights are real rights and collective rights are not. For it takes both collective rights and individual rights to allow for the realization of human rights. The notion of a conflict between freedom of expression and prohibition of hate speech stems from a misconception of what freedom of expression is. To put it boldly, freedom of expression does not include the freedom to utter hate speech.

Every right and every freedom must be understood in light of the interest it is meant to protect. Society guarantees freedom of expression for a reason, or rather, for several reasons. Speech that does not fit within these reasons falls outside the guarantee.

One reason we protect freedom of expression is to arrive at the truth. We have to allow old ideas to be replaced by new ideas. Ideas we believe to be true today may subsequently turn out to be false.

However, we cannot justify the right to utter hate speech on this basis. It is an absurd position to say that maybe it is true that Jews control the world, that blacks are less intelligent than whites, and so on. The mere suggestion that these utterances might be true gives credence to them, something we would not want to do.

Nonetheless, some speech, even though false, may lead to the attainment of the truth. We also encourage freedom of expression because we can get a better sense of what is true by knowing what is false.

However, again, here hate speech serves little purpose. We do not need to hear Holocaust denial to better understand the existence of the Holocaust, to hear that a minority controls the world to become more keenly aware of the disadvantaged situation of minorities. We do not heed to hear hate speech to keep our belief in equality alive. We show a deeper commitment to the truths of human equality and tolerance by prohibiting hate propaganda than by allowing it to flourish.

Using hate propaganda as a foil for the truth is playing with fire. The problem with hate propaganda is not so much that it is not true. Truth or falsity is almost irrelevant to the harm it causes. Hate propaganda is an attack on the truth-seeking process itself. It is directed to subverting and undermining the search for truth.

More generally, though, we protect freedom of expression to allow for the exposition of our thought, to explain our ideas, or to communicate information. The issue here is not truth or falsity, but simply the development of thought.

However, hate is an emotion not a thought. Insofar as there is an idea embedded in the emotion, it is the emotion that generates the idea. Jean Paul Sartre has written: "Antisemitism does not fall within the category of ideas protected by the right of free opinion. Indeed it is something quite other than an idea. It is first of all a passion."[2] As Sartre points out, antisemitism may be covered with a veneer of factual assertions and theoretical statements. However, the antisemite is immune to refutation from either facts or logic. An antisemite has chosen to live in hatred, without regard to either facts or logic.

Hatred is a vicious circle impervious to reality. If any fact could persuade an antisemite of the powerlessness of Jews, surely the Holocaust would. Yet, the very perpetrators of the Holocaust, as they led Jews to the gas chamber, continued to believe in world Jewish control and, indeed, justified their killings as the only way to end that control. Today, antisemites, starting from a premise of Holocaust denial, use the pervasive and overwhelming evidence of the Holocaust as yet further evidence of world Jewish control. Sarte writes: "The antisemite has chosen hate because hate is a faith; at the outset he has chosen to devaluate words and reasons."[3]

As the framers of the U.S. constitution recognized, freedom of expression is necessary for democracy. However, tolerance is also essential for democracy. Allowing hate propaganda to flourish will destroy democracy. Hate propagandists are no democrats. Even before they achieve power, their hate speech tears at the fabric of democracy by fomenting hatred of the majority against the minority. Hate propaganda is directed at excluding a minority from democracy, at rending apart the mutual acceptance in society necessary to make society function.

Alan Borovoy has called free speech society's grievance procedure.[4] We assert freedom of expression because, once limits to freedom of expression are in place, the power to enforce those limits is open to abuse by the state. The result may be inhibiting, even on legitimate speech.

Again here if the fear is tyranny, permitting hate speech is perverse. In a democracy, abuse of state power comes from a tyranny of the majority, by officials enforcing majority sentiment. However, hate propaganda encourages the majority to be tyrannical. Allowing hate speech gives licence to expression that increases the tyrannical danger in majority rule. Giving hate propaganda free rein does not protect against government tyranny. Rather it makes government tyranny more likely.

Free speech absolutists use the metaphor of the marketplace. They argue that just as in the marketplace for goods, where the better products win out and the shoddy products disappear, in the marketplace of ideas the soundness of tolerance will win converts and hate speech will be seen for what it is.

However, we have only to think of this market metaphor for a moment to see how unpersuasive it is. In the market, advertisers often persuade consumers to purchase inferior products. It is the advertising alone that persuades.

The 1965 Report of the Special Committee on Hate Propaganda in Canada[5] put it this way:

While holding that over the long run, the human mind is repelled by blatant falsehood and seeks the good, it is too often true, in the short run, that emotion displaces reason and individuals perversely reject the demonstration of truth put before them and forsake the good they know. The successes of modern advertising, the triumphs of impudent propaganda such as Hitler's, have qualified sharply our belief in the rationality of man. We know that under strain and pressure in time of irritation and frustration, the individual is swayed and even swept away by hysterical, emotional appeals. We act irresponsibly if we ignore the way in which emotion can drive reason from the field.

Using the notion of the marketplace of ideas to argue against banning hate speech is, in any case, circular. If the banning of hate speech is a better idea than untrammelled free speech, then it should win out in the marketplace of ideas. Indeed, the purpose of this book is to enter that marketplace with the hope that the ideas expressed in this book will win out. If the marketplace starts with the assumption that the ideas in this book must be rejected, then it is not a true open market. It is market rigged in favour of one side.

Hate speech laws are a form of group libel laws, laws against group defamation. Yet, libel laws, while they provide a variety of remedies, typically do not allow each and every member of a libelled group to sue the defamer for damage to reputation.

There is no question that civil liberties, including freedom of expression, are compatible with the law against defamation of individuals. Libel or slander can make a person a social and economic pariah. Part of respecting civil liberties means allowing people the freedom to maintain their individual honour and reputation.

The danger of defamation is not so much the slander by one individual. It is the weight of community opinion identifying with and agreeing with the person uttering the slander. Unless the target of slander has the opportunity of protection against the defamation, he or she becomes unjustly the victim of hostile community opinion.[6]

William Shakespeare put it most eloquently in *Othello*. After Othello sacks his lieutenant Cassio for taking part in a drunken brawl, Cassio bewails not so much the loss of his job as the loss of his reputation: "Reputation, reputation, reputation! O, I have lost my reputation! I have lost the immortal part of myself and what remains is bestial."[7]

Slander dehumanizes. It makes a person less than a person in society's eyes. A slander that is accepted and believed means that person, in the eyes of the community, has lost his soul.

All that is true of individual libel is true of group libel as well. Group libel dehumanizes as much as individual libel does. Group libel can turn a majority against a minority as much as individual libel can. Group libel may create social and economic pariahs out of whole communities in much the same way as individual libel may.

Accepting individual libel laws as compatible with civil liberties but rejecting group libel laws is a form of elitism. Only a few prominent individuals are the typical victims of individual libel. Masses of underprivileged are the typical victims of group libel.

It makes no sense to say that if you are libelled alone the libel is actionable, but that if you are libelled with others the libel is not actionable. It makes no sense to say to those who would defame that the more people you defame the less likely you are to be held accountable.

It is a perverse triumph of society's overly individualist focus on rights that individual libel laws are widely accepted, but group libel laws, that would allow any member of a vilified group to sue the defamer, are almost nowhere to be found. A hate promoter can denounce all Muslims and be immune from libel. Yet, anyone who calls the hate promoter a racist or neo-Nazi runs the risk of being sued for libel. When it comes to libel laws, the hate promoter is given free rein. The rights advocate is silenced by libel chill.

It should be obvious that a danger to an individual from libel is not lessened simply because the individual is part of a large group that is libelled. On the contrary, the danger is far greater. Group libel, run rampant, has led to far greater human rights violations than any individual libel.

Abandoning collective rights, ignoring attacks on collectivities, and concerning ourselves only with attacks on isolated individuals is to ignore the history of human rights violations. That history tells us that we cannot ignore the group in the name of the individual; that an attack on all is an attack on each and every one; that group libel can be even more dangerous than individual libel; that collective rights go hand in hand with individual rights.

One of the strongest rationales for freedom of expression is that it permits self-fulfilment for those expressing themselves. The opportunity for self-expression is an opportunity for self-realization.

However, for hate speech this means allowing incipient neo-Nazis to become fully developed neo-Nazis. It means allowing potential Ku Klux Klan to become actual Ku Klux Klan. Self-realization of Nazis in the bud is in the interest of neither society nor democracy.

Hate propaganda laws do more than help prevent racist acts. Hate speech laws enhance freedom of expression, the freedom of expression of the vilified group. Or, to put it another way, the flourishing of hate propaganda inhibits the freedom of expression of the vilified group. Members of minorities targeted by hate speech are less likely to feel free to express themselves in a society where hate propaganda directed against them flourishes.

Mr. Justice Quigley of the Alberta Court of Queen's Bench in the *Keegstra* case put it this way. He wrote that the harm of hate propaganda

> cannot rationally be considered to be an infringement which limits freedom of expression, but on the contrary it is a safeguard which promotes it. The protection afforded by the proscription tends to banish the apprehension which might otherwise inhibit certain segments of our society from freely expressing themselves upon the whole spectrum of topics, whether social, economic, scientific, political, religious, or spiritual in nature. The unfettered right to express divergent opinions on these topics is the kind of freedom of expression the Charter protects.[8]

Alan Borovoy is general counsel to the Canadian Civil Liberties Association, an organization which intervened in the *Keegstra* case at the Supreme Court of Canada on behalf of Keegstra. The answer Borovoy gives to this argument is that he does not consider the Jewish community inhibited in expressing itself on social, economic, scientific, political, religious or spiritual matters. Nor, he argues, in the United States where there are virtually no effective hate propaganda laws to speak of, is the Jewish community inhibited either.

That answer is not a satisfactory one. It defines away the problem by overgeneralizing it. The problem of hate propaganda is not that it inhibits all expression, but rather that it inhibits some expression in particular. The response of the Jewish community to antisemitism is not total silence. While, for some the response has been activism, for many others it has been avoidance. Antisemitism has inhibited the assertion of Jewishness, of Jewish identity, of Jewish rights.

The promotion of hatred run rampant against a victim group weakens self-assertion by members of that group. The Jewish community has only to look at its own experience, its own vocabulary, to see the effect antisemitism has on freedom of expression. The notion of *sh'a shtill*, "keep quiet," has been a political slogan, a byword in the Jewish community. The concept of *shanda fur de yidden,* "an embarrassment for the Jews," has permeated Jewish discourse. The Jewish community expresses concern about what other Jews say or do because of how it might reflect on the community.

The fear of stirring up antisemitism is a constant concern. There is apprehension that Jewish visibility, not perhaps in every arena, but in support of some people or some causes, will create resentment against the Jewish community.

An attitude exists within the Jewish community that Jews are guests in a non-Jewish society, and that the Jewish community should behave so as not to antagonize their hosts, even if it means curtailing words and deeds. There is a view that the Jewish community should not be criticising its benefactors; that the community exists in its host nation not as a right, but by dispensation from the majority, and must do nothing to antagonize or offend that majority.

The danger of racist speech is more than the inhibition of words or deed. Racist speech affects self-perception. Self-esteem depends on the esteem of others. When other think less of the community, the community thinks less of itself, and the very identity of the community, or at least of individual members of the community, is stifled. Avoidance grows to be become more than just a tactic. It becomes grafted on to the community's soul.

Mr. Justice Dickson, then Chief Justice of the Supreme Court of Canada in the *Keegstra* case, put the matter this way:

> In my opinion, a response of humiliation and degradation from an individual targeted by hate propaganda is to be expected. A person's sense of human dignity and belonging to the community at large is closely linked to the concern and respected accorded the group to which he or she belongs. . . . The derision, hostility and abuse encouraged by hate propaganda therefore have a severe negative impact on the individual's sense of self and acceptance. This impact may cause target group members to take drastic measures in reaction, perhaps avoiding activities which bring them into contact with non group members or adopting attitudes and positions directed towards blending in with the majority. Such consequences bear heavily in a nation that prides itself on tolerance and the fostering of human dignity through, among other things, respect for the many racial, religious, and cultural groups in our society.[9]

The repression within the vilified community reinforces the incomprehension of outsiders. When victims themselves evade the harm of hate speech, rather than confront it directly, the tendency of outsiders is to ignore it completely. If someone is murdered, it is easy for strangers to empathize, no matter what the public manifestation of distress of the family of the victim. Anyone can see himself or herself in the shoes of the victim of a crime of violence. Hate speech is different. For those not targets of hate speech, the invective seems to be meaningless gibberish best ignored. There is no immediate intuitive understanding of the harm.

The right to be free from incitement to hatred is a community right that belongs primarily to the community that is the target of the hatred. In a larger sense, it belongs to the whole human community. Hate speech, by dehumanizing components of the human family, by undermining the tolerance that keeps the community together, ultimately harms not just its victims but all of humanity. As one genocide after another has demonstrated, the banning of hate speech is something on which the survival of the whole human community depends.

Notes

1. At page 6.
2. *Antisemite and Jew.* New York: Schocken Books, 1948, p. 10.
3. Page 19.
4. *When Freedoms Collide: The Case for Civil Liberties.* Toronto: Lester & Orpen Dennys,1988.
5. *Report to the Minister of Justice,* Maxwell Cohen, Chair, p. 8.
6. Lee Bollinger. *The Tolerant Society: Freedom of Speech & Extremist Speech in America.* Oxford University Press, 1986.
7. Act II, Scene III.
8. *R. v. Keegstra* (1990) 3 S.C.R. 697.
9. (1990) 61 Canadian Criminal Cases (3d) 1 at page 36.

Chapter Four

What is Hate Propaganda?

ONE OF THE MOST FREQUENT CRITICISMS made against laws prohibiting hate propaganda is that the concept of hate speech is vague. For example, Mme. Justice McLachlin, in the *John Ross Taylor* case, asks:

> Where does dislike leave off and hatred begin? The use of the word hatred opens the door to investigation of matters which have more to do with dislike than discrimination. The notion of hatred does not send a clear and precise indication to members of society as to what the limits of impugned speech are.[1]

If the law is vague, there is a risk of catching within it expression falling short of hate propaganda. A vague law can also have a chilling effect, discouraging permissible speech out of fear the speech might be impermissible. Indeed many of the criticisms of anti-hate laws are built on an initial argument of vagueness. If the argument of vagueness falls, then these consequential criticisms fall as well.

The criticism of vagueness is different, however, from the criticism of overbreadth. A law can be both precise and overbroad.

An example of this distinction is the offence of vagrancy. The Criminal Code of Canada used to say that a person committed vagrancy if the person, having at any time been convicted of certain offences, was found loitering in or near a school ground, play ground, public park, or bathing area. The Supreme Court of Canada majority were able to define the concept of loitering in a sufficiently precise manner so as to avoid any problem of vagueness. Loitering was defined as standing idly around, hanging around, lingering, tarrying, sauntering, delaying, dawdling. The court majority nonetheless struck down the vagrancy offence as unconstitutionally overbroad, because it embraced all public parks and beaches no matter how remote; because the prohibition applied for life without any process for review to those convicted of the requisite prior offences; because of the large number of persons it encompassed; and because the prohibition could be enforced without any notice to the accused.[2]

The answer to the criticism of overbreadth, where it is valid, is to narrow the law so that the law ceases to be overly broad. The whole concept of overbreadth acknowledges the notion of a breadth that is acceptable.

Vagueness, where it exists, is a potentially more deadly flaw. Vagueness is not just a problem at the fringes. It is a problem at the core. Clarification may be impossible. If hate propaganda as a concept is vague, it is a legally unworkable concept.

Hate propaganda is not just a matter of emotion. The test of hate propaganda is not the feelings of members of the vilified group. Indeed, many members of vilified groups may view the propaganda as so ridiculous and removed from reality as not to merit attention. The test is, rather: is the contested speech likely to arouse hatred in third parties?

Anti-hate laws are not, after all, directed against stopping hatred. Hatred is a basic human emotion. Hatred will always be with us. What the laws are directed against is the communication of hatred, getting others who initially do not hate to join in the hatred. The ultimate focus of the laws is not the perpetrator, the vilified group, or even the message, but rather the potential convert. A message that is unlikely to lead to hatred in anyone is not hate propaganda at all.

Indeed, so central is the notion of generating hatred to the notion of hate speech, that for the one court in Canada that did decide hate propaganda laws are unconstitutional, the Alberta Court of Appeal in the *Keegstra* case, that was the basis of the decision. The Alberta Court of Appeal held that the law overly impaired freedom of expression because the law did not require proof of actual hatred in the listeners. The Supreme Court of Canada, in overturning that decision, noted that Parliament can use the criminal law to prevent the risk of serious harm, for instance by prohibiting drinking and driving. Studies show that the risk of harm from hate propaganda is real, and in view of the grievous harm to be avoided, proof of actual hatred in the listener is not required.[3]

While demonstrating that hatred resulted in the listener is unnecessary, there must be something to show that the material could lead to hatred, or otherwise it is not hate propaganda at all. Dr. Jean Ravault, a communications expert who testified in both the *John Ross Taylor* and *Terry Long* cases, has described the different ways in which a message intended to promote hatred actually succeeds in promoting hatred in those who receive it.

Who are the people who succumb to hate propaganda even in a free society? They are people not well-integrated in their communities, people who do not feel they belong and are in search of a new cause or a new group to join. Such persons are not well-informed generally about what is going on in society. They have uncertain self-images, a weak belief in who they are. Their relations with family and friends are not on a solid foundation. They see themselves threatened economically by international events beyond their control and beyond the control of the people around them. They are frustrated both in their personal and professional life. They may already have some mild prejudice against the vilified group that the propaganda reinforces. They are uncertain or confused about their own future and the future of their country. They are already disaffected from, and frustrated by, conventional solutions and are looking for more radical cures. They search out those who claim to have an answer for theirs and society's ills.[4]

Although the analysis provided by Ravault must be read in its entirety to see how hate propaganda targets, and persuades, these individuals, this excerpt of his analysis[5] of the pre-recorded messages of the Jesus Christ Aryan Nations in the *Terry Long* case, gives a sense of what is happening:

> Quite typical of the Nazi propaganda of the Thirties in pre-Hitlerian Germany, the inability of members of Parliament to deal with this crucial issue [refugees landing in Halifax] is pointed out.
>
> "But do you think that your Member of Parliament is gonna represent the concerns of their white electorate? Of course not!"
>
> And why?
>
> "Because white people have absolutely no say whatsoever in controlling their destiny—only racial minority pressure groups today call the shots. Whites are second-class citizens!"
>
> But the emergence of the situation for the white race which no longer is in control of its own destiny and has lost power over its own territory does not come alone from the arrival of third-world immigrants; there is a conspiracy to prevent it to reproduce itself!
>
> "Our birth rate in North America is at minus zero while non-white births are astronomically far ahead. Wherever will you find white babies in the maternity wards in New York, New Mexico, and California?"

Hate propaganda succeeds by addressing and exploiting circumstances surrounding its messages. Hate propaganda messages typically refer to well-publicized issues of concern to the general population such as unemployment or immigration. The general thrust of the messages is to scapegoat, to blame the group under attack for these general problems.

Hate messages also succeed by the imagery and references they contain. The use of quotations from or references to sources which may be seen as credible, references to the Bible, statistics and so on, give the messages a persuasive force. Positive sources such as these are juxtaposed with supposed admissions by members of the group attacked. The overall impression of the messages is one of research and reflection, normally by reference to sources that either are difficult or impossible to track down or verify.

Another measure of effectiveness is the medium used. In the cases where Ravault testified, the method used was taped telephone messages, a medium Ravault considered to be particularly effective. The listener must take a positive step to access each message. Telephone calls are more personal than radio or television, and for that reason are more likely to be listened to carefully.

In the case of *John Ross Taylor*, the Canadian Human Rights Act Tribunal described the system he used. Any member of the public, by dialing the relevant phone number, could listen to a pre-recorded message of approximately one minute in length. From 1977 to 1979 thirteen different messages were disseminated over the telephone lines in this fashion.

The telephone number in question was 967-7777. All the messages were drafted and recorded by Taylor himself, the acknowledged leader of the Western Guard Party. This telephone service was financed by the Western Guard Party or Mr. Taylor or his assistant Jack Prins. They distributed cards bearing only a maple leaf symbol and the words "Dial 967-7777" among individuals and crowds, and by slipping them under doorways. There was nothing on the cards which would indicate the nature of the message that a caller would receive. Secondly, they purchased a notation in the telephone book which read "White Power Message—967-7777." The name alone indicated to a prospective caller the nature of the message he or she would hear.

Although Ravault was testifying before the advent of the internet, much that Ravault said about pre-recorded, telephone hate messages can be said about internet hate websites. A hate website does not normally reside on a user's computer, rather the user must take a positive step to access the site.

Hate propaganda is not defined by the communications strategies and methodology hate propagandists use. Yet analyzing these methodologies distinguishes hate propaganda from other disturbing expressions. By looking at the strategies used we remind ourselves of the focus of the law, which is to prevent the *promotion* of hatred. As well, by looking at methodology, we can better understand how a message that may seem superficially silly or insignificant may, in reality, be quite effective in the promotion of hatred.

As a comparison, racial slurs are litigated in the context of workplace harassment and may constitute a violation of human rights statutes.[6] A racial slur is any utterance that is demeaning, disconcerting, and a profound affront to dignity and self-respect.[7] But, unlike hate propaganda, the focus is the victim rather than a third party. Also, unlike hate propaganda, the slur must be demeaning, whereas hate speech may well not be demeaning. A racial slur may be uttered only on one occasion and still be a slur. Hate propaganda, on the other hand, requires propagandizing, a continued course of conduct, rather than an isolated statement.

In Canada, a number of cases have discussed anti-hate laws in a constitutional context and defined what hate speech is. In the *Keegstra* case,[8] Mr. Justice Dickson, then Chief Justice of the Supreme Court of Canada, said that a dictionary definition may be of limited aid. By its nature a dictionary seeks to offer a panoply of possible usages. It does not give only the correct meaning of a word as contemplated by the legislators.

In the opinion of Dickson, the hatred contemplated by Canadian legislators connotes emotion of an intense and extreme nature that is associated with vilification and detestation. Justice Cory, in the *Andrews* case,[9] said "to promote hatred is to instil detestation, enmity, ill will, and malevolence in another." He added that an expression must go a long way before it qualifies as promoting hatred.

Mr. Justice Dickson said that hatred manifests insensitivity and bigotry. Its aim is destruction of the vilified group. It is an extreme emotion, without reason. The targets of hatred are to be despised, scorned, denied respect. Ill treatment is wished them. Hatred does not denote a wide range of diverse emotions, only the most intense form of dislike.

Hate propaganda can be identified by context. In this sense, hate propaganda relates to the concept of disadvantage.

The Canadian Charter of Rights and Freedoms prohibits discrimination on the basis of personal characteristics. The Supreme Court of Canada has held that this prohibition benefits only the disadvantaged.

Mr. Justice Hugessen, of the Canadian Federal Court of Appeal has said of the equality guarantee in the Charter: "Questions of stereotyping, of historical disadvantagement, in a word, of prejudice, are the focus and there may even be a recognition that for some people equality has a different meaning than for others."[10] In the words of Mr. Justice McIntyre of the Supreme Court of Canada, the beneficiaries of the equality guarantee of the Charter must be "a discrete and insular minority."[11]

To determine whether or not an act amounts to discrimination it is not enough to look at it in isolation. If the act is directed against a discrete, insular minority, a minority that has been historically disadvantaged and stereotyped, it may be discrimination. If, on the other hand, the act is directed against a group that has no history of disadvantage or of being stereotyped, the act may not amount to discrimination.

Much the same can be said about hate propaganda. In assessing whether or not speech amounts to hate propaganda, it is not enough to look at the content of the speech. One must also look to see against whom the speech is directed. If the speech is directed against a discrete disadvantaged and insular minority that has been historically stereotyped, the speech may well be hate propaganda. Otherwise, it may not be.

It is no coincidence that the hate speech in Canada which has led to convictions has in virtually every case been hate speech directed against Jews, although Jews have not been the only targets. Dr. Jean Ravault noted the similarity between the messages of Terry Long and John Ross Taylor, on the one hand, and the propaganda of Nazi Germany, on the other. In the *Taylor* case, Ravault wrote:

> All the themes and topics of the Western Guard party messages perfectly fit within the structure, framework, as well as the main ideological axes of the Nazi propaganda as elaborated by Rosenberg, Goebbels, and Hitler. . . . That German Nazi propaganda exposed persons to hatred and contempt is accepted. The demonstration of a strong parallel between German Nazi propaganda and Western Guard Party messages will be persuasive that these messages themselves expose persons to hatred and contempt.[12]

In the *Terry Long* case, the tribunal noted that Ravault felt that Long's messages have a strong similarity with Nazi propaganda.[13]

The point is not just that the verbal formulations are similar. It is also that the intended targets are the same.

Alan Borovoy suggests that under laws prohibiting hate speech some-one could possibly be prosecuted for saying that English Canadians have unfairly exploited French Canadians. He then proceeds to argue against those laws because the laws allow for this possibility.[14] The trouble with his argument is that he assumes the statement that English Canadians have unfairly exploited French Canadians is hate speech. Yet there are many rea-sons why it is not. Not the least of these is the contextual one. English Cana-dians have not been historically disadvantaged in Canada. It is ludicrous to suggest any analogy whatsoever between the way English Canadians have been treated historically in Canada and the way Jews have been treated historically worldwide. It is the horrendous and unparalleled history of vic-timization the Jews have suffered that leads both the experts and the courts to come to the conclusion that Nazi-like speech directed against Jews today is hate speech.

Courts have found specific hate messages to violate Canadian law. It is reasonable to assume that whatever else hate speech is, at the very least, those expressions found to be in violation of the law are hate speech.

In the *Keegstra* case, Jim Keegstra was a high school teacher in Eckville, Alberta from the early '70s until 1982, when he was dismissed. He taught his pupils that Jews were treacherous, subversive, sadistic, money-loving, power hungry, and child killers. Jews, he taught, seek to destroy Christianity. They are responsible for depressions, anarchy, chaos, wars, revolutions. They in-vented the Holocaust to gain sympathy. They are deceptive, secretive, and inherently evil. Keegstra expected his students to reproduce his bigotry in class and on exams. If they did not, they were marked down for it. He was convicted of promoting hate propaganda under the criminal code.

Donald Clarke Andrews and Robert Wayne Smith of the Nationalist Party of Canada promoted an ideology that the courts summarized this way: God conferred his greatest gifts on white people. All those who urge a race-mixed planet are working against God's will. Minority groups are responsible for increases in the crime rate. Coloureds do not believe in democracy and harbour a hatred for white people. America is being swamped by coloureds. There should be separation of races. Non-whites should be repatriated to their lands where their race is a majority. Zionists have fabricated the Holo-caust. They dominate the resources of the nation. Their domination means that the nation cannot remain in good health, because the interests of Zion-ists are alien to those of the nation.

Andrews and Smith were convicted under the Criminal Code of Canada's hate propaganda laws. Both the *Keegstra* conviction and the *Andrews and Smith* convictions were upheld by the Supreme Court of Canada.

John Ross Taylor, leader of the Western Guard Party, communicated a sequence of telephone messages summarized by a Canadian Human Rights Tribunal in this way: There is a conspiracy which controls Canadian society. The conspirators control our banks, our schools, our media. Because of this control it is difficult to find out the truth about this conspiracy. The conspirators cause unemployment, inflation. They encourage perversion, laziness, drug abuse, and race mixing, to weaken the rest of us. They steal property. They have founded Communism and control it in furtherance of the conspiracy. The conspirators are Jews.

The Canadian Human Rights Tribunal ordered Taylor to cease communicating the hate messages by telephone. By statute, the tribunal order had the effect of a court order. When Taylor persisted, he was convicted of contempt of court. This conviction was affirmed by the Supreme Court of Canada.

Terry Long of the Church of Jesus Christ Christian-Aryan Nations also used the telephone to communicate a sequence of telephone messages which a Canadian Human Rights Tribunal summarized in this way: A liberal, national immigration policy presents a threat to both the physical and moral welfare of the white race. The non-white races are intellectually and morally inferior. They are the dupes of the Jews who are bent on world domination. All of the country's and the world's ills are the workings of a Jewish conspiracy to which the liberal white political establishment is totally blind. Jewish cunning and deviousness are at every turn. Jews control merchandising for their own purposes at the expense of the general public. Judaism condones deception, neglect, and murder of Christians. Judaism is satanic and synonymous with international Communism. Jews are members of a worldwide Zionist banking conspiracy aimed at the collapse of the Western world. Jews conspire to rid America of the white race by manipulating immigration and subverting its racial purity by encouraging miscegenation.

The Human Rights Tribunal ordered Terry Long to cease communicating the hate message by phone. He complied with the order.

Hate speech takes a few common forms. One of these is unfounded allegations of atrocities directed against a whole people or nationality. It is this form of hate speech that has been so deadly recently in both the former Yugoslavia and Rwanda.

An important method of explaining hate propaganda is by counter definition, by stating what hate propaganda is not. Hatred is to be distinguished
from contempt, ridicule, and belittling. Hate propaganda is different from
blasphemy, offensive remarks, and racial slurs.

The Red Eye, a tabloid published by University of Saskatchewan engineering students in 1981, produced a number of issues that led to complaints to the Saskatchewan Human Rights Commission. The Saskatchewan
Human Rights Code prohibits any notice, sign, symbol emblem, or other
representation which exposes to hatred, ridicules, belittles, or otherwise of-
fends the dignity of any person.[15] A Saskatchewan Board of Inquiry found
that the tabloid ridiculed, belittled, and offended the dignity of women because of their sex.[16] That decision was eventually overturned by the Saskatchewan Court of Appeal, on the ground that the engineering tabloid was
not a representation, and therefore not within the prohibition contained in
the Saskatchewan Human Rights Code. However, it was common ground,
throughout the courts, that the tabloid ridiculed women, but it did not expose them to hatred.[17] Because of the court of appeal decision, the Saskatchewan legislature amended its Human Rights Code to cover newspaper
articles.

The book *The Satanic Verses*, by Salman Rushdie, was brought before the
British courts for blasphemy and not for inciting racial hatred. In Britain, as
in Canada, a prosecution for inciting racial hatred requires the consent of
the attorney general,[18] while a prosecution for the offence of blasphemy does
not. A blasphemy prosecution can be launched privately, and *The Satanic
Verses* blasphemy case was a private prosecution.[19]

The prosecution failed because the British law of blasphemy relates to
Christianity only. The allegation was that *The Satanic Verses* was a blasphemy
on Islam. Although, for the purpose of this discussion, the case went off on
a tangent, there is an extensive discussion in the judgment on what blasphemy is. The judgement refers to the case of *R. v. Lemon* and to *Stephen's
Digest of the Criminal Law*.

In the case of *R. v. Lemon*,[20] Judge King-Hamilton said that blasphemous
libel is an attack on religion so scurrilous, abusive, or offensive as to outrage
the feelings of any member of, or sympathizer with, the religion and would
tend to lead to a breach of the peace. *Stephen's Digest of the Criminal Law*[21]
says: "The test to be applied is as to the manner in which the doctrines are
advocated and not as to the substance of the doctrines themselves."

Because there are hate propaganda laws on the books, there are periodic calls by offended groups for seizure or prosecution of offensive material. The decision on what not to prosecute, when these calls for prosecution are made, tells us something about what is not hate propaganda.

The pro-Zionist novel *The Haj*, by Leon Uris, was investigated in Canada after Arab organizations said the book slurred and maligned Arabs. No charges were laid.[22] Canadian federal officials conducted a probe of the anti-Communist film, *Red Dawn*, without legal action. Canada Customs, in 1986, examined a film sympathetic to then jailed, black South African leader Nelson Mandela, and let it through customs. The phrase "Yankee go home" was not considered by Canadian authorities to be hate speech. Activists distributing pamphlets with those words were arrested in 1975 in Toronto, but after consideration, no charges were laid and the youths were released. In 1988, Salman Rushdie's *The Satanic Verses* was examined by Canada Customs and also found not to constitute hate propaganda.[23]

Critics of anti-hate laws point to these examples with dismay. They argue that the mere fact that charges in these cases were considered is, itself, an argument against the enactment of such laws. Mme. Justice McLachlin, in the *Keegstra* case, in dissent, said: "the record amply demonstrates that intemperate statements against identifiable groups, particularly if they represent an unpopular viewpoint, may attract state involvement or calls for police action."[24] Alan Borovoy, in his book *When Freedoms Collide*, writes: "even though no charges are laid in a case, official investigations tend to create a chill over the robust exercise of freedom of expression."[25]

There are two answers to this criticism. One is that a law will be a lot more uncertain when it is new and unused than when it is old and used. Through time and example we learn what law means. Uncertainty, even if it exists initially, dissipates. The texts that were questioned before will not be questioned later, because the questions have been answered. These answers not only tell us about those texts, but also about others like them.

The second answer is that to fear mere investigation without prosecution is to be altogether too fearful. An argument that there should be no hate propaganda laws because otherwise innocent acts might be examined to determine their compliance is not just an argument against hate propaganda laws. It is an argument against all laws. Once we have any law, everyone potentially becomes subject to scrutiny for compliance with the law.

Giving the authorities power to determine whether laws are broken cannot be improper if the law itself is proper. If a law is worth having, then it is worth giving the authorities power to investigate whether or not the law is broken. The mere power of investigation cannot throw into question the value of a law.

Of course, if the law is of little value, the power to investigate breaches of the law is a legitimate matter of concern. However, if the law is of little value, it is unnecessary to question the power of investigation to throw doubt on it. This argument from free speech absolutists is circular. If you do not believe in anti-hate laws, then for sure, you do not believe in giving authorities the power to investigate breaches of anti-hate laws. If you do believe in anti-hate laws, or are uncertain whether they should exist or not, the mere power of investigation that goes with them tells you nothing.

The same can be said of abuse of the law. To free speech absolutists, the examples, taken at their worst, are not mere mistaken applications of the law or potential mistakes, but rather malicious attempts to chill legitimate speech. A law, so it is argued, that lends itself to that sort of potential abuse is a bad law. A government that tolerates or itself propagates hate speech is likely to be an oppressive government that violates human rights in other ways as well. The tools of government are used by that sort of government as tools of oppression. To ask oppressive governments to ban hate speech may seem like inviting these governments to use yet another tool for oppression.

Any law, however, can be misused to chill legitimate dissent. A person can be falsely accused of murder for political reasons, just as a person can be falsely accused of propagating hatred for political reasons. In Canada and the United Kingdom, it is easier to charge a person falsely of murder than to charge a person falsely of propagating hatred. To launch a prosecution for propagating hatred in Canada requires the consent of the Attorney General of Canada. Any private individual can launch a prosecution for murder.

No one would argue against a law prohibiting murder simply because of the potential for abuse. Similarly we should not argue against a law prohibiting hate speech, simply because of the potential for abuse.

Like the criticism of potential abuse, much of the criticism of anti-hate laws for vagueness is criticism of a borderline variety. Hypothetical problematic examples are conjectured. The puzzlement these hypotheses generate is used to damn the law itself. Yet, that sort of criticism is unfair to anti-hate laws, as it would be to any law.

No law can be considered vague simply because one can construct hypothetical examples that pose legal problems. Dissents and reversals on appeal occur regularly in court cases without calling the laws themselves into question. The required clarity in the law is clarity at the core, not clarity at the edges. As long as there is a clear core meaning, the legal system is there to decide disputes at the edges of the law.

There is a disingenuousness about those who proclaim uncertainty. In other areas of the law, it is unusual for people to boast of their ignorance. The general advice one would give to someone who knows nothing is to keep quiet. When people make a point of saying they do not know what hate speech is, they are, in reality, pursuing another agenda.

The core concern of free speech absolutists is not clarity. Clarity is, after all, a concern in all areas of the law, not just speech laws. The concern for free speech absolutists is, of course, freedom of speech. A charge of vagueness is just a weapon they use in what they see as a battle over freedom of speech.

When I say that free speech absolutists are disingenuous when they charge anti-hate laws with vagueness, I do not mean to suggest they do not believe the charge. I simply point out that the adversaries of anti-hate laws are free speech advocates, not clarity advocates. Clarity in anti-hate laws would not satisfy free speech absolutists. Since clarity would not satisfy them, they are not particularly eager to find it.

Free speech absolutists seize on uncertainty, look for confusion, revel in opacity of anti-hate laws. Lack of clarity in anti-hate laws is, for them, a weakness in the opposing side, something to be highlighted and targeted. Free speech absolutists will insist on the existence of vagueness in anti-hate laws as long as it is remotely tenable to do so. If it ceases to be tenable, they will simply move on to other arguments, rather than abandon their opposition to anti-hate laws.

I believe in the value of anti-hate laws. All the same, I am quite prepared to concede that if anti-hate laws are vague, we should not have them. Vagueness would vitiate the laws, render them useless, and indeed threaten free speech unduly. Yet, that sort of concession is something free speech absolutists will never make. Free speech absolutists will never concede that, if anti-hate laws can be made precise, they are then unobjectionable.

For those who are genuinely undecided whether there should or should not be anti-hate laws, the charge of vagueness has to be taken seriously. However, when free speech absolutists say that anti-hate laws are vague, while their arguments should not be ignored, they should be taken with a grain of salt.

The charge of vagueness stems from an inability to appreciate subjectively the danger of hate speech. Critics will say that hate propaganda laws are vague because they are too subjective. My response is that the problem these laws face is the reverse: hate propaganda laws are not subjective enough.

With virtually every other law, the risk to the judge or the jury from the violation of the law is immediately obvious. Even if the gun is not pointed at the judge or jurors, even if the drunk driver is not bearing down on the judge or jurors, they can easily imagine themselves in the shoes of the victim or potential victim. They can feel subjectively frightened by the danger.

With hate propaganda, this leap of imagination is more difficult. Those susceptible to hate propaganda messages are not, one would hope, judges or jurors. Civil libertarians who argue against hate propaganda laws are, we can assume from their vocation as civil libertarians, impervious to hate messages. Because they have no subjective feel for the power of the messages, the whole notion of hate propaganda seems to them so vague as to be meaningless. Hate propaganda messages are to these people akin to communication in a foreign language they do not understand.

Of course, a foreign language can be learned; it can be interpreted. Interpreting hate propaganda messages to those who do not understand the dangers intuitively, immediately, means focusing on the impact of those messages. Hate propaganda is not going to make civil libertarians hate others, but it will lead some people to hatred, people who can be identified by a profile of characteristics.

It is understandable that when we talk about limiting speech, there is concern about what the limitation is. Certainly any limitation that is vague is an undue risk to free speech. One cannot fault those who ask us to define hate propaganda, to explain what it is. However, at the end of the day, explanations are available. Definitions can be given. The question: "What is hate propaganda?" can be answered.

Notes

1.   *C.H.R.C v. Taylor* (1990) 75 D.L.R. (4th) 577 at 626.
2.   *R. v. Heywood* [1994] 3 S.C.R. 761
3.   At page 59.
4.   *Terry Long* Decision, C.H.R.C., July 25, 1989, at page 24.
5.   October 1988 page 13.
6.   T. Cohen, "Race Relations and the Law," page 116.
7.   See *Mohammad v. Mariposa Storgg* 14 C.H.R.R. D/215, para 24 to 27, B.C. Council on Human Pights, December 18, 1990.

8.   (1990) 61 C.C.C.(3d) 1 at page 59.

9.   (1988) 43 C.C.C. (3d) 193 (Ont. C.A.).

10. *Smith Kline & French Laboratories v. A.G. Can.* (1986) 34 D.L.R. (4th) 584 at 591–2.

11. *Andrews v. Law Society of B.C.* (1989) 56 D.L.R. (4th) 1 at 24. See also Madame Justice Wilson at page 32.

12. At page 21.

13. Reasons, page 27.

14. *When Freedoms Collide*, p. 44.

15. Section 14(1).

16. 5 C.H.H.R. D/2074.

17. See *Sask.H.R.C. v. Engineering Students* (1989) 56 D.L.R. (4th) 1 at 602 (Sask.C.A., per Cameron J.A.).

18. Public Order Act 1936, Section 5A(5).

19. *R. v. Chief Magistrate ex. v. Choudhury* (1991) 1 All.E.R. 306 (Q.B.D.)

20. (1979) 1 AII.E.R. 898, 1979 A.C. 617.

21. Ninth Edition, 1950.

22. See Alan Borovoy, *When Freedoms Collide*, p. 43.

23. See *R. v. Keegstra* at page 120.

24. At page 120.

25. At page 43.

Chapter Five

Holocaust Denial

IS HOLOCAUST DENIAL HATE SPEECH? Should Holocaust denial be specifically prohibited by law?

As I mentioned in Chapter One, French National Front leader Jean-Marie Le Pen was convicted for calling the Holocaust a detail of history. For hate speech since World War II, the exact opposite is true. The issue of the Holocaust, in the form of Holocaust denial, has become central to the promotion of hatred in North America and Europe.

Holocaust denial is not just a current form of incitement of hatred against Jews. It has become the leading form of modern incitement of hatred against Jews. By examining Holocaust denial, we see who the hate promoters are. We see their techniques. We can understand their psychology and profile.

Hatred of Jews was the rallying cry of the Nazis. They incited this hatred to generate support and seize power in Germany. It became their justification for destroying democracy in Germany and invading the rest of Europe. The Nazi phenomenon was the individual hate-monger writ large, and like the individual hate-monger, the Nazi organizations did not incite hatred against Jews as an incidental, detachable part of their ideology. It was central to the Nazi core. It was the reason for the existence of the Nazi party, and the motivating force behind virtually all that it did. Without the incitement of hatred against Jews, the Nazi party would not have existed, would not have come to power, would not have started World War II, would not have invaded and occupied continental Europe and Northern Africa, would not have destroyed democracy wherever they went, would not have killed eleven million innocent civilians, including six million Jews.

Contemporary right-wing extremist organizations, which splinter in a thousand different ways, have this one belief in common. They have learned well from the initial success of the Nazis. The incitement of hatred against

Jews is a political tool for right-wing extremists which goes far beyond attacking Jews. That the road to power for these groups is whipping up hatred against Jews is illustrated by the phenomenon of virulent antisemitism in countries with no or virtually no Jewish populations. The incitement to hatred against Jews was and is, not just a threat to Jews, but a threat to peace, a threat to democracy, and a threat to all humanity.

The Holocaust, however, discredits right-wing extremists everywhere. Endorsement of the Holocaust, the belief that the Holocaust rightly happened, truly belongs to the lunatic fringe. Neo-Nazis well realize that they have no hope of building a mass movement or even significant support based on a defence of the Holocaust.

For contemporary right-wing extremists, Holocaust denial becomes a political necessity. Holocaust denial, for these extremists, serves a dual agenda. Denial co-opts the gullible into the extremists' ideology of Jewish fraud, Jewish world control, Jewish greed. As well, it legitimizes the very ideology which the Holocaust has delegitimized.

Holocaust denial is a particularly insidious form of hate speech because of its disguise as contested history. In an era of human rights discourse, upfront assertions of Jewish fraud, Jewish world control, Jewish greed find little or no audience, even amongst those who may be disposed to prejudicial views. Holocaust denial, at least superficially, appeals to ignorance rather than prejudice. By putting a thin veil of factual bafflegab over its appeals to racial prejudice, Holocaust denial caters to the desire for respectability of those who preach hatred and those who succumb to hatred.

While incitement of hatred against Jews has historically taken many bizarre forms, Holocaust denial is the one contemporary expression that encapsulates the whole phenomenon. Like most hate speech, the appeal of Holocaust denial is not apparent to those not inclined to hate. Like other antisemitic slurs, Holocaust denial seems absurd to those who are tolerant and grounded in reality. The denial may seem to reflect poorly on the deniers and no-one else. How Holocaust denial may lead to the hatred of Jews needs explanation.

The Holocaust, the World War II, Nazi-organized murder of six million Jews and the attempt to exterminate the whole Jewish people, is one of the best documented events of all history. There are many survivors still alive today who can testify to what happened. There are many perpetrators who have been accused, tried, convicted, and punished. Their trials have left extensive records from the testimony of witnesses and filings of exhibits.

There are museums and libraries throughout the world filled with documents and artifacts of the Holocaust, including Yad Vashem in Jerusalem, the Holocaust Museum in Washington, the Auschwitz Camp Museum in Poland, and the Berlin Documentation Centre in Germany. The remains of extermination camps still exist, such as Birkenau near Auschwitz and Majdanek. There are films, memoires, TV programs all grounded in the Holocaust. There are monuments where the victims were killed and the survivors now live, commemorating what happened.

One has to ask what Holocaust denial means, given this historical record. When a person says that the Holocaust did not exist, given all these court cases, all the monuments and museums, all the memoires and films, that person is alleging a fraud on a massive scale. Obviously, if the Holocaust did not happen, the survivors, the museum curators, the historians, the librarians, the prosecutors, the judges and juries, the movie and TV producers, the reporters are not just confused or forgetful. They are lying.

Holocaust denial, by its very nature, is an allegation of massive fraud. The allegation of massive fraud is not separate from the allegation that the Holocaust never happened but, by its very nature, implicit in it. Some forms of Holocaust denial actually assert this fraud. Others do not. However, it is not necessary to say the word "fraud"; the allegation of fraud is there even where it is unspoken.

One has to ask further who would be behind such a fraud, if one accepts the fraud in the first place. The answer of Holocaust deniers is the Jews. Although much Holocaust evidence comes from non-Jews and much of the documentation is Nazi German documentation, information from survivors and the organized Jewish community is essential to the memory of the Holocaust. Again, some Holocaust denial material explicitly accuses the Jewish community of perpetrating the fraud of the Holocaust. However, even the Holocaust denial material that says nothing about Jewish fraud implies this accusation. It is impossible to extricate Holocaust denial from this allegation of Jewish fraud, even where it is not explicit.

If we continue to follow this line of inquiry, one has to ask how such a fraud could be committed. How could the media, the libraries, the museums, the courts be filled with information about the Holocaust, if the Holocaust never happened? The answer deniers give or imply is Jewish control of the media, the libraries, the museums, the courts. Holocaust denial is a mutant of the standard, historical antisemitic smear that Jews control the world for their own evil interests. Here too, some forms of Holocaust denial state this explicitly. Even the forms of Holocaust denial that do not have this antisemitic conclusion out front have it hidden in the background.

On the descent to hatred, the largest movement a person has to make is the leap from the historical record to Holocaust denial. Once that leap has been made, the belief in Jewish fraud is just a small and inevitable step.

Finally, we have to ask, continuing to assume the fraud, why the Jewish community would carry out such a hoax. The answer Holocaust deniers give, sometimes explicitly, but otherwise implicitly, is for sympathy, for support for Israel, for reparations. Again, here we see Holocaust denial as a modern dress for a traditional antisemitic slur, the slur that Jews are greedy.

Deborah Lipstadt, in her book *Denying the Holocaust* has written:

> The central assertion for the deniers is that Jews are not victims but victimizers. They stole billions in reparations, destroyed Germany's good name by spreading the myth of the Holocaust, and won international sympathy because of what they claimed had been done to them. In the paramount miscarriage of injustice, they used the world's sympathy to displace another people so that the state of Israel could be established.[1]

I have heard it said that Holocaust denial is not hate speech because the true agenda of deniers is not hatred of Jews but legitimization of Nazi Germany. My response to that argument is that what deniers are attempting to legitimize by their Holocaust denial is the antisemitism of Nazi Germany, the incitement of hatred of Jews on which the Third Reich was built.

A person filled with racial hatred is never a thinking person with just a glitch in his thinking. Racial hatred is a world view that encompasses the relation of the individual with all his surroundings. A person who denies the Holocaust hates Jews. A person propagating Holocaust denial is spreading hate speech. There are no anodyne forms of Holocaust denial. No one believes, can believe, Holocaust denial in isolation from his other beliefs. Holocaust denial is an indicator of a world view that includes the belief in Jewish fraud, Jewish world control, Jewish greed.

I have been discussing Holocaust denial as a theoretical construct, Holocaust denial isolated from any other anti-Jewish statement. In addition, we must look at Holocaust denial as it actually exists.

It is impossible to separate Holocaust denial from Holocaust deniers. Every known Holocaust denier is a rabid antisemite, not just because he denies the Holocaust, but in other more patent, traditional ways. This tells us something about what Holocaust denial is.

Who are the Holocaust deniers? In Canada, the best known are Ernst Zundel, Jim Keegstra, and Malcolm Ross. In the United Kingdom, the most infamous is David Irving. In France, the most notorious is Robert Faurisson. It is stating the obvious to observe that Zundel, Keegstra, Ross, Irving, and Faurisson do not restrict their anti-Jewish utterances to Holocaust denial alone. This quintet are classic hard core Jew haters.

Four Canadian juries and a provincial human rights commission have found Holocaust denial to be hate speech. Because the juries made the findings in criminal prosecutions, the findings were that Holocaust denial is hate speech beyond a reasonable doubt.

Ernst Zundel was prosecuted under a provision of the criminal code that prohibited wilful publication of news that the publisher knew to be false and that caused or was likely to cause injury or mischief to a public interest.[2] The false news was Holocaust denial. The injury to the public interest was incitement of hatred against Jews. Zundel was convicted. The Ontario Court of Appeal struck down the conviction for errors in the admission of evidence and the charge to the jury. The court sent the case back for a new trial. In a second trial, Zundel was again convicted.

The Supreme Court of Canada struck down the provision of the criminal code under which Zundel was convicted as unconstitutional, because it violated the guarantee in the Canadian Charter of Rights and Freedoms of freedom of expression.[3] However, that decision did not and could not overturn the finding of fact of both juries that Holocaust denial was hate speech beyond a reasonable doubt.

The minority in the *Zundel* case at the Supreme Court of Canada, in dissent, but not on this point, said:

> [Holocaust denial] materials do not merely operate to foment discord and hatred, but they do so in an extraordinarily duplicitous manner. By couching their propaganda as the banal product of disinterested research, the purveyors of these works seek to circumvent rather than appeal to the critical faculties of their audience.[4]

Jim Keegstra, a school teacher, was prosecuted in Alberta under the criminal code provision banning the wilful propagation of hatred for what he had been teaching in the schools. One of his "lessons" was that the Holocaust did not happen and was created by Jews to gain sympathy for themselves. He was convicted in 1985 by a jury in a trial before Mr. Justice McKenzie of the Alberta Court of Queen's Bench.

That conviction went to the Supreme Court of Canada on the constitutionality of the law. The Supreme Court of Canada held the law constitutional in 1990, overturning a unanimous Alberta Court of Appeal. The case went back to the Alberta Court of Appeal and that court ordered a new trial because of flaws in choosing the jury.

A second jury convicted Keegstra in 1992 on the same charge. The Alberta Court of Appeal, in the third of a remarkable series of judgments siding with Keegstra, ordered a third new trial. The Supreme Court of Canada in February, 1996, eleven years after the original conviction, overturned the Alberta Court of Appeal a second time and reinstated the second conviction. The case went back to the Alberta Court of Appeal on sentencing alone.

Malcolm Ross taught elementary school in New Brunswick and outside of school hours conducted a hate propaganda campaign against Jews, including Holocaust denial. Professor Brian Bruce, as a Board of Inquiry appointed by the New Brunswick Human Rights Commission, wrote in 1991:

> The writings and comments of Malcolm Ross cannot be categorized as falling within the scope of scholarly discussion which might remove them from the scope of section 5 [of the New Brunswick Human Rights Act]. The materials are not expressed in a fashion that objectively summarizes findings and conclusions or propositions. While the writings may have involved some substantial research, Malcolm Ross' primary purpose is clearly to attack the truthfulness, integrity, dignity, and motives of Jewish persons rather than the presentation of scholarly research. As an example, much reference was made in evidence to the comments in Malcolm Ross' books regarding the numbers killed in the Jewish Holocaust. The facts as to the actual numbers killed was not questioned in a scholarly fashion, but rather portrayed in a fashion so as to buttress Malcolm Ross' position that there is a Jewish conspiracy to take over the world.[5]

This case went to the Supreme Court of Canada on the legality of the remedy ordered by Professor Bruce, that Ross must stay out of the classroom, and must stop his hate propaganda altogether if he wants to keep a job with the School Board. However, Professor Bruce's findings of fact were not challenged.

David Irving filed a libel lawsuit in the United Kingdom against Deborah Lipstadt, complaining that her book *Denying the Holocaust* accused him of being a Nazi apologist and an admirer of Hitler who has distorted facts and manipuled documents in support of his contention that the Holocaust did not take place. Mr. Justice Gray of the Queen's Bench Division, in giving judgment against David Irving in April, 2000 wrote:[6]

> [Irving's] words are directed against Jews, either individually or collectively, in the sense that they are by turns hostile, critical, offensive, and derisory in their references to semitic people, their characteristics and appearances. A few examples will suffice: Irving has made claims that the Jews deserve to be disliked; that they brought the Holocaust on themselves; that Jewish financiers are crooked; that Jews generate anti-semitism by their greed and mendacity; that it is bad luck for Mr. Wiesel to be called "Weasel"; that Jews are amongst the scum of humanity; that Jews scurry and hide furtively, unable to stand the light of day; that Simon Wiesenthal has a hideous, leering evil face; and so on. . . . The inference which in my judgment is clearly to be drawn from what Irving has said and written is that he is anti-semitic.

Robert Faurisson was convicted in April 1991 for violating the French Holocaust denial law and required to pay substantial fines and costs. He appealed unsuccessfully in December 1992 to the Paris Court of Appeal.

Faurisson then petitioned the United Nations Human Rights Committee claiming that France, by enacting the law and convicting him, had violated the International Covenant on Civil and Political Rights. The French government observed to the Human Rights Committee that:

> Under the guise of historical research, [Faurisson] seeks to accuse the Jewish people of having falsified and distorted the facts of the Second World War and thereby having created the myth of the extermination of the Jews. That Mr. Faurisson designated a former Chief Rabbi (Grand rabbin) as the author of the law of 13 July 1990, whereas the law is of parliamentary origin, is another illustration of the author's methods to fuel anti-semitic propaganda.[7]

The Human Rights Committee, in dismissing Faurisson's complaint in December 1996, ruled: "the statements made by the author, read in their full context, were of a nature as to raise or strengthen anti-semitic feelings."[8]

Holocaust denial is a form of camouflage racists use to hide their more explicit racism. If we look at the historical genesis of the obligation to prohibit hate speech in the international standards, and in Canadian law, the primary example drafters had in mind was the Holocaust and the hate speech that led to it.[9] While genocide occurred both before the Holocaust and since, the Holocaust genocide was unique in its dimensions, in techniques, and its political significance. It makes eminent sense to highlight in the general hate speech prohibition the very phenomenon that led to that prohibition.

Even for those who are prepared to accept that hate speech in general should be prohibited, one can ask whether, tactically, it makes sense to prohibit and prosecute Holocaust denial. The question of the truth as a defence bears on this issue. Depending on how the law is framed, if there is no specific prohibition of Holocaust denial, a prosecution of Holocaust denial as hate speech can be open to the defence that the Holocaust did not happen. Even though such a defence would presumably never succeed, it is important not to allow a court room to be used as an arena for racist propaganda.

Where the truth defence is allowed, any prosecution of Holocaust denial as hate speech is an invitation to the accused to use the courtroom as a platform for Holocaust denial. It is sometimes asked: Would not a more effective response to Holocaust denial be stripping the camouflage from the deniers outside of court, in the public arena?

There is a middle course, so this view goes, between debating deniers, which gives them legitimacy and suggests that their lies are tenable, and prosecuting deniers. That course is to show that quotes are misquotes, that the footnotes refer to sources that are not there or say nothing like what the footnotes suggest they say, to expose the lies, manipulation, the fraud. Deborah Lipstadt, in *Denying the Holocaust*, has done just that. Ken McVay has been fighting that battle on the internet.

In my view, exposure and prosecution are not alternatives. They are complementary activities, not just for Holocaust denial, but for all hate speech. It would be a mistake to prosecute in isolation from exposure outside the courtroom. It would be equally a mistake to abandon the remedy of prosecution. Out of court exposure shows the Holocaust deniers to be the frauds that they are. Prosecution and conviction are statements by society that Holocaust deniers are not just frauds but hate-mongers, not just wrong but destroyers of values democracy holds dear. Prohibition, prosecution, conviction and punishment are, themselves, part of the education effort.

Even if you are convinced both that Holocaust denial is hate speech, and that Holocaust denial should be specifically prohibited, can it be specifically prohibited? In Canada, would Holocaust denial survive a legal challenge that it is a violation of the guarantee of freedom of expression in the Charter of Rights and Freedoms?

Germany has an offence of Holocaust denial in its criminal law.[10] The majority in the *Zundel* case at the Supreme Court of Canada, in the course of striking down the provision under which Zundel was convicted, referred to the German offence and said that it was "a much more finely tailored provision [than the false news provision of the Canadian criminal code] to which different considerations might well apply."[11] Because a Holocaust denial prohibition is as specific as can be, its chilling effect on free speech is as limited as it can be. A Holocaust denial prohibition, by reason of the fact that it is specific, is ideally suited to survive a Charter of Rights, freedom of expression challenge in Canada.

Banning Holocaust denial as hate speech can be done, and should be done. It is more than the protection of the Jewish minority that is at stake, important as that is. If we who want to defend peace, democracy, and respect for all human rights have ourselves learned anything from the Nazi experience, it is the need to combat incitement of hatred against Jews. This is a lesson for all humanity.

Notes

1. A Plume Book, 1994, p. 23.
2. Section 181, Criminal Code, *Revised Statutes of Canada*, 1985, Chapter C–46.
3. *Zundel v. The Queen*, August 17, 1992, Court Number 21811, judgment of the majority, McLachlin J., p. 38.
4. Reasons of the minority, Cory and Iacobucci JJ., p. 41.
5. Decision of the Board of Inquiry, August 28, 1991, p. 54; Case on Appeal in the Supreme Court of Canada, p. 5069.
6. Judgement of April 11, 2000, paragraphs 13.101–105.
7. United Nations Document CCPR/C/58/D/550/1993, 16 December 1996, paragraph 7.6.
8. Paragraph 9.6.
9. See Stephanie Farrior, "Moulding the Matrix: The Historical and Theoretical Foundations of International Law Concerning Hate Speech," *Berkeley Journal of International Law 1* (1996) 14.
10. *Criminal Code*, article 185.
11. Majority judgment, p. 29.

Chapter Six

The Zundel Prosecution

THE PROSECUTION OF ERNST ZUNDEL for knowingly spreading false news has become, all on its own, an argument for not prosecuting promoters of hatred. Opponents of the banning of hate speech have zeroed in on this case as a prime example of why hate speech should not be banned. Any argument for the banning of hate speech has to confront the arguments against banning that the *Zundel* prosecution generated.

Alan Dershowitz in his book *Chutzpah* wrote:

> Prior to the commencement of the criminal prosecutions [against Zundel], the pamphlets and speeches of these neo-Nazis were limited in their impact. But the trials brought all the professional Holocaust deniers out from under their rocks. . . . Inevitably, criminal charges of this kind result in the Holocaust itself being put on trial. And so, in 1985, a Canadian courtroom became the platform for a legal debate that should never have taken place—a debate about an incontrovertible historical fact.

In a footnote, Dershowitz adds: "The defendant emerged as a victim, if not hero, in the eyes of many Canadians."[1]

Criminal lawyer Edward Greenspan has said:

> To challenge Zundel on the Holocaust is to meet him on his own terms. To do so is to give the allegation an aura of legitimacy. It also perpetrates the indignity. The evil is that ordinary people, decent Canadians forty or fifty years removed from the events of Nazi Germany will begin to believe the lies, have doubts, and again stroke the fires of antisemitism. If that is the real evil, then surely it is counterproductive to provide free of

67

charge the platform for the espousing of those views, through the legitimate media so that they almost take on an air of respectability.[2]

Alan Borovoy has said:

> There were solemn debates in court over the monstrous claim that
> Auschwitz was a Jewish country club rather than a Nazi death camp. The
> prosecutor, not the defendant, called a Gentile [non-Jewish] banker to
> the stand and asked him whether he was in the pay of a Jewish con-
> spiracy. This is not necessarily to blame the prosecutor for using those
> tactics. Understandably, he felt he had to meet every element of the
> accused's defence. It is simply to recognize that the risk of farce is en-
> demic to the very nature of the proceedings.
>
> Nor should we overlook what a criminal prosecution can do for a
> hitherto obscure propagandist. Outside of Jewish circles and a few gov-
> ernment offices, Zundel had been a virtual unknown. By the time his
> trial was in full swing, he had become a household name. . . . I do not
> raise this issue of publicity because of any fear that the trials will attract
> a significant following for the hate-mongers. I simply regard the trials as
> an affront to our dignity and common sense.[3]

What are the lessons to be learned from the *Zundel* prosecution? Are
they, as Borovoy, Dershowitz, and Greenspan have argued, that there never
should be any hate speech prosecutions? Or, is it merely that such prosecutions should be done differently? I would argue that the *Zundel* prosecution
was not a fair test of hate speech laws, that the failures of the *Zundel* prosecution are not inherent in hate speech prosecution generally and that hate
speech can be effectively prosecuted.

Sabina Citron, a Holocaust survivor, launched a private prosecution against
Ernst Zundel. He was prosecuted under a provision of the criminal code that
prohibited wilful publication of news that the publisher knew to be false and
that caused or was likely to cause injury or mischief to a public interest.[4] The
false news was Holocaust denial. The injury to the public interest was incitement of hatred against Jews. The Attorney General of Ontario took over the
prosecution and assumed conduct of it.

At the trial, the prosecution led evidence to prove the Holocaust did
happen. After the prosecution put in its case, and before the defence had
started its case, the prosecution asked that the court take judicial notice of
the Holocaust.

When judicial notice is taken of a fact, no formal evidence of that fact has to be introduced at the trial or hearing. Judicial notice is defined as "The court's recognition of certain facts that can be confirmed by consulting sources of indisputable accuracy, thereby relieving one party of the burden of producing evidence to prove these facts. A court can use this doctrine to admit as 'proved' such facts that are common knowledge to a judicial professional or to an average, well-informed citizen."[5]

The court in the first *Zundel* prosecution refused to take judicial notice of the Holocaust. Zundel was convicted, by a jury, and sentenced to fifteen months in jail and three years probation. A term of the probation order was that Zundel, during the three years, not publish anything about the Holocaust.

Zundel appealed to the Ontario Court of Appeal. The prosecution, on the appeal, contested the trial judge's decision on judicial notice, but the court of appeal refused to overturn the decision, saying that trial judges have a wide discretion as to matters on which they will take judicial notice.

Zundel also challenged the constitutionality of the law on the grounds of overbreadth and vagueness. The court of appeal said the law was constitutional. The false news that was criminalized must, according to the law, cause injury to the public interest. What, the defence asked, is the public interest? The court of appeal said the concept of public interest is not vague or overly broad bearing in mind it is used in relation to a statement known by the accused to be false. Furthermore, the court added, Zundel faced a charge limited to the public interest in racial and social tolerance. He was left in no doubt as to the manner in which his conduct was considered offensive.

The Ontario Court of Appeal nonetheless struck down the conviction for errors in the admission of evidence and the charge to the jury.[6] The court sent the case back for a new trial.

Zundel was convicted again, at his second trial. This time the prosecution asked for judicial notice of the Holocaust at the beginning, rather than in the middle, and got it. Specifically the court took judicial notice of the mass murder and extermination of Jews of Europe by the Nazi regime during the Second World War. However, the trial judge declined to take judicial notice of whether the mass murder of the Jews occurred by reason of any policy of the Nazi government; he did not take judicial notice of the specific numbers who died; and he did not take judicial notice of the use of gas chambers. All these last three issues remained factual issues before the court.

Zundel had made factual assertions in the material he published that there was no Nazi policy of Jewish mass extermination; that the number killed was not six million but less than 300,000; that the gas chambers did not exist. The prosecution attempted to prove that all of these statements were false. Counsel for Zundel attempted to prove they were true.

A jury convicted Zundel a second time. His sentence this time was nine months in prison. It was imposed May 13, 1988 by the trial judge, Justice Ron Thomas. Zundel appealed again first to the Ontario Court of Appeal and then to the Supreme Court of Canada. Pending appeal he was let out on bail. One of his bail terms was that he not publish anything in support of his view that the Holocaust did not happen.

In the court of appeal, the defence did not contest the fact of which the court took judicial notice, that many Jews were murdered by Nazis. The only concern of the defence was that taking judicial notice of mass killings, which was not in issue, might be confused by the jury with taking judicial notice of a policy of mass killings which was in issue. The court of appeal held that the trial judge, in his charge to the jury, was sufficiently clear in distinguishing between the two issues that there could have been no confusion in the minds of the jury.

In the second appeal, the Supreme Court of Canada struck down the provision of the criminal code as unconstitutional, because it violated the guarantee in the Canadian Charter of Rights and Freedoms on freedom of expression. According to the majority, the provision in the code about mischief to the public interest was overbroad. The provision was not appropriately measured and restrained regarding the evil addressed.[7] However, that decision of the majority did not and could not overturn the finding of fact of both juries that Zundel was guilty, beyond a reasonable doubt, of wilfully spreading news he knew to be false, that the Holocaust did not exist.

One has to wonder, given that the prosecution took the position that the public interest Zundel injured was the public's interest in preventing incitement to racial hatred, why the Attorney General of Ontario never charged Zundel under the hate propaganda provision of the criminal code. Sabina Citron did not prosecute Zundel for wilfully propagating hatred because legally she couldn't. A false news prosecution could be launched privately; a hate propaganda prosecution requires the consent of the attorney general.

If the Attorney General of Ontario felt that Holocaust denial was not hate speech, that would have been an understandable motivation, even if in my view not a good reason, why consent to a hate propaganda prosecution was withheld. However, once the attorney general took over the false news prosecution and proceeded to argue that the public mischief from Holocaust denial was hate speech, the refusal to consent to a hate propaganda prosecution became inexplicable. It remains a mystery to this day.

For those who oppose state prohibition of hate propaganda, the *Zundel* prosecution was a mistake from start to finish. Even for those who support the intervention of the state to prevent the dissemination of hate propaganda, as I do, there has to be severe reservations about the *Zundel* prosecution. If Zundel had been acquitted, his prosecution would have been a disaster for supporters of state prohibition of hate propaganda. Even his conviction leaves substantial grounds for dissatisfaction.

The mistakes made at the first trial were the least serious cause for concern for the prosecution or for the court. The mistakes made at the first trial were corrected at the second trial. Everyone learned from their mistakes. Yet, for the public at large, those mistakes were the most troublesome aspect of the trial.

The first trial was a tragedy of errors, errors by the prosecution, errors by the judge, and errors by the media. The most egregious mistake the prosecution made was failure to ask for judicial notice of the Holocaust at the beginning of the trial. The prosecution did ask for judicial notice of the Holocaust twice, once at the end of its own case, and again at the end of the defence case. Both times the request was refused. After the prosecution led evidence of the Holocaust, the judge refused judicial notice because he believed it would have the effect, in the eyes of the public, of not providing the accused with an opportunity to make full answer and defence. After all the evidence was in, the judge refused judicial notice because the allegation against the accused was that he had published something inherently false and the prosecution had the burden of proving that allegation.

In light of the refusal of judicial notice when it was asked, one cannot say for certain that, if the prosecution had asked for judicial notice at the beginning of the trial, it would have been granted. However, it might have been. The situation is significantly different after evidence has been led in part, or whole, from the situation where no evidence has been led.

One cannot say the delay in requesting judicial notice was a mistake in achieving a conviction, since the prosecution got a conviction. The prosecution may have thought that evidence of the Holocaust led in court would be more likely to result in a conviction than mere judicial notice of the Holocaust. If that was the thinking, it may well have been correct.

The mistake lay elsewhere, in the public dimension of the trial. Without judicial notice being taken of the Holocaust, the Holocaust became an issue. Instead of Zundel alone being put on trial, instead of his hate propaganda being put on trial, the Holocaust itself was put on trial.

While outside the courtroom the existence of the Holocaust was incontrovertible, within the courtroom, the existence of the Holocaust became a live issue. Witnesses were called for, and witnesses against. Documents were submitted for, and documents against.

I have called the trial a tragedy of errors and this is where the tragedy lay. The suffering of survivors was held up to ridicule, claimed to be a pretence. By providing a forum for the denial of the murder of millions, the victims were being assaulted twice over. The courtroom became the scene of the attempted murder of the memory of the victims.

Whether or not evidence of the Holocaust made a conviction more likely, it was not essential for a conviction. At the second trial, the prosecution asked for judicial notice of the Holocaust from the very beginning. The judge said to the jury:

> The mass murder and extermination of Jews in Europe by the Nazi regime during the Second World War is so generally known and accepted that it could not reasonably be questioned by reasonable persons. I directed you then and I direct you now that you will accept that as a fact. The Crown was not required to prove it. It was in the light of that direction that you should examine the evidence in this case and the issues before you.

Yet, Zundel was convicted all the same.

If Zundel had been prosecuted for propagating hatred, the legal issue would have changed. Instead of the issue being whether the news Zundel was spreading was false, or whether he knew it to be false, the issue would have been whether Zundel was wilfully promoting hatred against an identifiable group. More specifically, the issue would have been not whether Zundel's Holocaust denial was false, or whether he knew it to be false, but whether by his Holocaust denial, he was wilfully promoting hatred against Jews.

Even in a prosecution for promoting hatred, the Canadian criminal code now allows truth as a defence.[8] In a prosecution for promoting hatred, Zundel could have pleaded in his defence that the Holocaust never happened. So, even in that context, judicial notice of the Holocaust would be important. Alternatively, as I argue later in this book, truth should not be a defence to a charge of promoting hatred.

During the first appeal, the prosecution challenged the refusal of Mr. Justice Locke to grant judicial notice of the Holocaust. Normally the prosecution, which got the conviction it sought, would not challenge what the trial judge had done. Errors made in favour of the defence are of no consequence, since the accused was convicted anyways.

The issue was relevant because of the appeal raised by the defence. The defence argued that the evidence of Raoul Hilberg, an expert witness on the Holocaust for the prosecution, was inadmissible as hearsay. The court rejected that argument and held the evidence of Hilberg admissible.

The prosecution, however, did not know, that the court was going to come to this conclusion. So the prosecution argued, in the alternative, that if the evidence of Hilberg was inadmissible, the judge erred in refusing to take judicial notice of the Holocaust. Because of that error, Zundel suffered no real prejudice from the testimony of Hilberg, even if it was inadmissible.

Despite the fact that the court held the evidence of Hilberg admissible, it nonetheless went on to deal with the prosecution argument about judicial notice. The court said:

> If the trial judge had taken judicial notice of the existence of the Holocaust, he would have been required so to declare to the jury, to direct them to find that the Holocaust existed, which would have been gravely prejudicial to the defence insofar as it would influence the drawing of the inference concerning the appellant's [Zundel's] knowledge of the falsity of the pamphlet.

Because the court said taking judicial notice of the Holocaust would have been "gravely prejudicial" to the accused, the impression is left that taking judicial notice of the Holocaust is legally incorrect. However, the court also said that judges have "a wide discretion" as to matters of which they will take judicial notice. The court may merely have been saying that the judge was not required to take judicial notice of the Holocaust but was free to do so or not as he saw fit.

The error by the judge that looms large, in my opinion, was the recognition of Robert Faurisson as an expert witness. The trial judge made several errors which together resulted in the order for a new trial. The judge refused to allow defence counsel to put to potential jurors questions he should have allowed. The judge refused admission of some defence evidence which he should have allowed the defence to enter. As well, he misdirected the jury on the mental element necessary for the commission of the offence.

All these were legal errors which, in combination, justified a new trial. However, they pale in significance, in comparison with the acceptance in evidence of the testimony of Faurisson, which was never recognized as a legal error.

Robert Faurisson is a Holocaust denier like Ernst Zundel. He lives in France, and is, in many ways, the French equivalent of Zundel. Faurisson has been found guilty in France of group defamation of Jews for which he received a three-month suspended sentence. The trial judge in the *Zundel* case nonetheless qualified Faurisson as an expert witness on whether the German government from 1933 to 1945 deliberately embarked on a scheme to exterminate Jews in Europe.

Though the acceptance of the testimony of Faurisson was not recognized as a legal error, that does not mean it was not an error. On appeal the prosecution did not challenge the acceptance in evidence of Faurisson's testimony because it was not relevant to the prosecution's case. Unlike the argument on judicial notice, the issue of Faurisson's evidence never became relevant as a prosecution response to a defence challenge. So the court of appeal did not have to rule on the decision.

The defence argued that the evidence of Raoul Hilberg, who had been qualified as an expert witness on the Holocaust for the prosecution, should not have been admissible because it was hearsay. The court of appeal, in its response, referred to the rule that expert evidence based on hearsay has no weight. The court pointed out there are exceptions to this rule. One is that events of general history may be proved by accepted historical treatises on the basis that they represent community opinion or reputation with respect to an historical event of general interest. The court reformulated this exception to cover trustworthy evidence that, by necessity, can be presented only through hearsay. The materials on which Dr. Hilberg relied were trustworthy because they came into existence contemporaneously with the historical event in issue; and because they are part of the source material of history to which any careful and competent historian would resort. The second exception which the court applied to Hilberg was evidence based on material of a general nature which is widely used and acknowledged by reliable experts in the field.

Neither of these exceptions to the hearsay rule applied to the testimony of Faurisson. His material was not widely used. Aside from other hate propagandists like Zundel, no one uses it. It is not acknowledged as reliable by experts in the field. Experts in the field see it for what is, as a falsification. Faurisson's sources did not come into existence contemporaneously with the existence of the Holocaust. They are post-Holocaust concoctions of the neo-Nazi movement. They are not part of the source material to which any careful and competent historian would resort. Any careful and competent historian would not touch Faurisson's materials with a barge pole. As well, Faurisson's denial of the Holocaust does not represent community opinion or reputation.

So, by none of the tests the court of appeal proposed could Faurisson's testimony have been considered as admissible. Yet, it was admitted. The admission of that testimony, in error, compounded the original error of the prosecution in not asking for judicial notice. Not only were prosecution witnesses on the Holocaust held hostage to harassing cross-examinations. The court and the public were afflicted with the direct testimony of a Holocaust denier. The combination of the two, the failure to ask for and receive judicial notice, and the acceptance of Faurisson as an expert witness made the courtroom a theatre of the absurd.

The final difficulty I will mention is the problem posed by the reporting of the trial. That reporting was unbalanced in the extreme. When testimony of prosecution witnesses was reported, the cross-examination was highlighted. When testimony of defence witnesses was reported, the testimony itself was given prominence. Zundel and his cohorts were depicted in terms of their own fantasies, as historical revisionists defending the honour of the German people, instead of the reality, as falsifiers, antisemites, neo-Nazis. Extensive, and essentially positive publicity, was given to Doug Christie, the lawyer for Zundel, and to several Zundel disciples. Publicity about Sabina Citron, the complainant, and Peter Griffiths, the lead prosecutor, was muted or non-existent.

For example, in the final summation of the trial in the *Globe and Mail*, a large picture of a swimming pool was published with the caption, "This is the swimming pool that Zundel's defence claims visitors to former Auschwitz Camp are not allowed to see." There is no mention that Ditlieb Felderer, the photographer, is a photo-refinisher. Felderer is called a revisionist in the article, rather than a neo-Nazi. At no time during the trial were actual photos of the horrors of Auschwitz published.

In one *Globe and Mail* headline, the Nazi extermination is called a theory. The headline of January 12, 1985 read "Lawyer challenges crematoria theory." Another headline of February 12, 1984, above a story about the testimony of Felderer was "Camp Gas Chambers False, Holocaust revisionist says." The *Globe and Mail* story that ran February 6, 1985, the day after Faurisson testified was headlined "No Gas Chambers in Nazi Germany, Expert Witness Testifies."

This media imbalance can be explained in a number of different ways. One explanation is the "man bites dog" phenomenon. Asserting the Holocaust is not news because it is not new. Denying the Holocaust is out of the ordinary. So it becomes newsworthy.

Another explanation is the ignorance of the reporters themselves. The Holocaust is not well taught, if taught at all in Canadian schools. There is general Canadian ignorance of the Holocaust from which the journalistic corps also suffers.

A third explanation is ignorance of the danger of hate propaganda. The harm of hate propaganda is not immediately apparent to the superficial observer. The problem is partly one of perspective. It is difficult for an outsider to imagine him or herself in the shoes of a target of hate propaganda. It is as difficult for a Christian to imagine what it is like to be a Jewish target of hate propaganda as, for instance, a man to imagine what it is like to be a pregnant woman.

However, the problem is not only that. The real horror of hate propaganda is not the hurt sensibilities of the target group. It is the danger of intolerance, discrimination, and violence fomented by hate propaganda amongst the population, and within groups of hate promoters themselves.

The danger of individual libel, for example, is a good deal more accessible because libellous utterances made against individuals are easy to understand themselves. All that is at issue is whether the libel applies to the individual.

When I say "X" killed "Y," that is a libel if it is wrong. The concept of murder itself is easily understood. It is easy to see that the notion X killed Y would be harmful to X if believed and not true. It is also easy to see that, said often enough, by enough people, it might be believed.

The danger of hate propaganda is a good deal less accessible because the libellous statements made against groups are, to most people, hard to credit. The issue is not just whether the libel applies to the group. The issue is whether the libel can be taken seriously at all.

When I say that the Holocaust, one of the most documented events in history, never happened, or that Jews control the world, the statements seem like nonsense. The initial reaction is that it is hard to believe that anyone would accept them at all. It is not just farfetched that Jews control the world. It is farfetched that any minority ethnic group controls the world. It is incredible to say that any of the recent well-documented events of history never happened. Hate propagandists wallow in a category of discourse that is beyond most people's imaginings.

This inability to connect intuitively with the dangers of hate propaganda is not unique to journalists. It is even felt by human rights experts.

The Special Committee on Hate Propaganda in Canada chaired by Maxwell Cohen, in its report of 1965, wrote "we have had to ask ourselves whether we are dealing with a significant social problem at all." The Human Rights Tribunal appointed to hear the complaint against John Ross Taylor for promoting hatred by telephone said of Taylor's telephone messages: "As we listen to and read the messages, we frankly admit that we find it difficult to follow the thread of thought in most of them."

If these were the problems the Cohen Committee and the *Taylor* tribunal had, it is easy to see that journalists would have those problems as well. Because they do not see the danger, they have no reticence in repeating the message. Appreciating the harm of hate propaganda requires a study of history, an understanding of psychology, and an awareness of communications theory. The average journalist will not bring these tools to the reporting of a hate propaganda trial.

A further aspect of media coverage which interacts with the superficial inaccessibility of hate propaganda's harm is the penchant of journalists to expand the boundaries of free speech. It is generally accepted that some justifiable boundaries to speech exist, some utterances that are justifiably prohibited. However, where those boundaries lie is a matter of debate. In that debate, the journalistic corps is inclined, by profession, to want those boundaries to be as far away as possible. Limitations on freedom of speech, from a journalist's perspective, should be as few as possible, because any limitation that does exist will, in one way or another, impinge directly on journalists, on what they can say, on what they can write. Freedom of expression is a freedom that journalists exercise.

In the debate about whether or not hate propaganda should be prohibited, journalists are not neutral observers. They are a group with an interest.

In reporting on a hate propaganda trial, where freedom of speech is an issue, they are placed in a conflict of interest.

Normally, when a conflict of interest exists, the solution is to remove the person from the situation. For journalists reporting a hate propaganda trial, that is no solution. No reporting is not an answer to bad reporting.

The solution has to be an awareness of the conflict of interest. A conscious effort needs to be undertaken to make allowances for this conflict. In the *Zundel* case just the opposite happened. Journalists, by the sheer volume and prominence of their coverage of Zundel's claims that his free speech was threatened, used reporting of the trial to push forward their own agenda. Reporting Zundel's claims that he should be free to deny the Holocaust became an opportunity for journalists to promote their own beliefs in expanding the boundaries of free speech.

An important cause of the media circus around the *Zundel* trial had to do with the fact that it was a trial. Media errors interacted with the trial errors and compounded the overall effect. In any legal case, it is important to recognize the notion of *sub judice*, the fact that a matter is before the courts. When an issue is before the courts, it should not be argued out in the media. Arguing a court case out in the media can become contempt of court.

If the media called Felderer a revisionist rather than a falsifier, it was partly because whether Felderer and his gang were falsifiers or not was an issue in court. When the media called Faurisson an expert rather than a convicted hate promoter, part of the reason was that the court itself had recognized Faurisson as an expert.

As farfetched as the position of Zundel was in court, that the Holocaust did not happen, that was his position. The court had allowed him to argue that position. The prosecution had put that position in issue. The media presented a circus because the court itself was a circus. Once the incredible became a live legal issue in court, the media felt constrained to present it as a live issue, whether, in reality, it was one or not. To report the Zundel defence as the absurdity it was may have seemed to the media like prejudgment of the case before the court.

To blame the bad reporting of the *Zundel* trial on the media alone is to take too narrow a focus. Part of the blame lies squarely with the judge and the prosecution for the way the trial evolved.

Despite all its faults, the first *Zundel* trial did not lead to an increase in antisemitism. Conrad Winn and Gabriel Weimann, in *Hate on Trial*, found that those who were aware of the *Zundel* trial were less likely to doubt that six million Jews were killed in the Holocaust than those who were unaware of the trial.[9] After the *Zundel* trial, two-thirds of Canadians did not change their opinions of Jews. Of the one third who did, the vast majority became more sympathetic to Jews.

Ernst Zundel said: "[The trial] cost me $40,000 in lost work—but I got a million dollars' worth of publicity for my cause. It was well worth it." In reality, what Zundel got was one million dollars worth of notoriety. What he acquired was not so much fame as infamy, not so much publicity as exposure. Despite the grotesque nature of much of the reporting, it did not serve Zundel's cause.

However, to focus on majority attitudes to hate propaganda is misleading. In a free society, hate propaganda is bound to find adherents. They will not be a majority or even a significant minority, in percentage terms. However, they will be significant in terms of numbers. If hate propaganda is given free rein, society will be encumbered by a certain number of people who believe in, and act on the propaganda.

As long as the number of believers is small, the hate group will be in no position to control society and initiate another Holocaust. Nonetheless, violence does not have to be at the level of the Holocaust to be worrisome. Where hate propaganda is given free rein, as it is, for instance, in the U.S., we see a sequence of violent hate-motivated crimes perpetrated against totally innocent victims.

The publicity Zundel got in the course of the trial was awkward for him because his propaganda was presented in a context where it was refuted, and he, himself, was convicted. Even in that setting, there may have been some people who have become attracted to his views.

The *Zundel* case was dissatisfying not just for the errors that were made. Another ground of dissatisfaction was the risks that were run. Although the first *Zundel* trial appeared to be a trial of the Holocaust, that was not the only, nor legally, the most important issue. For the offence to be committed, the news must not only be false. The publisher must know it to be false. The prosecution must prove beyond a reasonable doubt that the publisher knows the news to be false.

Once Zundel and his counsel put the Holocaust in issue, an acquittal ran the risk of crediting Zundel's zany views. While denial of the Holocaust is not a tenable position, it was open for Zundel to assert that he honestly believed there was no Holocaust.

Most hate propagandists believe their propaganda, even if no one else does. The propaganda may be totally out of touch with reality. Yet, hate promoters develop a paranoiac world view that makes them impervious to reality. Hate propaganda is typically a self-delusional world system. The world view of the hate propagandist explains everything, rationalizes everything to fit in with the theories of the propaganda.

Two juries found that Zundel knew his own propaganda to be false. His propaganda activity was an elaborate fraud. However, there is no certainty that every false news, hate propaganda prosecution will reach that result. On the contrary, one can expect to find hate propagandists who evidently believe their material.

Part of the reason the case went to a second trial was that, in the first trial, the charge of the judge on knowledge was wrong. Mr. Justice Locke said the prosecution must prove that Zundel did not have an honest belief in the truth of his propaganda. The court of appeal said that proving that was not enough. A person with no honest belief in the truth of his propaganda may have no belief at all. The propagandist must actually believe his propaganda to be false in order to be convicted. Not believing it to be true is not, in itself, criminal.

Zundel failed at the second trial even to meet this lower test of belief set by the court of appeal. Because it is a low test, other hate propagandists will likely be able to meet it.

Of course, where judicial notice is taken that the slanders promoted by the propagandist are not true the issue of knowledge does not assume the same dimensions. With judicial notice, an acquittal based on no knowledge of falsity will not be seen as a vindication of the slander uttered by the hate promoter. In the second *Zundel* trial, the risks were less because judicial notice was taken.

However, when a prosecution is begun, whether or not judicial notice will be taken is never certain. Every hate propaganda trial for a false news prosecution runs the risk the *Zundel* trial ran. The slander of the propagandist may become an issue at the trial. An acquittal based on belief will be seen as a vindication of the slander.

There is a correcting mechanism at work. When the accused raises the truth of his slander as a defence, a conviction becomes more likely. The jury, itself, is aware of the stakes of the case. The jury will be unlikely to want to buttress the slander. If the hate promoter wants to make his slander the issue of the trial, he runs the risk that the jury will, itself, make it the issue of the trial and decide against him simply because it rejects the slander.

It would be wrong to count on that corrective mechanism always working. If it does not, the prosecution will be a disaster. Even when it does, as arguably it did in the first *Zundel* case, the trial itself can be a travesty.

The false news provision was removed from the criminal code after the Supreme Court of Canada decision on Zundel's appeal. While it was there, because of the requirement for the attorney general's consent for a hate propaganda prosecution, it was a safety valve. The problem was not just that the Attorney General of Ontario refused to consent to the *Zundel* prosecution. The problem was, and is, the very existence of the requirement of consent.

The hate propaganda provision of the Criminal Code of Canada needs to be reformed to remove the requirement of consent. If the requirement had not been there, the use of the false news section to prosecute hate propaganda would have been both unnecessary and ill-advised.

This is basically what the Law Reform Commission of Canada recommended in 1988. In a working paper on private prosecutions, the commission recommended that the right to prosecute privately ought to be extended to those offences where they are presently proscribed.[10] If the prosecution is abusive, the attorney general may intervene to stay proceedings. The commission also suggested the introduction of an effective costs system. An abusive prosecutor would have to pay the court costs of the accused.

In another working paper, the Law Reform Commission, anticipating the decision of the Supreme Court of Canada in the *Zundel* appeal, recommended that the offence of publishing false news be abolished.[11] The commission said that there should be a new offence designed to deal with causing public alarm. It should be defined in a precise enough manner to prevent its being used to prosecute hate messages.

I have no quarrel with these recommendations of the commission, provided they are viewed as a package. What is intolerable is the present situation in Canada where the false news offence has been removed as an avenue for hate propaganda prosecution and the attorney general's consent remains a requirement for the offence of hate propaganda. Now, attorneys general can effectively block prosecutions for hate propaganda.

Historically, attorney general refusal has been a real problem. *Zundel* is far from the only case where consent has been refused despite requests for prosecution where *prima facie* the offence has been committed.

The disappearance of the false news section from the criminal code, because of the decision of the Supreme Court of Canada, was not, when all is said and done, a great loss. Use of the false news offence to combat hate propaganda, even if it had remained on the statute books, would have been impractical. Its only value would have been as a potential outlet for those who wanted to mobilize the criminal law against a hate propagandist, but were frustrated by an obstinate attorney general who refused to consent to a hate propaganda prosecution.

Ultimately the problem with the *Zundel* prosecution was the offence for which he was prosecuted. While the prosecution against Zundel was, in essence a hate propaganda prosecution, the law on the books was not a hate propaganda offence. It was a false news offence.

Since what Zundel was doing wrong was promoting hatred, a false news prosecution was a distortion. Part of the reason the Holocaust was put on trial was that a central issue in any false news prosecution must be the falsity of the news. In a hate propaganda prosecution, the natural focus of the case is whether hatred is being promoted. That should have been the focus of a *Zundel* prosecution, rather than the existence of the Holocaust.

Even the second trial, where judicial notice was taken of the Holocaust, was misdirected. In the second trial, the issue became, did Zundel know what he was saying was false? This was not as offensive as asking whether the Holocaust really existed. However, it still missed the point. The point was, was Zundel promoting hatred? Only a hate propaganda prosecution could address that issue directly.

Critics of hate speech laws who rely on the *Zundel* case are criticising hate speech laws unfairly because it was not hate speech laws that were in use. A hate speech prosecution based on a law prohibiting incitement to hatred would not, could not, unfold the way the *Zundel* trial did. Front and centre would be the fact of incitement to hatred and the harm of incitement to hatred, not the falsity of news. Such a trial would put incitement to hatred on trial and not the Holocaust.

Notes

1. Little, Brown and Company, Boston, 1991, p. 172.
2. "The Criminal Prosecution of Hate Mongers and Holocaust Revisionists," text of a speech delivered to the Canadian Jewish Congress Plenary, May 21, 1992.
3. *When Freedoms Collide: The Case for Civil Liberties.* Toronto: Lester & Orpen Dennys, 1988, p. 48.

4. Section 181, Criminal Code, *Revised Statutes of Canada*, 1985, Chapter C–46.
5. John A. Yogis. *Canadian Law Dictionary*, 2nd ed., New York, 1990, p. 121; see also Osborne's *Concise Law Dictionary*, (seventh ed. 1983) and *Weighing Evidence*, Legal Services, Immigration and Refugee Board, December 31, 1999, posted at <www.irb.gc.ca>.
6. (1987) 58 O.R. (2d) 129.
7. *Zundel v. The Queen*, August 17, 1992, Court Number 21811, judgment of the majority, McLachlin J., p. 38.
8. Section 319(3)(a).
9. Mosaic Press, 1986, p. 73.
10. Working Paper 52, 1986.
11. Working Paper 50, 1986.

Chapter Seven

The Weimar Republic

FREE SPEECH ABSOLUTISTS argue that banning hate speech will not work, cannot work. They often point out that the German Weimar Republic after World War I had hate speech laws and yet the Nazis took power and perpetrated the Holocaust all the same. They assert that the Weimar hate speech prosecutions gave the Nazis a platform and helped the Nazi rise to power. Free speech absolutists conclude that if hate speech laws did not work in the Weimar Republic, there is no reason to expect them to work now.

That is the argument of Aryeh Neier, the former executive director of Human Rights Watch in the United States and which he raises in *Defending My Enemy: American Nazis, the Skokie Case and the Risks of Freedom*.[1] It is also the argument of Alan Borovoy, the Executive Director of the Canadian Civil Liberties Association raised in his book *When Freedoms Collide: The Case for Civil Liberties*.[2]

This is part of what Alan Borovoy wrote:

Remarkably, pre-Hitler Germany had laws very much like the Canadian anti-hate law. Moreover, those laws were enforced with some vigour. During the fifteen years before Hitler came to power, there were more than two hundred prosecutions based on antisemitic speech. And, in the opinion of the leading Jewish organization of that era, no more than ten per cent of the cases were mishandled by the authorities. As subsequent history so painfully testifies, this type of legislation proved ineffectual on the one occasion when there was a real argument for it. Indeed, there is some indication that the Nazis of the pre-Hitler Germany shrewdly exploited their criminal trials, in order to increase the size of their constituency. They used the trials as platforms to propagate their message.[3]

The Weimar Republic allowed both for civil liability and criminal prosecution for defamation or insult.[4] For civil liability, actual damage had to be proved. For criminal prosecution, it was not necessary to show actual damage.

Private prosecution for insult was possible under the German criminal code. However, those who prosecuted privately had to pay court costs and lawyers' fees. As well, a private prosecutor could not testify as a witness.

The offence of insult was punishable only if it could be shown that the insult was directed against a definite individual. A group libel against, for instance, all Jews, could not be prosecuted, but an antisemitic slur against an individual could be. The crime could be committed by either written or oral statements, and by statements either to the insulted person or to others. Truth was a defence to the charge. During the Weimar years, there were many convictions on insult charges for antisemitic attacks against individuals.

The criminal code in effect at the time of the Weimar Republic also prohibited incitement to violence against classes of people.[5] In one judgment, the German Supreme Court found that Jews were a class for the purpose of this provision. In another, the court found that the offence of incitement to violence was committed even if no one was incited to violence, as long as the target class acquired a justifiable fear because of the incitement.

In addition to the general prohibition against insult of individuals, the Weimar criminal code also contained a specific prohibition against insult of any religious community.[6] The potential sentence for this offence was the most severe of the lot, up to three years in jail.

There were also prohibitions against religious vandalism. It was a criminal offence to defile a grave or to engage in insulting behaviour at a grave. It was an offence to destroy any object of devotion of a religious community or anything dedicated to divine worship or any tomb.

So, superficially, there was a legal structure during the Weimar years capable of dealing with Nazi hate speech. Yet the Nazis rose to power in spite of those laws. What is more, Nazis actively used these laws to help their rise to power. They actively sought out prosecutions for the publicity the prosecutions gave to their cause.

Theodor Fritsch, editor of a violently antisemitic newspaper during the Weimar years, was convicted thirty-three times by 1926 for his antisemitic propaganda under one of these provisions. Julius Streicher, convicted at

Nuremberg, and Joseph Goebbels, later the Nazi Minister of Propaganda, were found guilty on many occasions under the Weimar Republic hate speech laws. Hundreds of Nazis were convicted under these laws.

There is no question that the Weimar hate speech laws failed. But did it have to be that way? Does that failure tell us that hate speech laws cannot work? I suggest not. There were a number of reasons why it would be wrong to draw this conclusion.

First, there were facets to the Weimar laws that made the laws unworkable. One was the availability of the defence of truth to the offence of insult. The accused and their lawyers used the insult prosecutions to deliver antisemitic tirades. Since truth was a defence to the charge of insult, Nazi accused inevitably attempted to demonstrate in court the "truth" of the antisemitic slurs for which they were prosecuted.

Second, there were the light sentences imposed on those convicted of insult. Most of the convictions led only to fines. Karl Holz, editor of the antisemitic *Sturmer*, was sentenced in 1931 to one year in prison for the offence of insulting, the maximum for that offence. However, it was his sixteenth conviction. Joseph Goebbels was sentenced to prison twice, once to three weeks and once to six weeks. Julius Streicher was sentenced to prison once for two months. Theodor Fritsch was sentenced to prison on one occasion for four months after a libel action that went on for years. Those sentenced for destroying Jewish tombstones or painting swastikas on synagogues and in cemeteries typically got light jail sentences if they got jail sentences at all.

Third, there were the amnesties and pardons which were granted frequently during the Weimar Republic. Streicher and Goebbels, though both sentenced to jail, never went to jail, because of these amnesties and pardons.

Similarly, there was the immunity of members of the Reichstag, the German Parliament. Nazi Members of Parliament became the editors in name of antisemitic publications, sometimes one deputy becoming an "editor" of several publications. These façades meant that no one could be prosecuted for the defamations in these publications. The Reichstag could waive immunity for its members, but did so rarely.

Additionally, the laws were interpreted in a technical manner. This meant that many accused went free although in substance it was clear that the offence had been committed. The law against insulting a religious community, for instance, was interpreted to exempt insults centering around the Talmud, on the ground that the Talmud is only a doctrine and not an institution of the Jewish community, or on the ground that the Talmud was not used for religious instruction.

An important reason why it would be wrong to jump from the Weimar experience to a rejection of all hate speech laws is the pervasive antisemitism of Weimar Germany. That antisemitism tainted both the public prosecutors and the judges. For instance, the Bavarian government issued a statement that it was its duty to repress excesses of antisemitism, "even though it does not have to take any position towards antisemitism as such." In another example, a prosecutor refused to prosecute the author of an article against the Jewish community on the ground that the article was against the Jewish race and not the Jewish religious community. To give an example from the judiciary, one judge justified a particularly light sentence against two Nazis guilty of destroying Jewish tombstones and painting swastikas because the convicts had been "seduced by the antisemitism preached by the group."

Daniel Goldhagen, in *Hitler's Willing Executioners: Ordinary Germans and the Holocaust,*[7] writes this about the Weimar Republic:

> A survey of the political and social life of Weimar reveals that virtually every major institution and group in Germany—including schools and universities, the military, bureaucracy and judiciary, professional associations, the churches and political parties—was permeated by antisemitism. . . . Antisemitism was endemic to Weimar Germany.

Antisemitism was so accepted, that it was not even a matter of debate. Goldhagen writes: "Because the party leaders knew that antisemitism permeated their constituencies, including the working class, at the end of Weimar, the political parties did not attack Hitler's antisemitism, although they attacked him on many other grounds."

Trying to enforce hate speech laws in the Weimar Republic was akin to the effort to enforce prohibition in the twenties and thirties in the U.S. Widespread violations, general public acceptance of lawbreaking, lack of any communal conviction of the value of the law, all meant that the law was impossible to enforce. No law can be effective without community support behind it, without a shared belief that the law is needed.

Hate speech laws in the Weimar Republic did not work because the German people, the German prosecutors, the German courts at the time did not want the laws to work. The failure of those laws then tells us nothing about whether similar laws would work now. All that the failure tells us is that no law can be effective if the community does not believe that the law should be there.

While in a general sense one can say that the Weimar hate laws failed, because they failed to stop the Nazi rise to power and the Holocaust, in the more particular sense of moderating hate speech, it would be going too far to say that the Weimar hate laws failed. As virulent and pervasive as antisemitism was in the Weimar Republic with its hate speech laws, matters would have been far worse without them.

This is certainly the view of Daniel Goldhagen who writes:

> Given the ubiquity and intensity of anti-Jewish feeling in Germany, sentiments that would later be activated and channelled by the Nazi regime into violent and murderous results, the restraints imposed by the Weimar government certainly prevented Germans' steady verbal assaults upon Jews from escalating still more frequently into physical ones.[8]

There was, at the time, a general failure to appreciate the seriousness of the Nazi threat. We have the benefit of hindsight. We can see where all this Nazi hate speech led. However, Weimar Republic judges and prosecutors had little idea where it was going. For instance, a pre-Weimar judgment ruled that a person charged with inciting violence against Jews should be acquitted on the ground that his immediate audience had not taken the accused seriously. Although this judgment was eventually overturned on appeal, it bespoke a common attitude in Weimar Germany.

The Weimar hate speech laws, such as they were, were not part of a coordinated community effort to combat antisemitism. Even when the laws were enforced, they were tiny islands of protection for the Jewish community in a raging sea of antisemitism.

This was the view of Chief Justice Brian Dickson of the Supreme Court of Canada in the *Keegstra* case.[9] The ineffectiveness of the Weimar hate speech laws became a matter of legal relevance in Canada when the Canadian prohibition of hate speech in the criminal code was challenged in the *Keegstra* case as a violation of the guarantee of freedom of speech in the Canadian Charter of Rights and Freedoms.

The Supreme Court of Canada held that the freedom of speech guarantee was indeed violated, but that the legislation was nonetheless saved because it was a reasonable limit to that freedom demonstrably justified in a free and democratic society. In order for a violation of a fundamental freedom to be a reasonable limit, there must be a rational connection between the challenged legislation and its objective. In the case of hate speech, the objective is protecting target groups and fostering harmonious social relations in a community dedicated to equality and multiculturalism.

The Canadian Civil Liberties Association intervened in the case and argued that there was no rational connection between the criminal code prohibition and its objective of protection and harmony by pointing to the Weimar experience. Put plainly, they argued that hate laws would not work in Canada, because they did not work in Weimar Germany. Further, they argued that because hate laws would not work in Canada, the limitation on freedom of speech they imposed was unjustifiable.

That was an argument accepted by Mme. Justice McLachlin in dissent. She said: "Historical evidence gives reason to be suspicious of the claim that hate propaganda laws contribute to the cause of multiculturalism and equality." She then proceeded to quote the passage from Alan Borovoy that I have reproduced.[10]

Chief Justice Dickson, for the majority rejected that argument. He stated:

> No one is contending that hate propaganda laws can in themselves prevent the tragedy of a Holocaust; conditions particular to Germany made the rise of Nazi ideology possible despite the existence and use of these laws. Rather, hate propaganda laws are one part of a free and democratic society's bid to prevent the spread of racism and their rational connection to this objective must be seen in such a context.

Hate speech laws can be likened to a dam against a flood. In the case of Weimar Germany, antisemitism was so ubiquitous, so deep that it overwhelmed the dam and flooded the country. However, one can no more argue from the Weimar experience that hate speech laws are useless than one can argue from one flood overflowing one dam that all dams are useless.

Rather, what Weimar tells us is that hate speech laws have to be part of an overall strategy to fight racist prejudice, along with education, training, multiculturalism, and promotion of equality. Weimar Germany may have had hate speech laws. But it did not have the necessary partners of promotion of tolerance and equality, education and training of human rights values, and respect for multiculturalism.

The Weimar Republic was a case of too little too late. Antisemitism in Germany did not start with the Weimar Republic. Goldhagen writes that by the eve of the First World War an antisemitic eliminationist discourse had for over thirty years been in place with regard to Jews. When the Weimar Republic began, there had already been decades of verbal, literary, institutionally organized, and political antisemitism.[11]

Hate speech laws dropped into a society where hate is the accepted norm are not going to make much headway. However, that is far different from the conclusion that hate speech laws do not work.

If the true lesson of the Weimar hate speech laws was indeed that they were ineffective, one would think that post-war Germany, at the very least, would have learned this lesson and avoided making the same mistake twice. However, post–World War II Germany, along with virtually every country that was a victim of Nazism now has hate speech laws on its books. As well, the international community has made the obligation to prohibit hate speech part of international human rights treaty law.

The argument of ineffectiveness is unhistorical, because it looks at only one aspect of the Weimar Republic, rather than the Weimar Republic in all its facets. The argument of ineffectiveness is also a logical fallacy. A truly effective effort against racist hatred requires a number of remedies, criminal prohibition being one of them. No one remedy will work on its own. The only way we can be confident of being effective in the battle against hate speech is to assemble and use all remedies available.

The argument that any one remedy is ineffective on its own is an argument that can be used not only against criminal prohibitions, but against any and all available remedies. If we are to accept the argument that we should abandon a remedy because it does not work on its own, then we would abandon any and every remedy, not just for hate speech, but for many other endeavours.

We should not jump to adverse conclusions about the Weimar experience because, in retrospect, too much is being asked of Weimar hate speech laws. The Weimar hate speech laws did not stop the Nazi rise to power, but it is asking too much of any law that it stop the rise to power of a political movement. The reality of Weimar Germany is that the rabid, obsessive eliminationist antisemitism of the Nazis represented and articulated German public will. There were other elements of the Nazi party program that were far more controversial in Weimar Germany than Nazi antisemitism. As I indicated earlier, Nazi antisemitism was so generally shared that it was not even a matter of public debate.

Cyril Levitt writes:

Had the administration of justice in the Weimar period functioned perfectly, and had all the draft amendments to the criminal code been enacted extending the legal protection further, it is hard to see what difference this would have made in a political culture which was, to a significant degree, anti-democratic. . . . If there is anything we can learn from the Weimar experience, I think it is this: The law can only be an effective instrument in containing, controlling, and discouraging racist expression if it is founded upon a sound democratic political culture.[12]

After all that, assume that I am wrong, and that it is indeed true to say that the Weimar hate speech laws were ineffective, that hate speech laws everywhere are ineffective. Does that mean that they should not exist?

In a general sense, it is wrong to say that simply because something can be done, it should be done. It is also wrong to say that simply because something cannot be done, it is not worth trying. Cannot does not imply ought not.

I would argue that hate speech laws serve a purpose even if they are ineffective in stopping hate speech. The criminal code is a statement of a country's values, the wrongs society considers most severe, the behaviour a country condemns outright. Because hate speech is so wrong, so dangerous, we should stand against it in the most clear cut way we can, by prohibiting it in the criminal code.

The reality is that in human endeavours, nothing is certain. A statement that something is ineffective is a statement about what the future will bring. However, the future in human affairs is never a pre-determined event that just arrives. It is something we create. If we do try to stop hate speech through every means available, including criminal prohibitions, we may or may not succeed. Of only one thing we can be sure. If we do not try, we are bound to fail. The only way we can hope to succeed is if we try. The evil of hate speech is so acute, so dangerous that we cannot afford to be immobilized by doubts that our efforts may fail.

The lessons I believe should be learned from the Weimar Republic are not that hate speech prohibitions are doomed to failure. There are three general lessons I believe can and should be learned from the Weimar experience. The first is that hate speech laws cannot bear the whole brunt of combatting hatred. Goldhagen writes that Jews, though ferociously attacked, found virtually no defenders in German society.[13] Franz Bohm, in a 1958 lecture about antisemitism said of the Weimar Republic: "For antisemitism hundreds of thousands were ready to ascend the barricades, to fight brawls in public halls, to demonstrate in the streets; against antisemitism hardly a hand stirred."[14] If hate speech prohibitions are to work at all, they must work in tandem with a coordinated effort for tolerance and against racism undertaken by every sector of society.

A second lesson from Weimar is the need to act on hate speech before it is too late. One argument that free speech absolutists use against hate speech prosecutions is that they give undue attention to a tiny lunatic fringe, that our time is better spent combatting the more widespread discrimination of polite racists who never utter a racist word, but who perform a whole series of racist deeds.[15]

The Weimar Republic experience I suggest is the best answer to that argument. The Weimar Republic shows us that the only time when we have a hope of being effective in combatting hate speech is at a time when it is the preserve of the lunatic fringe. Once hate speech becomes mainstream, it is too late. The Weimar Republic experience tells us that once hate speech becomes mainstream, laws alone will not work.

A third lesson we must learn from Weimar is the need for substantial sentences for hate crimes. Hate crime convictions must never be allowed to become just the cost of doing business for right-wing extremist groups.

It is generally true that an offence will not be an effective deterrent if there are no meaningful penalties attached to conviction. Because of the particular nature of hate crime offences, what is generally true in the criminal law, is especially true here.

The need for substantial sentences becomes crucial once truth is allowed as a defence to the offence of spreading racial hatred. In the case of hate speech prosecutions where truth is a defence, the accused, instead of wanting to avoid publicity, may actively seek publicity. That was the experience of the Weimar Republic with the Nazi accused. That was the Canadian experience as well with Ernst Zundel. Where truth is a defence, the only deterrence is conviction and sentencing itself. If the sentence is derisory, then the lesson of Weimar is that the law is bound to fail.

That is a lesson, I regret to say, that Canada is far from having learned. None of the best-known hate speech propagators in Canada has received a substantial sentence for his activities.

Ernst Zundel came closest, having been sentenced to a fifteen-month jail term after his first conviction and to a nine-month jail term after a new trial and his second conviction. However, he served neither term, because of his successes on appeal.

Jim Keegstra was sentenced to a fine of $5000 after his first conviction and to a fine of $3000 after a new trial and his second conviction. The prosecution appealed the sentence after the second trial because they considered the punishment derisory. The Alberta Court of Appeal, in its fourth judgment on the side of Keegstra, rejected the prosecution appeal and upheld the sentence. The only modification was the addition of a one year suspended sentence plus two hundred hours of community service.

Donald Clarke Andrews and Robert Wayne Smith were sentenced to one year and seven months in prison, respectively. On appeal, the sentences were reduced to three months for Andrews and one month for Smith. John Ross Taylor was sentenced to one year in jail, served his jail term, and repeated his behaviour. He was sentenced to a second one-year jail term.

On the other side of the scale, the Canadian Parliament in 1995 passed legislation which provides sentencing guidelines for judges.[16] One of those guidelines is that racial hatred as a motivation to a crime is to be considered an aggravating factor for sentencing purposes. So, a crime of violence motivated by racial hatred is more likely to receive a substantial sentence, now that the law has passed. However, the problem remains of imposing substantial sentences for hate speech offences alone. On balance, the Weimar lesson about the need for substantial sentencing is decidedly a lesson that Canada has yet to learn.

I mentioned earlier that Julius Streicher was convicted at Nuremberg. He was sentenced to death and executed for crimes against humanity. The crimes against humanity for which he was convicted were the propagation of hatred against the Jews. What weighed most heavily on the minds of the judges who convicted and sentenced him was that Streicher continued his hate propaganda in the midst of the Holocaust, after he knew it was going on. They wrote: "With knowledge of the extermination of the Jews in the Occupied Eastern Territory, this defendant continued to write and publish his propaganda of death."[17]

Today we all know the Holocaust happened. No one propagating hate speech today can claim ignorance of the consequences of hate speech. I do not advocate the death penalty, for hate promoters or for anyone. However, I would argue that, with the exception of the death penalty, today the crime of propagating hatred must be punished as severely as the International Military Tribunal at Nuremberg treated Streicher's crimes, that there are circumstances in which this crime is one of the most heinous known to humanity.

At the end of the day, we cannot be certain that we will never see hate-mongers in power again. The Nazis did not come to power on antisemitism alone. There were a whole set of historical circumstances that explained their rise to power. Circumstances may again put Nazi-like figures in power not because of their irrational hatred against a victim group, but for totally unconnected reasons.

I would like to feel that no matter who is in power, society contains a large group of people who have the courage to resist a state-sponsored hate propaganda. That means doing what we can to control hate propaganda now. If hate propaganda is tolerated in a free society, it becomes all that much easier to succumb to it should the unfortunate vagaries of history turn a society totalitarian.

Notes

1. 1979.
2. Lester & Orpen Dennys, Toronto, 1988.
3. At page 50.
4. Information about the Weimar hate speech laws is drawn from an article by Ambrose Doskow and Sidney Jacoby, "Anti-semitism and the Law in Pre-Nazi Germany," *Contemporary Jewish Record*, p. 498.
5. R. H. Gage and A. J. Waters, *Imperial German Criminal Code*, Johannesburg 1917, section 130.
6. Section 166.
7. Knopf, New York, 1996, p. 82
8. Page 84.
9. *R. v. Keegstra* (1990) 61 C.C.C. (3d) 1 at page 54.
10. At page 116.
11. At pages 80 and 81.
12. "Racial Incitement and the Law: The Case of the Weimar Republic" in *Freedom of Expression and the Charter*, edited by David Schneiderman, pp. 211–241.
13. At page 83.
14. Quoted in Goldhagen at page 84.
15. See for instance, Alan Borovoy, *When Freedoms Collide*, p. 48.
16. *1995 Statutes of Canada*, Chapter 22 adding section 718.2 to the Criminal Code.
17. "International Military Tribunal Judgment," *American Journal of International Law* (1947), Vol. 41, no. 172, p. 295.

Chapter Eight

Universities

FREEDOM OF EXPRESSION is more important to a university than to any other institution. A society without freedom of expression is still a society, albeit a repressive one. A newspaper, without freedom of expression, is still a newspaper, although a boring and dishonest one. A university without freedom of expression ceases to be a university.

Freedom of expression is integral to the very idea of a university. A university is a community of scholars joined together in the pursuit of truth. If the scholars at a university cannot pursue the truth wherever the search leads, cannot state the truth no matter how uncomfortable the results, then the university itself is at an end.

Because of the centrality of freedom of expression to a university, freedom of expression debates in a university loom large. Debates on the meaning and limits of freedom of expression in a university are debates about the very survival of the university. In a university setting, freedom of expression must be even more carefully guarded than in society at large. The existence of the university depends on it.

It is at a university that limitations on freedom of expression are at their lowest, must be at their lowest. In the days when blasphemy was prohibited in society at large, free-ranging religious discussions were tolerated at universities. Today, for national security considerations, universities will often refuse to do government work which prevents them from disclosing the results of their research to the world at large.

John Henry Newman, in his famous discourse delivered and published in 1852 in Dublin, said:

> An assemblage of learned men, zealous for their own sciences and rivals of each other, are brought, for the sake of intellectual peace, to adjust

together the claims and relations of their respective subjects of investigation. They learn to consult, to respect, to aid each other. Thus is created a pure and clear atmosphere of thought, which the student also breathes, though in his own case he only pursues a few sciences out of the multitude. He profits by an intellectual tradition, which is independent of particular teachers, which guides him in his choice of subjects, and duly interprets for him those which he chooses. He apprehends the great outlines of knowledge, the principles on which it rests, the scale of its parts, its light and its shades, its great points and its little, as he otherwise cannot apprehend them. Hence it is that his education is called "Liberal." A habit of mind is formed which lasts through life of, which the attributes are, freedom, equitableness, calmness, moderation, and wisdom; or what in a former discourse I have ventured to call a philosophical habit. This then I would assign as the special fruit of the education furnished at a university, as contrasted with other places of teaching or modes of teaching. This is the main purpose of a university in its treatment of its students.[1]

Can a university possibly achieve the pure and clear atmosphere of thought of which Newman spoke when it gives hate speech free rein? Can a university hope to form in its students the habits of freedom, equitableness, calmness, moderation, and wisdom when it permits an environment of hatred?

The special importance of freedom of expression to a university highlights the equal importance of prohibiting hate speech. We can see, more acutely at a university than anywhere else, that prohibiting hate speech is not a limitation on freedom of expression. It is a facet of freedom of expression. Prohibiting hate speech is not a hindrance to the realization of the idea of a university. It is essential to the realization of the idea of a university.

Of course, in one sense, prohibiting hate speech is a limitation on freedom of expression. However, prohibiting murder can also be a limitation on freedom of expression. Expression need not be by words; it can also be physical acts. Burning a flag is an expressive act. The murder of, for instance, Salman Rushdie for what he has written would also be an expressive act, communicating a particularly terrifying message.

It is, of course, wrong to assess anyone's life just in terms of freedom of expression: clearly the right to life supercedes the right to freedom of expression. The analogy with murder puts human rights topsy turvy, but the extremity of the example helps to make the point.

It is easy to see that it is essential in order for a university to function that it must not tolerate murder at university, not just as a reasonable limitation on freedom of expression, but as part of freedom of expression. It is essential to the working of a university that it be free from violence directed against its members.

For every wrong, there is a perpetrator and there is a victim. In assessing the impact on freedom of expression of prohibiting the wrong, we must not look only at the effect on the freedom of expression of the perpetrator and other would-be perpetrators. We must also look at the effect a *refusal* to prohibit would have on the freedom of expression of the victim and other potential victims.

If we take again the example of Salman Rushdie, we would have no hesitation in saying that the denial of freedom of expression to Rushdie and other writers caused by his murder would far outweigh the denial of freedom of expression that making every effort to prevent his death would cause his murderer and other killers. Freedom of expression values are best served by making every effort to keep Salman Rushdie safe, no matter how much this effort thwarts the expressive desires of his would-be assassins.

One can say the same of hate speech. Hate speech too has a victim: the target of the hatred. As we saw in chapter three, hate speech limits the freedom of expression of minorities targetted by its hate, not as dramatically as murder, but limits their freedom of expression all the same. Hate speech shuts its victims up.

Hate speech, of course, does not shut off all discourse. Nor does it shut everybody up. This book is proof of that. Hate speech stirs up discussion about the hate speech itself. But even while the propriety of the hate speech is debated, the stereotypes and dehumanization of hate speech work their insidious effects, undermining the assertion of identity of members of vilified groups, eroding the particular and unique contributions each can make to the university community. The self-censorship resulting from hate speech is destructive not only to the repressed individuals, but to the university community.

The prohibition of hate speech is grounded in the belief in human equality. Universities are institutions that have their own special commitment to equality because they are, or at least should be, institutions that promote scholarship on merit alone, regardless of race, colour, gender, or any other ground of discrimination. Prohibition of hate speech is a full-throated commitment to equality. Tolerance of hate speech is a rejection of the equality values essential to make a university work.

All hate speech is rooted in one big lie, the denial of the equality of all humanity. It is easy for purveyors of hatred to move from that one big lie to many more specific lies.

Hate-mongers are attracted to the ivory tower for the appearance of status it gives them. Once at a university, they put on a disguise of academic dress.

Holocaust denial is often so clothed. For example, the Institute of Historical Review in the United States, cloaks Holocaust denial in academic garb. Deborah Lipstadt has written:

> From the outset the Institute for Historical Review has camouflaged its actual goal by engaging in activities that typify a scholarly institution. It sponsors annual gatherings that are structured as academic convocations and publishes the *Journal of Historical Review*, which imitates the serious and high-brow language of academia.[2]

The very name "Institute of Historical Review" is a lie. The institute is not concerned with all history, but only the Holocaust. Its aim is not to review the history of the Holocaust, but to deny the history of the Holocaust.

The dishonesty of the Institute for Historical Review was established in a law suit. The Institute offered a reward of $50,000 to a number of survivors to prove that Jews had been gassed at Auschwitz. Mel Mermelstein accepted the challenge and provided the institute with proof, but they refused to pay the reward. Mermelstein went to court and got an order from the Los Angeles Superior Court in July 1985 that the institute must pay Mermelstein the reward.

Robert Faurisson, when he lost his university job and was convicted in France for Holocaust denial, complained to the United Nations Human Rights Committee established under the International Covenant on Civil and Political Rights and argued academic freedom. In his complaint, he stated that he was invoking, not so much a violation of the right to freedom of expression, which he accepted did admit of some restrictions, but a violation of his right to freedom of opinion and to doubt, as well as freedom of academic research. The latter, he contended, by its very nature could not be subjected to limitations.

The Human Rights Committee, in dismissing his complaint, found that Faurisson was not engaged in academic research, but rather in an attack against Jews, with pseudo-research as a smoke screen. The Committee stated:

> The notion that in the conditions of present-day France, Holocaust denial may constitute a form of incitement to anti-semitism cannot be dismissed. This is a consequence not of the mere challenge to well-documented historical facts, established both by historians of different persuasions and backgrounds as well as by international and domestic tribunals, but of the context, in which it is implied, under the guise of impartial academic research, that the victims of Nazism were guilty of dishonest fabrication, that the story of their victimization is a myth and that the gas chambers in which so many people were murdered are magic.[3]

Hate-mongers gravitate towards universities and pseudo-scholarship because of the credibility it gives their propaganda. Universities, as truth-seeking communities, have to be especially vigilant against those who would use university institutions to subvert university goals, those who would use the façade of scholarship to deny everything for which true scholarship stands.

Academic freedom does not mean freedom to perpetrate fraud. Indeed, academia, to be true to its ideals, has to stand steadfast against fraud. That is why plagiarism or falsified research are dealt with so harshly in universities. It is not just that plagiarism is theft. Even worse, in a university setting, plagiarism is a lie. No-one would defend plagiarism or the right to publish concocted laboratory experiments in the name of academic freedom. How, then, could anyone defend fraudulent hate speech in the name of academic freedom?

Fraud is not the only professional reason for university concern. Universities are institutions with standards. Whatever else can be said about hate speech, hate speech cannot meet academic standards of research and analysis. It has no place in academic discourse or academic institutions. For a university to give a forum to hate speech is to discredit the institution and to tarnish the values for which it stands.

I spoke at the Faculty of Law of the University of Western Ontario in March 1989 asking for the dismissal of J. Philippe Rushton from the psychology faculty of that university. Professor Rushton was conducting research purporting to show that the status of blacks and orientals at opposite ends of the socio-economic spectrum was a reflection of heredity and genetics.

Whether or not his research was hate speech, it was certainly racist. I argued then that a university medical faculty would not hire a witch doctor, nor an astrophysics faculty an astrologer. Similarly, a psychology faculty should not hire someone publishing and promoting racist research.[4]

Whether astrology is or is not good astrophysics should ultimately be for astrophysicists to decide. However, it is, to say the least, troubling when astrophysicists are agreed that astrology is nonsense and yet a university insists on keeping an astrologist on its astrophysics faculty.

Similarly, whether intelligence is genetic should ultimately be for geneticists to decide. But read what Rushton's peers write. Gary Atlin, a geneticist on the faculty of the Nova Scotia Agricultural College in Truro wrote in the *Globe and Mail* in 1994: "Philippe Rushton, the head-size comparer [who] is still, in defiance of reason and good science, on the faculty of the University of Western Ontario."[5] A. K. Dewdney, associate professor of computer science at the University of Western Ontario, in the *Winnipeg Free Press* in 1994, referred to Rushton's work as junk science: "By junk science we do not necessarily mean science that produces wrong conclusions, but science that does not follow the scientific process."[6] Dr. Rowland Chrisjohn, a researcher on intelligence at the University of Guelph, said that he did not think "there's any validity at all" to Rushton's research.[7]

Exposure and debate discredited Rushton's research, a crucial response to the work he had done. By arguing for his dismissal, I did not mean to argue against, or short cut, the refutation of his research. As I argued in the chapter on Holocaust denial, exposure and banning are complementary activities, not alternatives. Indeed, unless and until there is exposure, identification of writings as racist cannot be done.

In a later chapter, I argue for a gradation of responses to incitement of hatred, beginning always with the least-drastic remedy. The same is true for remedies for racism generally. In the university context, that would mean not giving any status to those promoting racism and other forms of discrimination. This is a distinction made and accepted even by civil libertarians.

Alan Borovoy writes:

A wise strategy must distinguish between those who have status in the community and those who don't. . . . If such people [more prominent individuals] vilify Jews, blacks or other minorities, they should be made to suffer political and social censure, including their removal from relevant positions of influence.

Borovoy noted with approval that "Following the reports of James Keegstra's anti-semitic preaching in Alberta's schools, for example, public censure triggered action. The education authorities discharged him as a teacher for abusing his pedagogical trust. The voters ousted him as mayor for disgracing his representative role."[8]

A university professor is a person with rank and authority at the university. Refutation of a professor's racist research is not a complete and satisfactory answer to the problem that his research poses. As long as the person maintains his position, the university gives his theories, no matter how convincingly refuted, a status they should not have.

In an earlier chapter I distinguished between hate speech and racial slurs and noted that racial slurs are litigated in the context of workplace harassment. The Rushton case identifies another form of harassment, student harassment. Giving a racist researcher university status poisons the environment in which students work.

Of course, there is an opposite extreme of political correctness, where every slight and slur is avoided for fear of giving offence. One can go too far in protecting against slurs as well as not far enough. In the university context, as elsewhere, a balance must be sought between the right to be free from wounding words and the right to freedom of expression. The chill to legitimate expression of those who might give offence is as much a concern as the danger of affront. In determining where that balance lies in a university context, it is important to keep in mind that staff are more powerful than students, that minorities run the risk of marginalization, that students are often young and vulnerable, and that retreat from a university environment is difficult.

Hate speech is a more egregious phenonmenon than racial slurs or racist research. If a university is a community of scholarship, then hate speech is antithetical to universities, because hate speech denies both scholarship and community. Hate speech is not the pursuit of learning. It is prejudice, the rejection of learning based on prior assumptions. Hate speech works to destroy the university community, by dividing the community, by fomenting hatred of one component of the community against another. Prohibiting hate speech, for a university, is a matter of self-preservation.

Because of the staff–student power relationship, the speech responsibilities of staff are greater than those of students or visitors. Every university hosts a variety of student associations where the students relate to each other as equals. The university student associations are a microcosm of the community at large with its different perspectives and interests. Statements by students, their associations, and guest speakers do not have the same status as statements by the university staff. However, even for the myriad of student associations and their guest speakers, there should be limits.

The speech of Hussein Hamdani, then President of the Muslim Student Association, in December, 1998 at the University of Western Ontario exemplified the problems that can arise. The general tenor of his speech was an example of what we see so often in contexts of armed conflict, allegations without evidence that the other side is guilty of atrocities of the worst sort.

Hussein Hamdani, in an e-mail to Jeffrey Clayman, the then President of the Jewish Students Association, wrote: "I believe the main accusation is that I invited hatred to the Jewish people. I am sure after you have heard the tapes, you will see that this is simply not the case. . . . Let's not a misunderstanding re-ignite the hostilities between the Arabs/Muslim/Jews on this campus."

Mr. Hamdani invites us to consider the tapes. The transcription of the tapes includes the following: "Right now there are twenty groups, twenty groups in Israel, Jewish groups, who have sworn in their declarations that they will [inaudible] who have made public their intention to destroy Islam." "This is what Palestinians have to go through . . . to be destroyed." "There is a benefit [to Jews] if you kill Muslims in prayer." "They are the only country in the world that has authorized the use of torture to elicit a confession." "Israel is developing an ethnic bomb that kills Arabs but leaves Jews unharmed." "The Israelis are looking for a chemical warfare drug that will attack only Arab DNA."

Each of these statements is elaborated at length. There are many more such statements. The allegations are not just directed against the state of Israel, but to Jews, generally, at least those Jews supportive of the state of Israel.

The Jewish Students Union of the University of Western Ontario wrote to the Race Relations Officer at the university complaining that Hamdani's speech violated the university's Race Relations policy. That policy asserts the right of every member of the university to study and work in an environment free from discrimination and harassment on the basis of race. Racial harassment is defined as: "engaging in a course of comment or conduct of a racially oriented nature that is vexatious and is known or ought reasonably to be known to be unwelcome." The term "race" is understood by the university to refer to race, ancestry, place of origin, colour, and ethnic origin.

In their letter, the Jewish Students Association said of the Hamdani speech:

> We have received complaints from members who felt personally threatened. The safety of all students on campus is of paramount concern to us all. The references to Jewish people cross the boundary between fair political comment against the state of Israel and antisemitism.... At least one incident of swarming occurred as a result of the speech.... Jewish students in attendance felt physically threatened and violated.

I wrote to the University of Ontario on behalf of B'nai Brith Canada stating:

> There are interspersed in that speech some criticisms of the government of Israel with which we would quarrel, which we think are wrong, but which, we concede, are within the legitimate realm of free speech. However, the overall drift of the speech as well as many of its specific statements cross the boundaries from the arguable to the disreputable, from debate to incitement, from criticism to hate. It is my view that speech inciting racial hatred constitutes harassment within the meaning of this [the university's] policy.

I never received a reply to that letter. Nor, to my knowledge did the university do anything in response to the Jewish Student Association complaint.

Hate speech is a form of harassment. In a university context, it is a harassment from which there is no escape. A university is a closed community with an all-enveloping atmosphere. In a general sense, one can say that if you do not like what you hear or see in a place, you can just go somewhere else. However, to say that to someone in a university is to end the university itself. When people who come to a university are told, if they do not like the hate speech they might encounter, they can leave, then the university community is dispersed and the university is over.[9]

What, then, is a university to do? There is a tendency amongst many institutions, not just universities, to shuffle off the responsibility for dealing with hate speech to the police and the courts. In Canada, where the criminal code prohibits the propagation of hatred, there is a tendency to say, if the contested speech is hate speech, let there be a prosecution; if there is a conviction, then we will deal with the contested speech, but not otherwise.

This passing the buck is inappropriate for a number of reasons. Requiring a criminal conviction before an institution reacts to hate speech puts the most drastic step first rather than last. It requires proof beyond a reasonable doubt. It allows defences which may be appropriate in a criminal context, but are inappropriate in a civil context. In Canada, it requires the consent of the attorney general of the province, which has been difficult to get, even in cases where there is overwhelming evidence that the offence has been committed. Prosecutions attack the person rather than the propaganda. They impose a punishment, when all that is needed is to end the propaganda.

From a university perspective, which must be a perspective of heightened sensitivity to freedom of expression, acting before the police and the courts act should be especially compelling. Calling in the police, or inviting others to call in the police is going to have a more chilling effect on expression than self-initiated action. Throwing someone in jail is going to have a more chilling effect on freedom of expression than throwing someone out.

It would have been unwarranted, a gross overreaction, for the University of Western Ontario to have called in the police and requested that Hussein Hamdani be criminally charged. However, that does not mean that nothing should have been done. The University of Western Ontario had an established race relation policy, and race relations policies are there for a purpose. Race relations work is not just confronting discrimination. It is also confronting incitement to discrimination. For universities to ignore their race relations policies and to decline to apply them to hate speech on campus is an abdication of university governance, destructive of the institutions, and a denial of the ideals for which universities stand.

Proceedings before civil tribunals, rather than prosecutions in criminal courts, are another option available to institutions like universities, and there is something to be said for first resort to state-sponsored civil remedies. They often bring a specialization to bear on the complaint.

In Canada, for example, there are state-sponsored civil remedies for hate speech communicated by telephone, under the Canadian Human Rights Act; for imported hate speech, under the Customs Tariff Act; for broadcast hate speech under the Canadian Radio-television and Telecommunications Commission Act; for mailed hate speech, under the Canada Post Corporation Act. Provincially, there are general prohibitions against hate speech in Saskatchewan and British Columbia, in their human rights codes.

Patrick Lawlor in 1984 recommended for Ontario a general provision for its Human Rights Code akin to what are now the Saskatchewan and British Columbia provisions.[10] This recommendation has yet to be accepted.

Civil remedies are also worth invoking because they make the statement that hate speech concerns the whole community. However, as is apparent, state-sponsored civil remedies can be a patchwork quilt. They exist for hate speech communicated in some forms and not in others; for hate speech generally in some provinces and not in others.

Universities have their own special reasons for being directly involved in combatting hate speech. And for the same reasons that internal resolutions are preferrable to criminal prosecutions, universities should not leave combatting hate speech to outside human rights commissions. Where state-sponsored civil remedies do not exist, the only remedy for hate speech at a university is direct university involvement.

While at the end of the day for the most egregious cases of hate speech, trial, conviction, and punishment may be the best remedy, it is surely going too far to say that, for every example of hate speech, it should be the only remedy. A free-speech sensitive response to hate speech would try to discourage prosecutions, by resorting to other less chilling remedies.

The prohibition of hate speech is not just a society value; it is a university value. Making the prohibition work must not be left to the general institutions of society at large, the human rights commissions, the police, the prosecution, the courts. University governing institutions must themselves work to make the university hate speech free. It is part of their responsibility to make certain the university functions effectively as a university. Even more acutely than in society at large, at a university freedom of expression values are best served by making every effort to prohibit hate speech.

Notes

1. "Knowledge Its Own End," in *The Idea of a University.* New Haven: Yale University, 1996, p. 77.
2. *Denying the Holocaust.* New York: Plume, 1994, p. 142.
3. United Nations Document CCPR/C/58/D/550/1993, 16 December 1996, Communication No. 550/1993, Views of the Human Rights Committee.
4. See David Helwig "B'nai Brith lawyer calls on university to rid itself of controversial professor," *Globe and Mail,* March 8, 1989.
5. "Don't cite geners to explain the gap in IQ test scores," *Globe and Mail,* November 1, 1994.
6. "IQ test is junk science," *Winnipeg Free Press,* November 12, 1994.
7. Shelley Page. "Scholars dismiss Canadian's racial theory," *Toronto Star,* January 21, 1989.

8. *When Freedoms Collide: The case for our civil liberties.* Toronto: Lester & Orpen Dennys, 1988, p. 53.

9. See Charles L. Lawrence III "If He Hollers Let Him Go," in *Words That Wound.* Boulder, CO: Westview Press, 1993, pp. 70–71.

10. Patrick D. Lawlor, Q.C. "Group Defamations: Submissions to the Attorney General of Ontario," March 1984.

Chapter Nine

Libraries

LIBRARIES ARE, LIKE UNIVERSITIES, repositories of knowledge and vehicles for access to knowledge. Indeed, for disciplined and highly motivated readers not formally enroled in a university, a well stocked and serviced library can provide an education all on its own. How should the hate and free speech debate be resolved for libraries?

In June 1998, the Juan de Fuca branch of the Greater Victoria Public Library system, in Colwood British Columbia rented its meeting room to Doug Christie and the Canadian Free Speech League. The Law Society of Upper Canada, in a 1993 report, described Christie as a person who "has made common cause with a small lunatic antisemitic fringe element of our society." The Victoria Public Library Branch in Saanich B.C., on June 5, 1999, allowed a meeting of the Canadian Free Speech League to sponsor a fund raiser for Doug Collins, whom the British Columbia Human Rights Commission had found, in February of that year, had promoted hatred in his column for the *North Shore News*.

The Vancouver Public Library also rented a meeting room, on September 30, 1999, to Doug Christie and the Canadian Free Speech League. This meeting attracted the former head of the British Columbia Ku Klux Klan; Jud Cylorn, author of a racist book titled *Stop Apologizing;* Marc Lemire, the Ontario webmaster for racists; as well as Doug Collins.[1] The public purse incurred an estimated expense of $30,000 to provide security and policing for the event.

Are British Columbia libraries in the vanguard of freedom of expression, or are they bringing up the rear on human rights? The Universal Declaration of Human Rights provides: "All are entitled to equal protection against any discrimination in violation of this Declaration and against any incitement to such discrimination."[2] The International Covenant on Civil and Political

Rights provides: "Any advocacy of national, racial, or religious hatred that constitutes incitement to discrimination, hostility, or violence shall be prohibited by law."[3] The Covenant is a treaty which Canada has signed and ratified. The United Nations Convention on the Elimination of All Forms of Discrimination provides that states: "shall not permit public authorities or public institutions, national or local, to promote or incite racial discrimination."[4] The Convention is also a treaty that Canada has signed and ratified.

These standards are binding on Canada as a state. That means they are binding, not just on the federal government, but on all government institutions, federal, provincial, and local. The Vancouver Public Library has a duty to protect against incitement to discrimination. Compliance with that duty means that the library, as a public institution, should not rent meeting-room space to any person or organization likely to use the space for the purpose of inciting discrimination.

The June 1998 meeting of the Juan de Fuca library prompted a complaint to the British Columbia Human Rights Commission which was dismissed in October 1999.[5] However, the complaint was not about the June meeting, or any meeting, but only about the meeting policy of the library board. The letter of dismissal noted that the complainants did not complain about any specific incidents.

At issue in the complaint was the library board's policy not to "knowingly permit any individual or groups to use its facilities in contravention of the Criminal Code of Canada."[6] The board of the library had given the library the right to refuse bookings at its discretion.[7] So there was no obligation to rent rooms to every applicant who appeared to be behaving in a legal manner. The substance of the complaint was that the library policy mentioned the criminal code, but not the British Columbia Human Rights Code.

The board defence to the complaint raised a number of legal issues. The board noted that its staff lacked the experience to assess the legal behaviour of groups and would have to rely on outsiders. What seemed to be of most practical concern to the board was the availability of police, prosecutorial and judicial resources to investigate and determine a complaint regarding a violation of the criminal code and a lack of resources in the British Columbia Human Rights Commission to investigate, prosecute, and determine a human rights complaint. The policy that seemed most capable of practical application to the library board was one that relied on the police, prosecutors, and courts using the criminal code.[8]

In the very same month as the meeting in Juan de Fuca, the Ottawa Public Library refused the use of its meeting rooms to Paul Fromm and the white supremacist group the Alternative Forum. The decision to refuse was made by the library administration.

Paul Fromm used to be a school teacher in Ontario. He was fired from his teaching position after he spoke at a memorial symposium for a white supremacist, despite a warning from the Ministry of Education not to engage in activities contrary to the Peel Board of Education multicultural and human rights policies. According to the 1999 Audit of Antisemitic Incidents of the League for Human Rights of B'nai Brith Canada, "Fromm continues his connections with the extreme right" in speaking tours across Canada.[9]

The Ottawa Public Library refusal become a matter for discussion at an Ottawa Public Library Board meeting on June 16, 1998. The board was concerned that the library might "receive another request to rent public meeting space to the Alternative Forum."[10] Paul Fromm and two other representatives of the Alternative Forum attended the meeting.

Board member Jeffrey Simpson proposed a motion, seconded by Naiana Sloan, that until the board had more fully debated the issue, "the Ottawa Public Library be directed to reject applications from the Alternative Forum to rent public meeting space at the library." Chief Librarian Clubb stated that "the staff are clear on the policy, have received sufficient instruction this evening from the board on how to proceed, and that the motion would not be necessary for the staff's protection." The motion was withdrawn. The Ottawa Library, since that meeting, has not, on any occasion, rented public meeting space to Paul Fromm or the Alternative Forum.

A memorandum from Madeleine Aalto, Director of the Vancouver Public Library, to the Internal Operations Committee dated October 18, 1999 states: "our practice and that of virtually all public libraries is to rent to anyone who meets the terms and conditions of our rental procedures . . . regardless of the content of the meeting." However, as far as I can tell, the practice, outside of British Columbia, is the opposite. I am not aware of any library in Canada outside of British Columbia renting a meeting-room to an extreme right-wing group, a white supremacist group, or a Holocaust denial group. The only time when a refusal to rent a meeting-room to such a group was challenged at a library board, in Ottawa, that refusal was upheld and continued.

The Canadian Library Association policy is absolutist. Free speech is the only human right that matters. The policy says: "It is the responsibility of libraries to guarantee the right of freedom of expression by making available all the library's public facilities and services to all individuals and groups who need them." The policy goes on to say: "Libraries should resist *all* efforts to limit the exercise of these responsibilities . . ." (my emphasis). Encouraging resistance to all efforts is as absolutist a position as you can get.

This meeting-room policy of the Library Association is consistent with its book acquisition policy. The policy states that "libraries shall acquire and make available the widest variety of materials."

The Canadian Library Association policy raises two issues. One is whether there should be a linkage between the acquisition policy of the library and its meeting-room policy. The other is, if there is a linkage, what the overall policy should be.

It is by no means obvious that there should be a linkage between a meeting-room policy and a book acquisition policy, although the Canadian Library Association statement assumes that link. Libraries have to have books, or videos, or discs, or other collected items available to its users in order to be libraries. Libraries do not have to have public meeting-rooms in order to be libraries, and, in fact, many libraries do not have them.

A library could have a broad policy for acquisition and another narrower policy for the use of meeting-rooms. Some librarians may feel that restricting access to any books is antithetical to the nature of a library. However, granting access to meeting-rooms has, in principle, nothing to do with the work of libraries. Libraries can have whatever meeting-room policy they choose without it affecting in any way their core library work.

The meeting-room policy for the Canadian Library Association has been caught up in the tail of the book acquisition policy. Even that book acquisition policy is open to question. Within professional librarian circles, the views espoused in the Library Association policy are far from universal. There is an attitude within librarian thought that argues librarians should show community intellectual leadership; that they should exercise judgment and taste; that they should provide the community with literature and not with a random sampling of everything produced, regardless of its content.

For instance, the American Library Association president, Joseph Nelson Larned, in an address to the annual gathering of the association in 1895 said: "defend [your] shelves against the endless siege of vulgar literature."[11] American Library Association president, Arthur E. Bostwick, in his address to the annual gathering in 1908 said:

Books that distinctly commend what is wrong, that teach how to sin and tell how pleasant it is, sometimes with and sometimes without the added sauce of impropriety, are increasingly popular, tempting the author to imitate them, the publishers to produce, the bookseller to exploit. Thank heaven they do not tempt the librarian.

More recently, in October 1999, professional librarian Mark Herring wrote that we should construct our libraries around four cardinal virtues— courage, justice, temperance, and patience—and three theological virtues— faith, hope and charity—"collecting only what exemplifies these." Herring referred to these seven virtues as his "Marshall Plan for library restoration."

There is a middle ground between collecting examples of everything and collecting only that which the good taste of librarians allows. That middle ground is to guarantee freedom of expression, as the current Library Association policy does, but within the context of promoting respect for all human rights. The holders of this middle ground would not collect only books which exemplify virtue, or literature, or good taste. They would, however, refrain from collecting books which incite to hatred, which exploit children in pornographic performances, and generally all materials which violate human rights.

The Canadian Library Association makes no distinction between types of libraries. Yet, libraries are not a single set of institutions. They are a variety of institutions which need varying policies on freedom of expression. Rather than one freedom of expression policy, there should be a continuum of freedom of expression policies.

Freedom of expression concerns should be at their highest at university and college libraries. They should be at their lowest at elementary school libraries. Both the rights of children and the rights of adults are based on the same individual right to dignity. In the case of children, their physical and mental immaturity means this right is best effected by special safeguards and care. Children are entitled to a higher level of protection from the state; that approach should also extend to libraries for children.

Along the continuum, between university libraries at one end and elementary school libraries at the other, are junior high-school libraries, high-school libraries, specialized libraries and public libraries. Because public libraries are public facilities, public library policies should be congruent with public facility policies generally. A public library should reflect the community it serves.

It is striking that the behaviour of the British Columbia libraries is incongruent with community policy. For instance, the City of Vancouver adopted a policy in May 1998 which proclaimed the objective that "all residents should be able to conduct their daily lives free from evidence of prejudice on the part of their fellow residents and public services." The policy instructed city staff to ensure that this objective was met in the performance of their duties. Renting a public library meeting-room to a hate-monger contradicts and undermines this policy objective.

The Vancouver Library convened a forum for February 9, 2000 to address the issue: "Is it ever appropriate for the library to censor free speech?" However, that is not the issue the library faces and characterizing it that way is misleading and tendentious. It suggests an answer, that there should not be censorship, when censorship is not put in question by a meeting-room policy. Hate-mongers denied library meeting rooms can still meet elsewhere. The forum was postponed from February 9th because of criticism that the question showed a bias.

One has to ask, why have hate promoters sought a library out in the first place? It is not the need for meeting-room space. Many hotels in Vancouver have meeting rooms available for rent. Indeed, the size of the groups attending these meetings is such that they could easily meet in a private residence.

Hate-mongers seek out libraries for the same reason they seek out universities, because of the respectability it gives their cause, because of the aura of credibility it bestows their propaganda. A library location gives hate promoters legitimacy.

For some hate promoters, though not all, hate propaganda is an exercise in fraud, the uttering of statements contradicted incontrovertibly by the sources which they quote. Like any fraud artist, hate promoters want a cover the better to fool their audience. They seek out libraries because it gives them that cover.

Libraries do not tolerate copyright fraud or plagiarism. No library would knowingly purchase the work of someone who is trying to make a fast buck by passing off the writings of another person as his own. Why should a library tolerate fraud about the Holocaust or other sorts of fraud which are motivated not by greed but by a far baser instinct, the desire to exterminate?

Libraries are expected to collect books but not to provide meeting rooms. If libraries are concerned about copyright fraud or plagiarism in performing their core task of collecting books, why should they show no concern for hate speech fraud in the peripheral activity of renting out rooms?

Fraud is more than just falsity. Fraud is a deliberate attempt to deceive. Fraud is not an essential component of hate speech, however, it is often part of the hate speech mix. When it is, it makes no sense at all to say that other sorts of fraud are wrong, but this sort of fraud is entitled to a library platform.

Furthermore, public space exists because of public expense. The public expense for the Canadian Free Speech League meeting at the Vancouver Public Library in September 1999 was exorbitant because of the policing and security costs. However, putting those costs aside, any use of public space means the public purse is subsidizing the event. Tax money pays for library buildings. Tax money pays the salaries of library staff. It is an abuse of community funds to use that money to give a forum to those who would tear the community apart.

It is also striking that what the Vancouver Public Library did bears little relationship to its meeting-room policy. The practice of the library appeared to be anything goes, without distinction. The policy of the library sets out a number of distinctions.

The general policy statement of the library is that preference for meeting rooms will be given to library programs and to non-profit activities and programs consistent with the Vancouver Public Library Board Mission and Vision Statement.[12] The vision of the library is to "enrich lives and inspire the human spirit by encouraging exploration of the broadest range of ideas, wisdom, and culture." Providing a forum for the promotion of hatred hardly enriches lives and inspires the human spirit. It does quite the opposite.

The library policy then goes on to set out priorities for the use of meeting rooms.[13] The first priority is library programs. The second priority is groups affiliated with or programs sponsored by the library. It would be consistent with library policy to limit its meeting-room use to its first two priorities or to scrutinize more closely groups or events which do not meet these priorities. However, the practice, it seems, is to have no priorities.

Finally, the policy says "The Library reserves the right to refuse bookings at the discretion of the director."[14] Yet, when it comes to hate groups, that discretion is abdicated. There is no exercise of discretion.

The print media provides a useful point of comparison. The press, like libraries, feel duty-bound to uphold freedom of expression. The press, like libraries, see it as their responsibility to provide access to a wide variety of views and information. The press, like libraries, are free from a regulatory environment, other than regulations and laws that apply to the community generally. The press, if anything, are more free than libraries, since the vast majority of newspapers and magazines are privately owned whereas public libraries are, by definition, publicly owned.

Yet, the B.C. press do not see providing a platform to hate-mongers as part of their defence of freedom of expression and commitment to providing a variety of views. Rather they have adopted a specific policy to the contrary. The Code of Practice of the British Columbia Press Council says "Unless the information is directly relevant to the story, newspapers should not publish material likely to encourage discrimination on grounds of race, colour, sex, sexual orientation, age, or mental or physical disability, and should avoid reference to the above in prejudicial contexts."

The B.C. Press Council has a chair and eight directors. Four directors are drawn from the newspaper industry and four from the public. Any member of the public can complain to the Press Council about a violation of the code of practice. Council directors decide on the merits of complaints.

The renting of meeting rooms to hate groups by British Columbia libraries appears then to be in contravention of international standards binding on libraries as public institutions, in violation of the community policies where the libraries are found, and out of step with the libraries' own policies. It is also in contrast to what is happening elsewhere in Canada and to the behaviour of newspapers in British Columbia.

The Vancouver Public Library Board, at a meeting in April 2000, decided to ask renters not to contravene the criminal code and British Columbia human rights legislation. If a group refused to sign to their acceptance of this request, the room could not be rented. If a violation occurred, the group would not be allowed to rent again. Signs would be posted outside meeting rooms stating that the views expressed are not endorsed by and do not necessarily represent views of the library.

This policy, while a step forward, is unsatisfactory because it remains the policy of the library to rent a room to a group even where it can be demonstrated, in advance, that in spite of their signing the rental agreement, the group is likely to contravene the criminal code and British Columbia human rights legislation. Furthermore, the library, as can be seen, foists determination of violations of its own policy on the criminal courts and the British Columbia Human Rights Commission. There is no internal mechanism proposed to assess and resolve complaints that a meeting room is likely to be used or even has been used to incite hatred.

The British Columbia library practice is anomalous. It would have been a simple matter for libraries in B.C. to refuse to rent meeting rooms to extreme right-wing groups, exercising the discretion library managers have to refuse to rent rooms to anyone. That is what has happened elsewhere, without its causing problems to anyone. Even fringe groups that sought library meeting rooms outside of B.C. were able to meet elsewhere after being denied.

B.C. library managers, by declining to exercise the discretion they have and insisting that a meeting room can be refused only through the application of some specific policy, such as a previous breach of the criminal code, have backed their libraries into a corner. What could have been a matter of discretion has, through the failure to exercise that discretion, become a matter of policy. A policy decision has to be made. Will libraries rent rooms to groups likely to incite hatred or not?

In my view, B.C. libraries should follow the B.C. Press Council model. B.C. libraries should have a rule that a meeting room will not be rented to persons or groups likely to use the room to encourage discrimination on grounds of race, colour, sex, sexual orientation, age, or mental or physical disability. Any refusal of a rental application based on this rule, or any acceptance of a rental application that may violate this rule, could be the subject of a complaint to the board of the library, which would adjudicate the complaint.

The concern of the Victoria Library Board that the application of a content-based rule for the renting of meeting rooms would require their staff to acquire an expertise they do not have can be answered in two ways. One answer is that library expertise does not have to be in-house, any more than newspaper libel expertise has to be in-house. Newspapers do not publish libellous articles, but are not necessarily experts on libel law. Rather, they hire experts on a case-by-case basis to give them advice. Libraries could easily do the same, hiring experts to give them advice on incitement to hatred on a case-by-case basis.

The second answer is that a complaint-driven procedure puts the onus on the complainant to provide the necessary expertise. Library boards that are adjudicating complaints would not sit as expert tribunals, but only as impartial ones. The expertise would be brought to the boards by the complainants and intervenors.

Professed incompetence may be an understandable explanation for doing nothing, but it is never a proper justification. One would hope that libraries in particular would operate under the assumption that what can be known will be known, that libraries would not operate under an assumption of their own ignorance. If we operate under the opposite assumption, that it is possible to determine whether a meeting room is likely to be used for incitement to discrimination or not, then a primary objection that B.C. libraries have to a content-based meeting-room policy melts away.

Because conveying information and knowledge are central to the purpose of libraries, libraries must themselves resolve the hate speech–free speech debate. Failure to come to grips with hate speech is an abdication of their position not just generally as community institutions, but specifically as communications institutions. If libraries fail to make their own decisions on matters central to their purpose, then others will make those decisions for them. If libraries fail to exercise a discretion given to them others will exercise that discretion for them. The decisions of outsiders can not possibly be as sensitive to library values as the decisions libraries themselves would make.

Notes

1. "1999 Audit of Antisemitic Incidents," League for Human Rights of B'nai Brith Canada, p. 28.
2. Article 7.
3. Article 20(2),
4. Article 4(c).
5. Letter from Mary O'Byrne Duffy, Delegate, Commissioner of Investigation & Mediation, British Columbia Human Rights Commission, to Robert N. Friedland and Timothy Schober, October 5, 1999.
6. Meeting Rooms Policy of December 17, 1996, paragraph 10.
7. Paragraph 5.
8. See paragraphs 34 to 55 of the response to the complaint.
9. "1999 Audit of Antisemitic Incidents," League for Human Rights of B'nai Brith Canada, p. 31.
10. Minutes of the meeting of June 16, 1998, p. 7.
11. Mark Herring. "Reading between Librarians' Lines," *Society*, September/October 1999, p. 26.
12. Paragraph A.
13. Paragraph C. 7.
14. Paragraph C. 9.

Chapter Ten

The Ross Case

FOR A TEACHER TO TEACH antisemitism as fact and to examine his students on it is clearly unprofessional. James Keegstra was fired from his teaching job in Eckville, Alberta for doing just that. He was also prosecuted and convicted for promoting hatred. While the prosecution and conviction were legally controversial, his firing was not. There was no significant constituency arguing that Keegstra should have been allowed to keep his job and to keep teaching antisemitism as part of that job.

Malcolm Ross represented a different and more subtle problem. Like James Keegstra, Malcolm Ross taught school. Like James Keegstra, Malcolm Ross promoted antisemitic beliefs. Unlike James Keegstra, Malcolm Ross kept his antisemitism out of the classroom. Despite that forbearance, he was removed from the classroom. Should he have been?

If a person does his job, does it matter that he uses his spare time to incite hatred? Is disciplining or even firing an employee for promoting hatred outside of work hours an unwarranted intrusion in the employee's freedom of speech? As the two previous chapters have argued, a university or library should not be platforms for hatred. Where an employee of one of these institutions promotes his hatred outside of the institution, should the institution cease to care?

Malcolm Ross believes in a Jewish conspiracy to control the world. He is certain that the Holocaust never happened, that it is a hoax and part of a world Jewish conspiracy. He claims that the Jewish religion is worship of the devil.

For him, this hatred was not just a private opinion; it was a public cause. He wrote books on his opinions; he gave television and radio interviews; he wrote letters to the editor to newspapers setting out his hate fantasies.

Yet, from 1971, Malcolm Ross taught school, elementary school, in the public school system in New Brunswick. He did not teach his hatred in school. However, his mere presence in the classroom as a highly visible symbol of antisemitic bigotry caused a stir. The school board, in New Brunswick School District 15, received complaints from parents about leaving a known bigot in the classroom.

The school board did virtually nothing. The board monitored Ross' class from time to time to ensure that Ross was not preaching his hatred in the classroom. The board appointed a review committee that went nowhere. In 1986, the school superintendent warned Ross against further publication of his views. In March 1988, the school board issued a similar warning, saying further publications or public discussion of his views or work could lead to dismissal. This warning remained on Ross' file until September 1989.

David Attis, a parent of three Jewish students in the school district in which Ross taught, filed a complaint with the New Brunswick Human Rights Commission in April 1988 claiming that the school board, by its tolerance of Ross, had discriminated against his daughter on the basis of ancestry or religion. The commission appointed a Board of Inquiry in September 1988, consisting of one member, Brian Bruce. Professor Bruce, in August 1991, found that the school board had discriminated against the Attis children by creating a poisoned environment in the school district.

Bruce ordered the school board to remove Ross from the classroom, to place him on an eighteen-month leave of absence, to appoint him to a non-teaching position during the leave period if one became available, to terminate his employment after the leave period if no non-teaching position became available, and to terminate his employment in any event if at any time he published, sold, or distributed his anti-Jewish hate propaganda. A non-teaching librarian position did become available during the leave period and Ross took it up.

Ross challenged the order of Bruce in the Queen's Bench of New Brunswick as a violation of the Canadian Charter of Rights and Freedoms. He claimed that the order violated his right to freedom of expression and freedom of religion guaranteed under the Charter. Mr. Justice Creaghan of the Trial Division of the Queen's Bench of New Brunswick held in December 1991 that the order removing Ross from the classroom was constitutionally valid, but the order restraining Ross from disseminating his hatred was not. Furthermore, the Board of Inquiry did not have the statutory authority to issue such an order, regardless of what the Charter allowed.

Ross appealed the Creaghan judgement to the New Brunswick Court of Appeal. The court of appeal, in December 1994, allowed the appeal and quashed the order of the Trial Judgement. Ross was allowed to return to the classroom. Mr. Justice Hoyt for the majority found that both the restraining order and the order keeping Ross out of the classroom violated the Charter. Mr. Justice Ryan in dissent found both components of the order to be legally valid.

Any prohibition of speech is, according to the Canadian courts, a violation of the Charter of Rights and Freedoms' guarantee of freedom of expression. The sole issue is whether prohibition nonetheless survives Charter scrutiny on the grounds that it is a reasonable limit, prescribed by law, and demonstrably justified in a free and democratic society. The courts have said that a prohibition that violates a Charter guarantee may nonetheless be a reasonable limit if it is motivated by an objective of sufficient importance; if there is a rational connection between the objective and the means chosen; if it impairs as little as possible the right under question; and if the objective and helpful effects of the prohibition outweigh its harmful effects.[1] The courts have held that the banning of hate speech is an objective of sufficient importance to justify overriding the constitutionally protected right to freedom of expression.[2]

Justice Creaghan in the first Trial Division hearing held that the restraining order against Ross did not survive Charter scrutiny because it did not meet the tests of rational connection and minimal impairment. He found that the rational connection between the restraining order and the anti-discrimination objective of the New Brunswick Human Rights Act to be tenuous, and that there was too great an impairment of Ross's constitutional rights. Justice Hoyt for the majority in the court of appeal affirmed the decision and reasoning of Creaghan on this point.

Justice Ryan in dissent found that the restraining order was rationally connected to the objective of the Human Rights Act to ensure a discrimination-free environment. The remedy was also minimal impairment of the right. Other possible remedies that Professor Bruce considered such as an apology or classroom monitoring would have been insufficient to protect the victims. Firing Ross, instead of keeping him on with a restraining order, would have been a greater impairment of his rights. Finally, the objective and helpful effects of the restraining order, by promoting the inherent dignity of the human being, a commitment to social justice, equality, and respect for cultural and group identity, outweighed the harmful effects on

Ross. Ross was free to quit work and say whatever he wanted without restraint.

David Attis, the New Brunswick Human Rights Commission, and the Canadian Jewish Congress, which had been given intervener status at the original Board of Inquiry, applied for leave to appeal to the Supreme Court of Canada. The court granted leave and heard the appeal in October 1995. The court permitted the League for Human Rights of B'nai Brith Canada to intervene in the case. I, Marvin Kurz, and Jacqui Chic represented the League.

The International Covenant on Civil and Political Rights requires states to prohibit advocacy of national, racial, or religious hatred that constitutes incitement to discrimination, hostility, or violence. Hostility in this context means an act, and not just an attitude. Like discrimination and violence, it is something harmful likely to be done to the victim as the result of the advocacy of hatred. An act of hostility is an aggressive act of enmity. In determining whether or not a prohibition of a particular form of advocacy of hatred fits within the Covenant requirement, there must then be a determination that the particular advocacy incites either discrimination or hostility or violence.

The Board of Inquiry had found that Ross held those of the Jewish faith and ancestry in contempt[3] and that this incited hostility towards Jews.[4] His advocacy of hatred resulted in an atmosphere where anti-Jewish sentiments flourished and where Jewish students were subject to a poisoned environment within the school district which greatly interfered with the educational services provided to the complainant David Attis and his children.

Students gave evidence to the board of repeated and continual harassment in the form of derogatory name-calling of Jewish students, carving of swastikas by other students into their own arms and into the desks of Jewish children, drawing of swastikas on blackboards, and general intimidation of Jewish students. The complainant's daughter, Yona Attis, herself a student in the school district, gave evidence of an occasion when she planned to attend the school where Malcolm Ross taught to watch a gymnastic competition. She was advised that she could not go to the school because that was "... where the teacher who hates Jews works." Yona Attis attended the competition, but testified that she felt scared while there, and anxious "... that someone was going to come up behind [her] and grab [her] and beat [her] up or something."

Further evidence of taunting and intimidation of the Jewish students was disclosed in her testimony, including incidents of shouting and signalling of the "Heil, Hitler" salute. The Supreme Court of Canada observed: "What this evidence discloses is a poisoned educational environment in which Jewish children perceive the potential for misconduct and are likely to feel isolated and suffer a loss of self-esteem on the basis of their Judaism."

The testimony of the students did not establish that the off-duty conduct of Ross had a direct impact on the school district. Nonetheless, the board concluded:

> Although there was no evidence that any of the students making anti-Jewish remarks were directly influenced by any of Malcolm Ross's teachings, given the high degree of publicity surrounding Malcolm Ross's publications it would be reasonable to anticipate that his writings were a factor influencing some discriminatory conduct by the students.

The Supreme Court of Canada had previously held that contempt is a subset of hatred. In the case of *Taylor*,[5] the court accepted the distinction of the Canadian Human Rights Tribunal in *Nealy v. Johnston*[6] that hatred is a broader concept than contempt, hatred being extreme ill will, and contempt being extreme ill will plus looking down.[7] In other words, all contempt is hatred, although not all hatred is contempt. That Ross was engaged in advocacy was not in dispute. Therefore, Professor Bruce had found as a fact that Ross had committed all of the elements of the activity that Canada by international law was bound to prohibit: Ross was advocating hatred of a national, racial, or religious group, and that advocacy incited to hostility. There was, accordingly, an obligation to prohibit that activity, and, by the order of the Board of Inquiry, it had been prohibited.

The Board of Inquiry found that the writings of Ross were *prima facie* discriminatory,[8] and had a discriminatory effect,[9] that the climate he had created by his writings interfered with the desired tolerance required by the school system.[10] In addition to inciting hostility, the writings of Ross also incited discrimination. Here too, Professor Bruce had found as a fact that Ross had committed all of the elements of the activity that Canada by international law was bound to prohibit.

The prohibition order of the Board of Inquiry, prohibiting Ross from disseminating his hatred, was not just something that could be done. It was something that had to be done. The International Covenant on Civil and Political Rights and the Convention on Elimination of All Forms of Racial Discrimination do not just allow prohibition. They require prohibition. The

Board of Inquiry, by the prohibition order, was doing something that it had a duty to do at international law.

At the Supreme Court of Canada, the League for Human Rights of B'nai Brith Canada argued that the court of appeal erred when it decided that the Charter prevents the making of an order which under international human rights law there was a duty to make. There exists a presumption that domestic law will not be interpreted, where possible, as violating international obligations imposed by a treaty signed and ratified by the government.[11] The Supreme Court of Canada has said that the content of Canada's international human rights obligations is an important indicator of the meaning of the full benefit of the Charter's protection. The Charter should generally be presumed to provide protections at least as great as that afforded by similar protection in international human rights documents which Canada has ratified.[12]

The European human rights system has dealt with a similar case. The Government of the Federal Republic of Germany dismissed Rolf Kosiek in 1974 as a lecturer at the Nurtingen Technical College because he was a prominent official of the National Democratic Party of Germany, a neo-Nazi party. He appealed his dismissal eventually all the way to the European Commission on Human Rights and to the European Court on Human Rights which considered whether his dismissal was a violation of the guarantee of freedom of expression in the European Convention on Human Rights.[13]

The European Commission on Human Rights noted that Kosiek, in his writings, referred at some length to the "naïveté" of the concept of racial equality and the allegedly inherent differences between races. He advocated that the appropriate consequences should be drawn in the field of education from the "undesirable" and "deleterious" consequences of racial intermarriage and the biological "fact" of the inferior intelligence of blacks compared with whites. He considered that the ideal of a pluralistic society was based on a misconception of the nature of man and of peoples.[14]

The commission, in May 1984, held that the dismissal of Kosiek was not a violation of the convention because it was necessary in a democratic society for the protection of the rights of others.[15] In coming to this conclusion, the commission took into account the importance we must attach to the opinion and influence of lecturers who, in a free society, have a key role in the development and dissemination of ideas. Mr. Kosiek was a lecturer some of whose student may have been at a stage of intellectual development when their vulnerability to indoctrination was a factor which could not be ignored.

In these circumstances, Kosiek was subject to special duties and responsibility relating to his opinions and their expression, both directly at the college and to a lesser degree as a figure of authority for students and other members of staff at other times. This responsibility was highlighted by Kosiek's considerable political experience and the inevitable notoriety that this would have generated.[16] Mr. Tenekides of the commission, in a separate opinion, found that the dismissal of Kosiek was justified by relying on the United Nations Convention on Elimination of All Forms of Racial Discrimination.

The European Court of Human Rights, in August 1986, held that there was no violation of the European Convention on Human Rights in the dismissal of Kosiek because his dismissal lay within the sphere of the right of citizens to have access to employment in the civil service, a right that is not secured in the convention. The responsible ministry took account of the opinions and attitude of Mr. Kosiek merely in order to satisfy itself as to whether he possessed the necessary personal qualifications for the post.[17] Judge Cremona, in a concurring opinion, held the guarantee of freedom of expression in the European Convention on Human Rights was violated by Kosiek's dismissal, but it was justified as a restriction prescribed by law and necessary in a democratic society.[18]

Doug Christie, counsel for Malcolm Ross, argued in the Supreme Court of Canada that the offence of hate propaganda under the criminal code was not proved because the writings of Malcolm Ross were an expression of religious opinion, and expression of religious opinion is a defence to the offence of propagating hatred.[19] The answer I gave, in my capacity as counsel for the League for Human Rights of B'nai Brith Canada, was firstly that the defence of expression of religious opinion is not a constituent part of the definition of hate propaganda. It is an affirmative defence, once the offence is made out. A matter does not cease to be hate speech simply because it is an expression of religious opinion. All that happens is that it ceases to be criminally punishable.

Second, there is no comparable relief from punishment in the International Covenant on Civil and Political Rights or the Convention on Elimination of All Forms of Racial Discrimination. The obligation in these instruments is not limited in the same way as the criminal code. A criminal prohibition must fall within the confines of the criminal code. But Ross was not facing a criminal hate promotion charge. A civil prohibition need fall only within the ambit of the international instruments to meet international standards.

Third, it is not sufficient for a person to say that his expression is an opinion on a religious subject for it to be so. The Board of Inquiry found that there was insufficient evidence to prove that Malcolm Ross's writings are required by his religion.[20] Justice Creaghan, however, found that Ross's writings reflect religious expression.[21] The League submitted that the suggestion of religious opinion by Malcolm Ross was a mask for prejudices which intrinsically have nothing to do with religion. Religion was not the cornerstone of Ross's advocacy. Rather, the beliefs and teachings of a religion were being twisted and construed to condone the prejudice.[22]

Christie, for Malcolm Ross, argued that "Antisemitism in a religious context is meaningless."[23] Yet, surely that must be wrong, or any person can avoid the consequences of propagating hatred simply by what label he or she puts on the speech, i.e., "I say that this is my religious opinion."

The Supreme Court of Canada said in the *Taylor* case that the conciliatory bent of human rights statutes renders limits on freedom of expression imposed under these statutes more acceptable than is the case under criminal provisions.[24] Even if criminalizing hate speech without the defence of religious expression is not constitutionally acceptable, that does not mean allowing the defence of religious expression is necessary to make the order of the Board of Inquiry constitutionally acceptable. In fact, there was no such defence in the statute upheld in the *Taylor* case.

The same can be said of truth. Christie argued at many points that what Malcolm Ross said may be true. Truth is a defence to the criminal offence of propagating hatred. However, even for the criminal offence, the Supreme Court of Canada has expressed doubt as to whether the Charter mandates that truthful statements communicated with an intention to promote hatred need be excepted from criminal condemnation.[25] For an order made under the authority of a human rights statute, these doubts are even stronger.

David Attis, the complainant, never asked for the restraining order imposed on Ross at the Board of Inquiry, or at any level. He was satisfied with the order removing Ross from the classroom. At the Supreme Court hearing, the court wondered whether the restraining order could properly be made or its striking down properly appealed, when the complainant never requested it. The League answer was that the Human Rights Commission was a party before the board, and they wanted the restraining order. Their request for the order was sufficient to give the board power to order it.

As well, what was at issue before the board was not just how the children of Attis were to be treated, but the poisoned atmosphere created by Ross within the school district and the school board's acceptance of Ross's behaviour generally. The Board of Inquiry had a legitimate interest in the general issue of discrimination independently of the specific complaint.

Thirdly, the jurisdiction of the board to order a remedy did not depend on what remedy the complainant requested. The complainant made the allegation of discrimination. Once the allegation was found to be true, it was up to the board to fashion the appropriate remedy.

The Supreme Court, at the hearing, also wondered what the restraining order had to do with the poisoned atmosphere in the classroom, if Ross was out of the classroom. The restraining order applied when Ross had a non-teaching position, and even when he was on a leave of absence, doing nothing for the school board. Did the Board of Inquiry have the power to issue a restraining order to anyone in their employ, even a person who had never been in the classroom? The purpose of the Human Rights Act of New Brunswick is to combat discrimination in the provision of services. Yet, if Malcolm Ross was providing services to no-one, or was not discriminating in the services he was providing, what mandate did the Board of Inquiry have to interfere in what the school board was allowing Ross to do?

The League answer was twofold. Once Ross worked for the school board, the reputation of the school district as a non-discriminatory service provider was inevitably undermined, and it was in fact undermined, as long as Ross was allowed to disseminate his hatred from no matter what position in the school system. If the school system was to be consistent and credible in its commitment to promoting non-discrimination, it could not turn a blind eye to the hate propaganda activity of Ross.

Regulations promulgated under the Schools Act of New Brunswick provides that a teacher shall maintain a deportment becoming his position as an educator of the young.[26] Even though Ross was out of the classroom, he remained employed as a teacher so the obligations regarding teacher deportment continued to apply to him. A deportment as a hate propagandist and Holocaust denier is not a deportment becoming a position as an educator of the young.

As well, the school board, as a service provider, should not be helping to foster discrimination in society at large by providing a haven to a hate propagandist. A hate propagandist does not have to be in the classroom to create a poisoned environment in the classroom. Hate propaganda poisons the general environment, outside and inside the classroom. Simply because Ross was not in the classroom, that did not mean that the insidious effect of his hate speech stopped at the classroom door. Preventing the classroom from degenerating into a hostile environment meant more than just getting Ross out of the classroom. It meant shutting Ross up.

However, the court wondered, is not a restriction on what an employee can say, when what he says has nothing to do with the job he does, an overbroad restriction on freedom of expression? Can the state require an employer to insist that an employee not disseminate his views where the dissemination of his views is done on his own time, and the dissemination of those views does not affect his job performance? The answer the League gave was that the state can indeed impose that restriction when the views being disseminated are hate speech. The requirement is not overbroad, because hate speech itself is a limited category of discourse that the Supreme Court of Canada has already held, in the *Taylor* and *Keegstra* cases, is not overbroad.

The British Columbia government intervened in the *Ross* case to argue this very point. British Columbia human rights legislation uses language prohibiting hate speech similar to that found in the Canadian Human Rights Act. In the *Taylor* case, John Ross Taylor had had a restraining order issued against him by the Canadian Human Rights Commission, prohibiting him from using the telephone to disseminate hatred. That order was held by the Supreme Court of Canada to be constitutionally valid.[27] Yet John Ross Taylor worked for no one. The order against Taylor was not keep quiet or lose your job. It was keep quiet or go to jail, a much more severe order. In fact, Taylor did go to jail. If that harsher order against Taylor was constitutionally valid, why would not the milder order against Ross be constitutionally valid?

British Columbia intervened in part to defend its own legislation. Formally, the order against Taylor was an order not to use the telephone for the purpose of disseminating hatred. The British Columbia government argued that the precedent could not and should not be limited to telephone use because the Supreme Court had not relied on that fact to decide that it was constitutionally valid. In 1993, the B.C. legislature, in reliance on the *Taylor* decision, legislated a general civil prohibition on hate speech. An amendment to its Human Rights Act provides that no person shall publish, issue or display, or cause to be published, issued, or displayed any statement, publication, notice, sign, symbol, emblem, or other representation that is likely to expose a person or a group or class of persons to hatred or contempt because of the race, colour, ancestry, place of origin, religion, marital status, family status, physical or mental disability, sex, sexual orientation or age of that person or that group of persons.[28] Counsel for B.C. argued that, given the province's close and careful reliance on the court's decision and reasons in *Taylor*, the authority of that case should in no way be attenuated.[29]

The Supreme Court of Canada, on April 3, 1996 upheld the order of the New Brunswick Human Rights Board of Inquiry removing Malcolm Ross from the classroom, but overturned the restraining order, that, even in a non-teaching job, he could not propagate hatred. The court ruled that both orders infringed both freedom of expression and freedom of religion, but that removing Malcolm Ross from the classroom was justified. The Court's reasoning had more to do with the structure of the Canadian Charter of Rights and Freedoms than with the substantive contents of those freedoms.

In Canada, the Supreme Court of Canada has interpreted the guarantee of freedom of expression in the Canadian Charter of Rights and Freedoms to encompass all verbal, visual, and written expression. This general and broad definition is a consequence of, and relies on, section one of the Charter, which subjects the rights in the Charter to such reasonable limits as are demonstrably justified in a free and democratic society. The Supreme Court of Canada has held that, in light of the reasonable limits provision, the guarantee of freedom of expression should be interpreted as broadly as possible and laws which limit expression should be judged by section one of the Charter.

United States offers a different model and different jurisprudence. The United States Bill of Rights has nothing equivalent to section one of the Canadian Charter of Rights and Freedoms. As a result, substantive rights, including the right to freedom of expression, are read in a more limited fashion.

Take, for instance, a law prohibiting a false cry of "fire" in a crowded theatre. Both Canadian and U.S. law hold that such a law is in conformity with basic rights. Canadian law would hold that the law violates the guarantee of freedom of expression but is a reasonable limit to that guarantee. U.S. law would hold that the law does not violate the guarantee of freedom of expression.

Mr. Justice La Forest for the court in the *Ross* case stated that while it is not logically necessary to rule out internal limits to freedom of expression or freedom of religion, it is analytically practical to do so where the context requires a detailed contextual analysis. In these circumstances, the detailed analytical approach developed by the court under the reasonable limits section of the Charter provides a more practical and comprehensive mechanism to assess competing interests.[30]

In a "section one" or "reasonable limits" analysis, the onus is on the state to justify the infringement of the right. How heavy that onus is depends on the nature of the rights under consideration. When the form of expression allegedly impinged by a ruling or law lies far from the core values that justify a right, a low standard of justification is applied. Hate propaganda strays some distance from the core values of freedom of expression and consequently restrictions on expressions of hate speech are easy to justify.[31]

The same is true for freedom of religion. Where the manifestations of an individual's freedom of religion are incompatible with the very values the Charter seeks to uphold, then an attenuated level of justification is appropriate. The religious views of Malcolm Ross serve to deny Jews respect for dignity and equality and these are among the fundamental guiding values of the Charter. Malcolm Ross could not be permitted to use the Charter as an instrument to roll back advances made by Jewish persons against discrimination.[32]

The Supreme Court's rejection of the restraining order against Ross was, in the end, a finding on the evidence, rather than a finding on the law. The court noted that the Board of Inquiry did not, in fact, find that the presence of Malcolm Ross in a non-teaching position and preaching hate would compromise the ability of the School Board to create a discrimination-free environment.[33] If the board had indeed found that, the Supreme Court of Canada may well have allowed the restraining order to stand. Because the board had not shown that the restraining order was warranted, the court was not prepared to uphold the order restraining Ross from preaching hate while in a non-teaching position with the school board.

Employers, especially in public institutions, must commit to combatting incitement to hatred as much as to freedom of expression. It is easy to fire someone who is spending time promoting hatred instead of doing their job. Firing someone who is promoting hatred off the job requires a stronger commitment to combatting hatred.

It would violate freedom of expression to fire or discipline someone for expressing views outside of work that the employer does not share. If the right to be free from incitement to hatred is to be placed at the same level as the right to freedom of expression, then it is equally wrong to do nothing when an employee outside of work promotes hatred. The Supreme Court of Canada in the *Ross* case tells us that it, in some circumstances, something can be done about employees who promote hatred off the job. The positive human rights obligation on all of us to combat the promotion of hatred means that when it can be done, it should be done.

Notes

1. *R. v. Oakes* (1986) 1 S.C.R. 103.
2. *Canada Human Rights Commission v. Taylor* (1990) 3 S.C.R. 892; *R. v. Keegstra* (1990) 3 S.C.R. 697.
3. Case on Appeal in the Supreme Court of Canada, Vol. 27, p. 5067, lines 10–15.
4. Case on Appeal in the Supreme Court of Canada, Vol. 27, p. 50969, lines 5–11.
5. *Canada Human Rights Commission v. Taylor* (1990) 3 S.C.R. 892.
6. *Nealy v. Johnston* (1989) 10 C.H.R.R. D/6450 at D/6469.
7. At page 927.
8. Case on Appeal in the Supreme Court of Canada, Vol. 27, p. 5067, line 5.
9. Case on Appeal in the Supreme Court of Canada, Vol. 27, p. 5070, line 55.
10. Case on Appeal in the Supreme Court of Canada, Vol. 27, p. 5069, lines 10 and 11.
11. *A.G. v. B.B.C.* (1980) 3 W.L.R. 109 (H.L.); *Ernewein v. M.E.I.* (1980) 103 D.L.R. (3d) 1, per Pigeon J., at page 17.
12. *Davidson v. Slaight Communications Ltd.* (1983) 93 N.R. 183 (S.C.C.), per Dickson, C.J.C., at pages 199–200.
13. *Kosiek Case* Eur.Ct. H.R. (1986) Series A, No. 105.
14. At page 42, paragraph 104.
15. At page 45, paragraph 115.
16. At page 43, paragraph 108.
17. At paragraphs 36 and 39.
18. At page 23.
19. Response to Attis, paragraph 137; response to CJC, paragraph 137; response to NBHRC, paragraphs 31 and 59.
20. Page 5053, lines 29 to 35.
21. Case on Appeal in the Supreme Court of Canada, Vol. 27, p. 5103.
22. See Gordon Allport *The Nature of Prejudice* (Cambridge, MA: Addison-Wesley, 1954); Elisabeth Odio Benito, United Nations Centre for Human Rights, "Elimination of all forms of intolerance and discrimination based on religion or belief," Study series 2 (1989), p. 40, paragraph 163.
23. Response to New Brunswick Human Rights Commission, paragraph 58.
24. Pages 928, 929.
25. *R. v. Keegstra* (1990) 3 S.C.R. 697 at 781.
26. Section 37(1)(a), School Administration Regulations, under the Schools Act R.S.N.B. c. S–5.1.

27. *Canada Human Rights Commission v. Taylor* (1990) 3 S.C.R. 892.
28. Section 2(1)(b) Human Rights Amendment Act, 1993, S.B.C. Chapter 27.
29. Factum of the A.G. of B.C., paragraph 29.
30. Reasons, page 44.
31. Reasons, page 51.
32. Reasons, page 49.
33. Reasons, page 60.

Chapter Eleven

South Africa

SHOULD COURTS PENALIZE politicians for not telling the truth? The question sounds more satirical than real. One might quip: "If the courts penalized politicians for lying, they wouldn't have time for anything else," or "If politicians could tell only the truth, they'd be left speechless."

However, for the South African election of April 1994, the question was real. The Electoral Act of South Africa binds every political party, every party leader, office bearer, member, supporter, and candidate to an Electoral Code of Conduct.[1] And it requires them all to tell the truth.

Most of this book examines speech laws that do not go far enough and argues that they should go farther. This chapter examines speech laws that go too far and argues that they should be pulled back. It steps through the looking glass and looks at speech issues from the other side.

Because protection from incitement to hatred is part of a total human rights package that includes freedom of expression, it is not enough for human rights advocates to promote only protection from incitement to hatred. There must also be promotion of freedom of expression. What would that promotion look like coming from someone who believes in protection from incitement to hatred? This chapter is an attempt to answer that question.

A later chapter in this book argues that truth should not be a defence to hate speech. Truth is irrelevant to determining whether advocacy is incitement to hatred. The converse is also true. Falsity should not be prohibited where there is no incitement to hatred. Falsity in itself does not justify banning.

The South African Electoral Code of Conduct requires all those bound by the code to refrain from publishing or repeating false, defamatory, or inflammatory allegations concerning any person or party in connection with the election.[2] Those who infringe the code can be penalized, according to the Electoral Act, with a formal warning and a fine not exceeding 100,000 rand (today about $14,000 U.S.).[3] Parties can potentially lose their election deposits.[4] In addition parties, but not individuals, can be prohibited from conducting various listed campaign activities.[5]

Legislation establishes an Election Monitoring Directorate in an Independent Electoral Commission to investigate[6] and an Electoral Tribunal[7] to adjudicate breaches of the code. Regulations provide that an order issued by an Electoral Tribunal shall be deemed to be an order issued by the Supreme Court of South Africa.[8] Accordingly, a formal warning issued by an Electoral Tribunal would have the same effect as a formal warning issued by the Supreme Court of South Africa. Disobedience of the warning would be contempt of court, a criminal offence.

Furthermore, the regulations provide that an Electoral Tribunal may order against parties and individuals a prohibitory interdict, ordering the discontinuance of the violation; a mandatory interdict, ordering the rectification of the violation; damages to compensate for violation of the code; and removal of an individual offending the code from his or her party position.[9] There is an emergency jurisdiction in the Electoral Tribunals, which, when invoked, allows a tribunal to make a prohibitory interdict only.[10] So, these tribunals have substantial powers, akin to a superior court.

In addition to Electoral Tribunals, the law creates Electoral Appeal Tribunals,[11] to hear appeals from the Electoral Tribunals. Finally, there is a Special Electoral Court,[12] to serve as a final level of appeal for the system.

I was part of a legal team sent by the Canadian Bar Association, the Lawyers for Social Responsibility, and the International Commission of Jurists to help determine whether the 1994 South African elections were free and fair. One question we had to answer was whether this particular power given to specially established Electoral Tribunals to penalize politicians for false, defamatory, or inflammatory statements was conducive to free and fair elections.

The Canadian legal team was dispersed throughout South Africa. Linda Lock, a British Columbia lawyer, and I were assigned to the Eastern Cape province and stationed in Port Elizabeth. In Port Elizabeth, we attended two Electoral Code trials.

In one, the National Party accused Bantu Holomisa of lying, defaming them, and inflaming voters. Holomisa is a former head of the black homeland, Transkei. He was number thirteen on the national list of African National Congress candidates for the election. At a speech he gave to students at the University of Port Elizabeth on March 24, 1994, he accused the National Party of planning to rig the vote during the election. The National Party, he said, would get hold of blank ballot papers, mark the ballots in favour of themselves, and inflate their vote count in farm areas and at South African Embassies abroad. He also said that the National Party would try to get blacks to eat *pap-en-vleis* (porridge and meat) tainted with the ink to be used to identify those who voted. Blacks who ate the tainted food would not be allowed to vote, because the ink would still be on their hands.

The National Party, through Johannes Wessels Maree, a director of their Federal Council, swore in an affidavit that none of that was true. The party asked for formal warning, a fine of 100,000 rands, and an interdiction order restraining both Holomisa and the African National Congress from breaching the code.

Holomisa claimed that what he said was true. He claimed that he had been informed by a confidential source that the truth of what he said could be shown by the Steyn report.

The National Party government on November 18, 1992 had asked Lieutenant General Pierre Steyn, a former chief of staff of the South African Defence Forces, to investigate allegations of covert activities by the forces.[13] As a result of an interim report filed with the government, State President F. W. de Klerk, on December 19, 1992, announced the early retirement of sixteen members of the forces, and the placement on compulsory leave of seven others.[14] De Klerk said that the report showed that a limited number of members, contract members, and collaborators of the forces had been involved and were still involved in illegal and/or unauthorized activities and malpractices, including political murders. The report was never released.

The failure to release the report had become a bone of political contention. In the one nationally televised debate between F. W. de Klerk and Nelson Mandela, on April 14, Mandela raised several times the government failure to release the Steyn Report.

At the Holomisa hearing, on April 18 in Port Elizabeth, counsel for Holomisa, Silus Nkanunu, a Port Elizabeth attorney, asked the tribunal to order the release of the report so that Holomisa could show that what he said was true. The tribunal adjudicator, Lex Mpati, an advocate with the Legal Resources Centre in Grahamstown, refused the request on the grounds that the report was in the hands of the government, not the National Party. In his view, the National Party could not release the report.

On the merits, counsel for the National Party, Ben Niehaus, an East London attorney, argued that what Holomisa said was defamatory of the National Party. There is a defence of truth to a claim of defamation, but it is a defence that must be established by the defaming party. The onus rested on Holomisa to establish the truth of what he said. That onus was not discharged, claimed Niehaus, merely by referring to an unnamed confidential source.

All the allegations of Holomisa, so Niehaus argued, were inflammatory. The allegation of feeding blacks tainted *pap-en-vleis* was inflammatory because it implied that all blacks were hostile to the National Party, that whites wanted to trick blacks into voting contrary to their true intentions.

Nkanunu, for Holomisa, argued that Holomisa should not be penalized unless the National Party could show that what Holomisa said was false, and further that either Holomisa knew it to be false or had no reasonable grounds for believing it to be true. The Electoral Act legislates a criminal offence of disseminating false information with the intention of influencing the election which has the defences Nkanunu raised.[15] The Electoral Code is part of the Electoral Act. The Electoral Code prohibition on false statements, Nkanunu argued, should be read to be subject to the same restrictions as the criminal offence. Further, counsel argued that the tribunal should take into consideration that the very evidence that might establish the truth of what Holomisa said was in the hands of the complaining party, the National Party. Even if the tribunal did not have the power to order the release, the fact that the report was in the hands of the National Party and was not disclosed should be taken into account.

Finally, Nkanunu argued, the tribunal had no power to order an interdict. The power to order an interdict against an individual was in the regulations only. The Electoral Act gave the tribunal power to issue a formal warning, but said nothing about an interdict. The regulations could not expand the powers of the tribunal given by the act.

The adjudicator Mpati, on April 20, found the allegation of ballot rigging, as well as the allegation of feeding black voters with tainted *pap-en-vleis*, to be allegations of intentional fraudulent activity.[16] As such they were *per se* defamatory. As well, the allegations of feeding blacks tainted *pap-en-vleis* had a racial connotation. They were intended to stir up trouble, and were accordingly inflammatory.

The ruling of the adjudicator was that, because the allegations of ballot rigging and the feeding of tainted *pap-en-vleis* were defamatory, the onus fell on Holomisa to show that they were true and in the public interest. If the allegations were true, it was undoubtedly in the public interest to disclose them. So the only issue was whether or not they were true.

A mere statement in an affidavit that Holomisa had heard from a confidential source that the Steyn Report contained evidence of these dirty tricks was not enough, according to the adjudicator, to discharge the onus that rested on Holomisa. So the onus was not discharged.

What is more, the adjudicator continued, even if the Steyn Report said what Holomisa said it said, the onus would still not be discharged. The Steyn Report was filed with the government some time before December 19, 1992. The Electoral Code of Conduct was promulgated by regulation, after agreement by all parties, including the National Party, on January 14, 1994. Even if the Steyn Report showed that the National Party, in December 1992, intended to perpetrate the dirty tricks alleged by Holomisa, the agreement to the Electoral Code by the National Party in January 1994 showed that they no longer intended to engage in such perfidy. For Holomisa to discharge the onus on him, he would have to show that the National Party was still intent, since January 1994, on perpetrating these dirty tricks. This Holomisa did not even attempt to do.

Having found Holomisa in violation of the code, the adjudicator nonetheless refused to order either a fine or an interdict. He found, as counsel for Holomisa had argued, that he had no power to order an interdict. An inferior tribunal, such as the Electoral Tribunal, has no power to decide that regulations are beyond the authority of a statute, that is something only the Supreme Court of South Africa can do. However, every inferior tribunal has both the power and the duty to determine its own jurisdiction and act only within its jurisdictional powers. Adjudicator Mpati found that his jurisdiction was limited to the powers given to him by the Electoral Act. He could not use the Electoral Act regulations to broaden his jurisdiction beyond that given to him by statute. Accordingly, he issued a formal warning only. He felt that, in any case, a formal warning would have the same effect as an interdict. He was also of the view that a formal warning, on its own, was sufficient, that an additional fine was unnecessary. Finally, the adjudicator awarded costs to the National Party.

The second Eastern Cape truth trial we attended was a complaint by the Democratic Party against the National Party. The National Party had circulated a pamphlet in the Eastern Cape claiming that the Democratic Party was "not prepared to take up seats in the Central Cabinet or in the East Cape

Provincial Cabinet." The Democratic Party complained to the Independent Electoral Commission about the pamphlet. The commission was of the view that the pamphlet was false, defamatory and inflammatory and, accordingly, an infringement of the Electoral Code of Conduct. The commission formally warned the National Party against further distributing the pamphlet.

After the warning, the Democratic Party, believing that the violation was continuing, invoked the jurisdiction of the Electoral Tribunal. The standard procedure requires that the hearing must be at least five days after the day the summons was served.[17] The emergency procedure allows the tribunal to dispense with the five day limit.[18] Since the election was fast approaching, the Democratic Party invoked the emergency procedure.

In their summons, the Democratic Party asked for an interim interdict to be granted at the emergency hearing, ordering the National Party to refrain from distributing the pamphlet. The Democratic Party further asked, subject to a final hearing, for a formal warning; a fine of 100,000 rand; a forfeiture of the National Party's election deposit; and a final order of interdict. The Democratic Party also asked for an order to the National Party to retract the statement, acknowledge it was incorrect, publish the retraction in the newspapers and distribute the retraction in all post boxes in which the National Party had distributed the pamphlet.

Prior to the first hearing, the National Party filed an affidavit in their defence claiming that the statement under complaint was true. At the hearing, in Port Elizabeth on April 23, the National Party filed a further affidavit swearing that they had ceased distribution of the controversial pamphlet after being warned by the Electoral Commission.

At the hearing, Rayn Wade, a Port Elizabeth advocate acting for the Democratic Party, withdrew the request for all remedies except the interim interdict. He was of the view that the tribunal would have no jurisdiction to grant the other remedies at a later date. A hearing where the other remedies could be granted would require a new summons that fulfilled the five day notice requirement.

Wade then proceeded to argue that the contentious statement in the pamphlet was false, because it was not the whole truth. Democratic Party spokesmen had not said that the party would not serve in the national or Eastern Cape cabinets. They had said only that the party would not serve in cabinet if they were bound by cabinet solidarity and unable to criticise cabinet decisions. The party would be quite happy to serve in cabinet as long as the party cabinet members were free to criticise government policy.

The statement was defamatory, so Wade argued, because the notion of not being prepared to serve in cabinet had a double meaning. One sense of the phrase was that the party admitted that its members did not have the ability to serve in cabinet. When the phrase was interpreted in that sense, the pamphlet was defamatory.

For the National Party, Dup de Bruyn, a Port Elizabeth advocate, argued that the contentious statement was true, because it was a fair conclusion that could be drawn from Democratic Party policy read in conjunction with the new constitution, which was to come into effect after the elections. According to that constitution, for cabinet, both at the national and provincial levels, there is collective accountability.[19] De Bruyn reasoned that collective accountability was incompatible with allowing criticism by a cabinet minister. Although the Democratic Party was conditionally willing to serve in cabinet, they had a imposed a condition that could never be fulfilled. Therefore, what the National Party had said was in substance true.

De Bruyn further argued that the National Party was under no obligation to repeat word for word what was stated by the Democratic Party. The National Party was entitled to draw its own conclusions from Democratic Party policies, where those conclusions were logical and fair comment. De Bruyn urged that latitude must be allowed in debate on public issues.

Advocate de Bruyn rejected that the interpretation Wade had proposed, that the Democratic Party did not have the ability to participate in cabinet, was conveyed by the pamphlet. Such an interpretation was, to de Bruyn, strained and not reasonable.

In order for an applicant to succeed in an emergency proceeding, the applicant must show that a right had been infringed, that there is reasonable fear he or she will suffer irreparable harm if the order sought is not granted, and that the balance of convenience favours granting an order.[20] De Bruyn submitted that it was not necessary for the tribunal to determine whether the code had been infringed, because there was no apprehension of irreparable harm. The National Party had ceased publication and distribution of the pamphlet and undertook not to recommence publication and distribution. That alone should be enough to justify dismissal of the application.

Adjudicator Belinda Hartle, a Port Elizabeth attorney, on April 22, ruled that the National Party had violated the Electoral Code.[21] The statement in the pamphlet about the Democratic Party was false. A half truth is not the truth. The failure of the National Party to qualify their bald statement that the Democratic Party was not prepared to serve in cabinet rendered the statement false. The statement was not made in the context of a debate where there was an opportunity to respond. The wide distribution in a pamphlet compounded the infringement.

The adjudicator further held that the statement was inflammatory. It was a statement that was capable of inflaming passions.

Moreover, the statement was defamatory. The reading that advocate Wade gave the statement, regarding the ability rather than the willingness to serve in cabinet, was the reading made by the Democratic Party supporters or potential supporters. Their reading of the statement in that way was sufficient to make the statement defamatory.

The Democratic Party had established that a right of theirs was infringed, because the Electoral Code was violated. However, in light of the undertaking by the National Party not to continue distributing the pamphlet, there was no reasonable apprehension of irreparable harm. So the request for an interim order was refused.

In closing, Adjudicator Hartle pointed out that there was a gap in the regulations. The emergency procedure provides, in the regulations, for prohibitory interdicts, but not mandatory interdicts. The Democratic Party did not need what the adjudicator could give, a prohibitory interdict, since the National Party had already ceased publication of the pamphlet. Additionally, the adjudicator could not give what the Democratic Party needed, a mandatory interdict for corrective action, namely, to order the National Party to retract the false statement by newspaper ads or a further pamphlet. The regulations did not allow the adjudicator to make such an order in emergency proceedings.

Were this law and these cases conducive to free and fair elections? Certainly, penalizing politicians for not telling the truth or arousing passions is not conducive to free elections. It violates the principle of freedom of expression. Freedom of expression means the right to be wrong. Freedom of expression is not limited to freedom to speak official truth. On the contrary, it is particularly what society views as false that needs the protection of the guarantee of freedom of expression.

The Electoral Code of Conduct, in other provisions, penalizes intimidation and any language which may lead to violence or intimidation.[22] So the prohibition against inflammatory allegations is a prohibition against language that is not necessarily intimidating, that may not lead to violence or intimidation.

Freedom of expression is not just a freedom to express that which calms or soothes. Arousing passions by speech does not put the speech outside the guarantee of free speech. Getting people stirred up during elections may strengthen rather than weaken democracy.

Defamation is a legitimate and generally accepted exception to the principle of freedom of speech. However, it is also generally accepted that defamation law has little application to political debate. What would be defamatory of a private individual is not necessarily defamatory of a politician. Defamation law must not be applied so as to inhibit robust political exchange.

The issue becomes whether what is lost in freedom is gained in fairness. Did the truth provision of the Electoral Code of Conduct make the South African election fairer than it otherwise would have been? If so, did the increase in fairness justify the decrease in liberty?

The justifications that have been raised in defence of the truth provision in the Electoral Code of Conduct are various. One is that the political parties voluntarily agreed on the code amongst themselves. Even if it is wrong to impose a prohibition on freedom of speech in an election, there is nothing wrong with political parties voluntarily accepting it for themselves.

In an Electoral Tribunal case in Cape Town, Adjudicator Lee Bozalek, articulated this viewpoint. He said: "real content must in my view be given to the restraints which the parties have accepted on their electioneering activities in terms of the code which they have negotiated and subjected themselves to, failing which it becomes a mere set of empty promises."[23]

Secondly, the notion of penalties for not telling the truth has traditionally been part of South African law. It used to be an offence to publish any false information concerning the experience in prison of any prisoner or ex-prisoner or relating to the administration of any prison. And it used to be an offence in South Africa to publish any untrue matter about the police force, or any part of it, or about any member of the force in relation to the performance of his functions, without having reasonable grounds for believing the statement to be true. The onus of establishing reasonable grounds fell on the publisher.[24] The truth provision in the Electoral Code of Conduct is not that far different from these other truth provisions.

Additionally, the times were troubled. There had been thousands of political killings in South Africa before the 1994 election. Apartheid generated a discourse of repression and revolution, a discourse of violence. The legacy of apartheid had far from dissipated. It was necessary to do everything possible to lower the political temperature in order to avoid a continuation of this political violence during the election period.

South Africa had been plagued by political dirty tricks, covert activities, and the operation of a destabilizing third force. This skulduggery had led to suspicion and distrust. The parties were not prepared to believe that everyone, on his or her own, would show forbearance and tolerance. There had been no history of respect for the rules of democracy. To generate trust, it was necessary to set up a system with legal sanctions behind it.

For most voters, this was their first election. Over the course of elections, voters become used to forming their own judgments on political rhetoric. They learn to sort out the true from the false. They become less ingenuous, even cynical. However, for this election, which was the first election for the majority of South Africans, it was necessary to take every step possible to ensure that political rhetoric was honest and dispassionate.

Many of the voters were also illiterate. Political debate through newspaper stories, advertisements, and pamphlets would not have been sufficient to correct untruths once told. In an illiterate community untruths are much more likely to be accepted, at least in the short run.

South Africa is a country of many languages. Very few people know every South African language. It would be difficult to correct quickly an untruth spread in one language about the politics of those who speak another language. It is far better to prevent such untruths from being spread in the first place.

Judicialization moves the debate about truth from the heat of the political arena to the calm of the courtroom. Tribunals can conduct investigations, hear witnesses, summon documents, and come to deliberated determinations about what the truth is. Voters would not be left with just bald competing assertions of truth, and little or no information with which to assess them.

These were justifications that were made for the law. Do they make any sense?

The argument that the code is voluntary, and is therefore not an imposition on anyone, made sense for the National Party and the African National Congress, the major parties to the negotiations that led to the code. For the other political parties involved in the negotiations, the code was inevitable.

The code, however, did not apply only to the parties who participated in the negotiations. It applied to every party and candidate that wished to contest the election, even parties formed after the code was legislated. To say that the code was freely self-imposed was highly artificial.

Reference to the former provisions in the Police Act and the Prisons Act is also unpersuasive. Penalizing the telling of untruths in these acts was part of the state apparatus of oppression during the height of apartheid. These laws were repealed when the legal superstructure that supported apartheid was dismantled. It was hardly appropriate to use the laws of apartheid as a model for the laws for fair and free elections. Many wrongs, of course, do not make a right. The fact that a provision penalizing falsehood can be found in many laws does not make the provision right or sensible or fair in any law.

The notion that judicialization will take the heat out of the political process and bring us closer to the truth ignores the limitations of the courts, and the danger posed to the courts by bringing politics into court. Courts do not necessarily or always determine the truth with accuracy. Court judgments are sometimes wrong. One has only to look at the number of reversals on appeal to see that this is so.

What courts give us is a peaceful way of resolving disputes. Facts are not so much determined as they are decided for the purpose of the dispute. While, in court, every effort is made to determine the truth, at some time there must be finality to litigation. At the end of the day, the parties must accept the results, right or wrong.

Courts are not the only or even the best way for resolving disputes, particularly political disputes. The traditional way to resolve political disputes is through democratic elections. The traditional court for resolving political disputes is the court of public opinion. Taking disputes away from the public and putting it into the courts is undemocratic. It leaves the resolution of political disputes to a few, rather than to the many.

The atmosphere of a courtroom may be calm and cool. However, that does not mean to say that the litigants are calm and cool. Litigation hardens attitudes. It forces the parties into fixed adversarial positions. It can add fuel to any fire. Litigation may itself be inflammatory.

There is also the danger that the courts become misused for political purposes. If the courts are offered as a forum for political parties during elections, the parties will be glad to take up the offer. Court proceedings offer publicity and a chance of victory. The possibility of court proceedings may generate or exaggerate disputes that would otherwise not have existed, or have gone unnoticed.

Asking the courts to resolve political disputes politicizes the courts. Once the courts enter into the political arena, there is a danger that their impartiality will be questioned, not only in the interpretation of election laws or codes, but in all areas.

In South Africa, Electoral Appeal Tribunals and each Special Electoral Court must have a chairperson who is a judge of the Supreme Court.[25] So the regular court system is drawn into this specialized electoral adjudication. If electoral adjudication becomes politicized, so does the whole South African court system.

The notion that first-time voters need some special protection others do not need is condescending. In every election, in every country, there are many voters who vote for the first time.

Democracy is not the rule of those who have voted before. It is not the rule of the literate. It is not the rule of those who know every language in a multilingual society. It is rule of the people, first time voters as well as experienced voters, illiterate as well as literate, unilingual as well as multilingual. Restricting freedom of speech during elections because voters are voting for the first time, because voters are illiterate, because voters are unilingual in a multilingual society means denying voters the full measure of democracy. It means a refusal to accept, completely, the rule of the people.

When political leaders of South Africa or of any country talk about a fair election, they mean there must be a level playing field. There is an assumption, however, that what is fair to the parties will be fair to the voters. That assumption is not necessarily valid. In general, when parties agree about matters of public interest, the agreement can reasonably be said to reflect the public interest. However, when political parties agree about political party matters, the agreement may reflect only the parties' own self-interest. Such agreements must bear close scrutiny.

It may be fair to the parties to set up a policing system for themselves, to prevent false, defamatory, or inflammatory statements, and yet be unfair to the voters. Freedom of speech is a value both for the speaker and the listener. For the listener, freedom of speech means the listener can decide for himself or herself what the truth is. Even if we put aside the value of freedom of speech to the speaker, as the South African political parties have done with their agreement, the value to the listener remains.

The history of dirty tricks and political violence in South Africa is a different matter. It is not so easy to dismiss out of hand concerns based on this history. The parties, not that long before the 1994 election, viewed each other as criminals. It would be unfair to suggest any symmetry whatsoever between the crimes of the apartheid regime and the crimes of its opponents. Nonetheless, there was reason for each of the parties to be fearful of the others. It would have been all too easy to relapse into the rhetoric and from there, into the violence of the bloody past.

The question became, given this history and the dangers it signalled, were the restrictions found in the Electoral Code of Conduct fair to the parties and the voters? In order to answer that question, regard must be given to general principles and standards.

The Universal Declaration of Human Rights,[26] the International Covenant on Civil and Political Rights,[27] the African Charter on Human and People's Rights,[28] and the new South African Constitution[29] all guarantee the right to freedom of expression. This guaranteed right is subject to exceptions.

For the International Covenant on Civil and Political Rights, there is an exception for those restrictions necessary for the respect of the rights or reputations of others.[30] There is also an exception to the guarantee of freedom of expression in the International Covenant that relates to hate speech.[31] The Electoral Code of Conduct prohibition overlapped with, but did not coincide with, this hate-speech standard. Not all inflammatory language is advocacy of national racial or religious hatred. Language may be inflammatory even when it is not advocacy of hatred and speech may be advocacy of hatred whether it is true or false. The Electoral Code of Conduct refers specifically to false speech. The International Covenant also allows for derogation from the right to freedom of expression in times of public emergency which threaten the life of the nation.[32]

The African Charter provides that the rights and freedoms of each individual shall be exercised with due regard to the rights of others. The rights of other includes collective security, morality, and common interest.[33]

The new South African Constitution provides that all rights guaranteed in the constitution can be limited, but only by a law that is reasonable and justifiable in an open and democratic society based on freedom and equality. Further, any limitation specifically to the right to freedom of expression as it relates to free and fair political activity, must in addition to being reasonable, also be necessary.[34]

The Constitution further provides that the right to freedom of expression, amongst other rights, may be suspended in consequence of the declaration of a state of emergency. However, the suspension must be only to the extent necessary to restore peace or order.[35]

The international, as well as the South African, standards require us to decide not just whether the truth provision of the Electoral Code of Conduct is conducive to free and fair elections. Rather, we must decide whether the provision is *necessary* for free and fair elections.

Certainly in Port Elizabeth and the Eastern Cape the provision was not necessary. One newspaper columnist called Port Elizabeth the boredom capital from an electoral perspective.[36] Another columnist wrote about the Eastern Cape: "the revolution is largely over here. Reconciliation, which does not make for good television pictures, is well under way."[37] There was only one reported incident of physical violence during the campaign. A loud, drunk National Party supporter was stabbed in the arm during an African National Congress rally at Humansdorp on April 20.[38]

There were only five cases that went to adjudication in the Eastern Cape. There were only two in Port Elizabeth, the truth cases about Holomisa and the Democratic Party. If the truth provision had not been in the Electoral Code, there would have been no adjudications in Port Elizabeth at all.

Of the other three cases in the Eastern Cape, one was in Adelaide, on April 14. The second was in Barkly East, on April 19. The third was in Mdantsane, on April 26. The Adelaide and Mdantsane cases were settled on the court doorstep.[39] In Barkly East, the adjudicator dismissed the complaint.[40]

All told, in the Eastern Cape, as of April 23, the Friday before the election, there were 105 complaints. Six were sent to mediation. Twenty-four warnings were issued to individuals by the Independent Electoral Commission. Five warnings were issued to political parties. The Democratic Party case was the only case that went to litigation after a warning.

The situation was different in Natal. There it was far from peaceful. Political violence was so extensive that the President F. W. de Klerk announced a state of emergency for the province on March 31. The state of emergency continued throughout the election, even after the Inkatha Freedom Party decided to contest the election.

However, even in Natal, political violence diminished, once Inkatha decided to participate in the process. Four weeks into the state of emergency, in the week following Inkatha's decision to join the election, the political death toll in Natal fell from fifty-one to twenty.[41]

It is a compliment to South Africa, I believe, rather than a criticism, to say that the truth provision in the Electoral Code of Conduct was not necessary for there to have been free and fair elections. Things were not so bad that the provision was needed. At the time agreement on the code was achieved it may have seemed so, but in spite of continuing violence in parts of South Africa, the willingness of South Africans, generally, to resolve their differences through peaceful and democratic means was so widespread, that the truth provision in the Electoral Code of Conduct amounted to an excess of caution.

Repeal of the truth provision in the Electoral Code of Conduct would not leave South Africa defenceless against the dangers of wild rhetoric. The provision in the Electoral Code against language which might lead to violence or intimidation would remain.[42]

The offence in the Electoral Act which penalizes those who disseminate false information with the intention of influencing the election would also remain.[43] Because that offence has a requirement of intention, and because it is a criminal offence with all the accompanying safeguards of the criminal process, it is not as problematic as the Electoral Code of Conduct provision.

The power to declare a state of emergency, as in Natal, would also remain. In a state of emergency, derogation from the right to freedom of expression may be justifiable.

The Eastern Cape adjudication cases demonstrated a number of different ways the process could be improved. There should be a closer match between the types of orders adjudicators could issue under the act and under the regulations; the power of adjudicators to issue orders in emergency situations should be expanded to cover, at the very least, mandatory interdicts; and Electoral Commission warnings should require the person warned to inform the commission about future compliance in order to avoid unnecessary litigation.

These reforms may be useful to make the system work for other sorts of violations of the Electoral Code of Conduct. However, making the truth provision in the code more effective would only compound the problems the provision now poses.

Heinz Klug, in an article in the *South African Journal on Human Rights*, warns of the need to make a clear distinction between the electoral process and genuinely democratic elections. He writes:

Although a formally fair and transparent electoral process may take place, in order to conduct a genuinely democratic and free election it is imperative that there be genuine freedom of expression and association so that those participating in the election are able to organise politically and express their positions on all issues of relevance to the electorate. [44]

In general, the Electoral Code of Conduct and the adjudication of disputes under the code were conducive to free and fair elections. However, there was not complete freedom of expression during the election, because the Electoral Code of Conduct prevented it. The truth provision in the code was not necessary to make the election fair. It should not have been there.

The parliament of South Africa passed a new Electoral Act with a new Code of Conduct for the May 1999 elections.[45] The prohibition against inflammatory allegations disappeared. The prohibition against false allegations remained.[46]

Free speech absolutists argue that any restriction of free speech puts us on a slippery slope leading to ever greater violations of the right to free speech. Practically, this argument is rebutted by everyday reality. The few speech restrictions we see are not leading to ever greater restrictions.

That argument is wrongheaded conceptually as well. Being in favour of the prohibition of hate speech does not knock the intellectual underpinning out from the defence of free speech. It is possible, as this chapter has attempted to show, both to defend the right to free speech and to argue for the banning of hate speech.

Support for the banning of hate speech does not leave us defenceless in the assault against free speech. The arguments for the banning of hate speech are not arguments that can be transferred holus bolus to justify the banning of any speech. On the contrary, the right to free speech and the right to protection from incitement to hatred mesh together as a human rights whole.

Notes

1. Electoral Act, *Statutes of South Africa* (1993), Act 202, Section 69(1)(b).
2. Electoral Act, Schedule 2, Section 4(d).
3. Section 69(2)(c)(i).
4. Section 69(2)(a)(iii).
5. Section 69(2)(a)(iv)–(vi).
6. Independent Electoral Commission Act, *Statutes of South Africa* (1993), Act 150, Section 24(1)(d).
7. Section 28.
8. Electoral Regulations, *Government Gazette*, February 17, 1994, Section 81(5).

9. Regulation 81(1)(b).
10. Regulation 82(1)(b).
11. Section 30.
12. Section 32.
13. "Hierarchy dismayed over axing of generals," *Eastern Province Herald*, December 21, 1992.
14. "De Klerk axes six SADF top brass," *Eastern Province Herald*, December 19, 1992.
15. Section 63(b).
16. *N.P. v. Holomisa*, Case NO. PTE 1/94.
17. Regulation 77(4)(b).
18. Regulation 82(1)(a).
19. *Constitution of the Republic of South Africa* (1993), Act 200, Sections 92(1) and 153(1).
20. Regulation 82(2)(b).
21. *D.P. v. F.P. Smith*, Case No. PTE 2/94.
22. Sections 4(a) and (b).
23. *A.N.C. v. N.P.*, CT/2/94.
24. Police Act, *Statutes of South Africa* (1958), No. 7, Section 27B(1); inserted by section 9 of Act 64 of 1979 and repealed by section 4 of Act 23 of 1992.
25. Independent Electoral Commission Act, *Statutes of South Africa* (1993), Act 150, Sections 30(2)(a) and 32(1)(a).
26. Article 19.
27. Article 19(2).
28. Article 9(1).
29. Article 15(1).
30. Article 19(2).
31. Article 20(2).
32. Article 4(1).
33. Article 27(2).
34. Article 33(1).
35. Article 34(4).
36. Patrick Cull. "Elections Imperative," *Eastern Province Herald*, April 16, 1994, p. 4.
37. Simon Barber. "All Quiet on the Eastern Front," *Eastern Province Herald*, April 22, 1994, p. 6.
38. Traci Mackie "Loud Nat stabbed in scuffle," *Eastern Province Herald*, April 21, 1994, p. 1.
39. *Meyer for the NP v. Maclean for the ANC*, Case No: ADL 1/1994; *ADM v. ANC*, Case No. MDA 1/1994.
40. *ANC v. Pretorius for the NP*, Case No: BKE 1/1994.

41. Human Right Commission, *Weekly Report*, from Week No. 17 (20/04/94 to 25/04/94).
42. Section 4(a).
43. Section 63(b).
44. "Guaranteeing Free and Fair Elections" (1992) 8 SAJHR 263 at page 269.
45. Law 73 of 1998.
46. Schedule 2, section 9(1)(b).

Chapter Twelve

The Internet

THE ADVENT OF THE INTERNET has given a new and powerful tool to hate-mongers. Hate speech, because of the internet, is circulating as it never was before.[1] It is accessible to adults and children alike, at the click of a button.

Hate speech, unlike pornography, is not something that is obvious at first sight. Hate speech combines in a volatile cocktail incitement to violence and fraud. It is insidious, devious. While one can say, at least for adults, that they can choose to click on, or not click on, pornography, the same cannot be said for hate speech. Those susceptible to the messages of hate-mongers are those with little appreciation of the danger of the messages.

Hate speech on the internet cannot be ignored. It represents a threat that needs to be combatted. How it should be combatted, however, requires sensitivity to the medium.

It is important, first of all, to consider the general boon the internet has become. The internet offers a great advantage for communicating information worldwide. It is quick; it is cheap; and it is accurate, in the sense that the data received reproduces the data sent.

Marshall McLuhan over thirty years ago wrote: "After three thousand years of specialist explosion and increasing specialism and alienation in the technological extensions of our bodies, our world has become compression-able by dramatic reversal. As electronically contracted the globe is no more than a village."[2] What was compressionable in 1964 when those words were published, has, through the internet, become compressed. The internet has made Marshall McLuhan's global village an electronic reality.

The internet has made global freedom of expression a practical mundane fact for anyone with a computer and a phone. Today, because of the internet, anyone and everyone can disseminate their thoughts, their feelings, their research, their discoveries, their analyses, their opinions world-wide to millions at virtually no cost.

Even at this early stage, it is not too early to say that the internet is important for democracy. To take an example, in Serbia, there was a direct connection between freedom of speech on the internet and the reinstatement of the municipal election results of late 1996, which President Slobodan Milosevic tried to thwart. When protests began against Milosevic's refusal to recognize the election results, the response of the authorities was to jam the signal of radio station Radio B92, which was broadcasting information about the protests. Eventually the authorities shut down Radio B92 completely.

Drazen Pantic of Radio B92 responded by sending audio reports of the protests over the internet using RealAudio. The Radio B92 reports continued to be available to anyone on the internet, all over the world, including Serbia. Radio Free Europe used transmitters to broadcast the Radio B92 stories back into Serbia. The only way for Milosevic to shut down internet access for Radio B92 would have been for him to shut down the whole Serbian telephone system. When it became apparent to the authorities that they could not stop the Radio B92 protest reports, they allowed the radio station to switch its transmitter back on. The reports of the protests, and the abandonment by the authorities of their censorship of B92, encouraged the protesters, added to their numbers, and led to the authorities backing down from their reversal of the municipal election results.[3]

The right to freedom of expression must be respected on the internet. So must the right to be free from incitement to hatred. For most countries of the world, there is little or no censorship on the internet. There are, in contrast, substantial violations of the right to be free from incitement to hatred.

In the internet hate speech–free speech debate, there is a tendency for advocates to divide. Free speech absolutists are on one side. Advocates of prohibition of hate speech are on the other.

This divide is inevitable in some contexts. However, it is not intrinsic to the internet. Because the internet has much less regulation than other media, there is the danger that anti-hate activists will leave the impression that free speech limitations are not their concern.

Supporters of the prohibition of hate speech must not abandon free speech values to free speech absolutists. We must embed our activity in a complete human rights framework, and show not only when, where, and why hate speech should be prohibited, but must also show how and why free speech should be protected.

Many countries try to grapple with the internet to maintain some semblance of respect for the right to be free from incitement to hatred. It is important to point out that these countries are all democracies with a human rights tradition that respects the right to freedom of expression and make the effort to square control of the internet with that freedom.

Other countries, however, approach the internet from the opposite end of the spectrum, not as democracies attempting to respect the right of everyone to be free from incitement to hatred, but as autarchies attempting to repress dissent. Repression today means shutting down the internet.

In Burma, use of the internet is outlawed. So is ownership of an unregistered computer with networking capabilities, or membership in an unauthorized computer club. Linking up with the rest of the world on the internet in Burma can lead to a prison sentence of seven to fifteen years. Neither of Burma's two local internet servers is available to the public. A Burmese willing to risk violation of the law to access the internet has to call an international provider. In Burma international telephone calls are billed at five dollars U.S. a minute.

There are similar restrictions in Cuba, Singapore, and China. The government of Cuba allows only a few scientists and government employees to use the local internet access provider. All others have to get access through long distance calls paid for in hard currency. In Singapore, anyone downloading material of which the government disapproves is subject to huge fines.[4]

In China, anyone sending e-mail must register with the authorities. Through China Telecommunications Ltd., established under the authority of the Ministry of Information Industry, the Government of China has a monopoly over all telecommunications. Every internet service provider in China connects to the internet through China Telecommunications Ltd.

It is possible to circumvent China Telecommunications Ltd. by using a foreign internet service provider. However, to do so would mean incurring long distance charges, an impractical cost for many internet users.

The Government of China uses its internet monopoly to prevent the posting, in China, of websites that are critical of the government. It shuts down internet accounts of users who send out e-mail critical of the government. The government blocks access to foreign websites the government considers objectionable. Amongst the websites blocked are Amnesty International, Human Rights Watch, and Cable Network News (CNN). This blocking has the effect of shutting out criticism of the Government of China for internet users in China.

To circumvent this blocking, various offshore services determined to get the truth about China to the Chinese have resorted to e-mail from offshore. Most notably amongst these is VIP Reference. VIP Reference is an e-mail service which spams information about China to China from the United States. (Spamming is the practice of sending high-volume unsolicited e-mail.) VIP Reference sends out about 250,000 messages daily to e-mail addresses in China that VIP Reference has collected. The service changes its home site address every day to circumvent blocking.

Since VIP Reference is outside China, it is beyond the grip of the Government of China. In order to function, VIP Reference nonetheless needs the cooperation of people in China in two crucial ways. It needs information from China, and it needs e-mail addresses from China.

The Government of China has rolled its machine of oppression over individuals who have supplied both. Wang Youcai, on December 21, 1998 was sentenced in Hangzhou China to eleven years in prison for subversion. Amongst the crimes with which he was charged was sending out e-mail from China to foreigners which the government considered subversive, and accepting money from a foreigner to buy a computer.

Lin Hai, on January 20, 1999 was sentenced in Shanghai to two years in prison, also for subversion. He was released in March 2000, after serving over one year of this sentence. His sole crime was providing, free of charge, Chinese e-mail addresses to VIP Reference.

Wang Youcai is a political activist. He was one of the leaders of the Tiananmen Square protest of 1989, and more recently in 1998, he was part of a group attempting to launch a democratic opposition party, the Chinese Democratic Party. The activities for which he was convicted were partly but not exclusively internet activities.

Lin Hai is an internet businessman without a political past. Before his arrest in March 1998 he ran an internet firm called Key Soft, which helped people in China set up websites. The firm engaged in internet job searches for hire. As part of his business and in order to build up its e-mail list for job searches, Lin Hai engaged in e-mail list swaps and sales. Lin Hai gave 30,000 e-mail addresses to VIP Reference. It was this activity alone for which Lin Hai was sentenced to two years in jail.

The trial and sentencing of Wang Youcai and Lin Hai were unfair proceedings. They were closed trials before courts that were not independent from government.

In principle, there is nothing wrong with the blocking of hate websites, either foreign or domestic. There is everything wrong with blocking political criticism, whether domestic or foreign.

There is nothing wrong with penalizing spamming. Spamming is, by definition, the mass sending of unwanted e-mail. However, there is everything wrong with penalizing the mass sending of e-mail to willing recipients.

There is nothing wrong with penalizing the use of mass e-mailing to incite hatred. There is everything wrong with penalizing the use of mass e-mailing to criticize the government.

The internet began through the efforts of private individuals working on their own communicating with each other to solve the problems thrown up by the developing technology. Like the pioneers of the Wild West, these pioneers have developed an ethic of libertarianism, a belief that internet users, and not governments, should solve internet problems, that the internet should not be so much unregulated as self-regulated.

However, the internet, like the West, has now been occupied and settled by a population far larger than the original pioneers and far different from them. Now the internet needs law and order. The internet should not be a law-free zone. Neither should it be a special domain for Big Brother where an all powerful state holds sway. Just as one can say that crimes off the internet should also be crimes on the internet, one can also say that freedom of speech off the internet should also be freedom of speech on the internet.

What is wrong with the blocking and penalizing that is going on in China is not that there is blocking and penalizing, but rather what is blocked, what is penalized. China represses political dissent on the internet because it represses political dissent generally. Its denial of political dissent on the internet is part of a larger denial of political dissent wherever and however that expression surfaces.

Looking to other examples around the world, it may be difficult to hold out any one country as a model, to say the law should be exactly as it is in the United Kingdom, the United States, Germany, Canada, or Australia, for example. However, it is easy to say what we do not want. We do not want to be like Burma or Cuba or Singapore or China.

If human rights are to be truly protected, then there must be protection on the internet both for freedom of expression and from hate speech. At the level of principle, the issue of hate speech on the internet raises no new questions. The issue of balancing rights remains.

What is new, however, with the internet is the question of technology. Given this technology, is it at all possible to ban hate speech on the internet?

As Marshall McLuhan has reminded us, in many ways the medium is the message. Electronic technology is an extension of our senses.[5] The internet gives an extension to the senses of hate-mongers far beyond what had been earlier technologically feasible. This extension, the empowerment of hate propagandists through the internet, rather than sapping our will, should mobilize it.

The internet has made hate speech accessible to those who would have never come into contact with it before. It has brought hate speech to children, to the suburbs. Those most prone to the messages of hate speech are the marginal and the alienated. Prior to the internet, it was relatively difficult, for hate-mongers to seek these people out. The marginal and the alienated, by their very nature, are disconnected socially and politically. There are no organizations for the marginal, clubs for the alienated, connections amongst the disconnected. The internet allows hate-mongers to reach into the privacy and isolation of people's homes, to find the vulnerable who are prone to the message of hate speech wherever they happen to be.

Before the internet, hate speech was accessible to thousands, those on mailing lists, those who called in to telephone hate lines, those who could be pamphleteered on the street or in parking lots. Now, through the internet, hate speech is accessible to millions. The random chance that those susceptible to the siren songs of hate-mongers will now hear those songs has increased exponentially.

McLuhan distinguishes between hot and cool media. Hot media are high definition and filled with data; cool media are those that give a meagre amount of information.[6] McLuhan observes that a hot medium used in a cool or non-literate culture has a violent effect.[7] The internet is a hot medium that reaches non-literate or semi-literate individuals even where those individuals are found within generally literate cultures. Like McLuhan's description of radio, the internet can be a medium for frenzy.[8]

The internet has rapidly become the medium of choice for hate-mongers both because of its broad reach and its low cost. Norman Olson, commander of the Michigan Militia Corps, one of the many extreme right-wing groups using the internet, has said "Thank God for high tech."[9]

Teenagers Eric Harris and Dylan Klebold shot and killed twelve class-mates and a teacher, wounded twenty-three others, and then killed them-selves at Columbine High School in Littleton, Colorado on April 20, 1999. They were enthusiastically involved with Nazi hate sites on the internet.[10] Brian Levin, the director of the Center on Hate and Extremism at Stockton College in Pomona, New Jersey said: "The internet now allows kids to sculpt their own antisocial ideology from a buffet of harmful messages . . . When you have a troubled kid, and you get them into something like this, the messages they can latch onto can exacerbate their violent tendencies."

Gail Gans, a hate monitor with the Anti-Defamation League observed that online screeds can attract middle-class teenagers—kids like Harris and Klebold—that no Klan rally would ever draw. She said: "In the '80s, if I wanted to find out about a hate group, I'd have to do something proactive. Today, all you have to do is go into your den or living room, turn on your computer, and they come into your home."

Hate promoters admit they go after the young. Tom Metzger, the leader of White Aryan Resistance, based in Fallbrook, California stated: "I concen-trate almost totally on young people."

The rise of the internet has coincided with a rise in hate crimes, a low-ering of age for the commission of hate crimes, and the existence of hate crimes where they never existed before. Hate crimes have spread to subur-bia, because the internet, carrying hate speech, has spread to suburbia. The 1996 League for Human Rights of B'nai Brith audit of antisemitic incidents showed that anti-semitic incidents have increased in Ontario's smaller com-munities, the bedroom suburban communities of the Greater Toronto Area. The majority of hate crimes are now committed by people under the age of twenty.[11] Isolated, opportunistic hate crimes are becoming more and more prevalent. For these crimes there are no signs of organized hate crime gangs. The only plausible explanation for these crimes is the advent of the internet.

Marshall McLuhan said: "The threat of Stalin or Hitler was external. The electric technology is within our gates, and we are numb, deaf, blind, and mute" to its dangers. "I am in the position of Louis Pasteur telling doctors that their greatest enemy is quite invisible, and quite unrecognized by them."[12] "The new media and technologies by which we amplify and extend ourselves constitute huge collective surgery carried out on the social body with complete disregard for antiseptics. If the operations are needed, the inevitability of infecting the whole system during the operation has to be considered."[13] Though he was talking more generally about electronic communication, what he wrote applies eloquently to hate on the internet.

Free speech absolutists will tell you that banning hate speech on the internet will not work, that it cannot work. They will further argue that because the internet makes a mockery of hate speech prohibition laws, there is no point any more in having any such laws.

This is the point of view, for instance, of Adam Clayton Powell III, vice president for technology programs with Freedom Forum, a non-partisan foundation for media education; Shabbir Safdar, co-founder of Voters Telecommunication Watch, dedicated to preserving free speech on the internet; and Stanton McCandlish, program director of the San Francisco–based Electronic Frontier Foundation, which also fights for free speech on the internet. They have all argued that the internet is essentially uncontrollable.[14] Jim Carroll, who wrote the *Canadian Internet Handbook*, said "It's like passing a law that makes mosquitoes illegal, or banning winter from Canada."[15]

It is noteworthy that the United States Supreme Court, which has been sympathetic to the free speech absolutist cause, rejected this argument of ineffectiveness. The court heard in 1997 a constitutional challenge to the Communications Decency Act, a statute which penalizes the display of indecent material on the internet. Bruce J. Ennis argued on behalf of a coalition of civil-liberties and computer-industry groups that the law was bound to be ineffective. Ennis told the court that over thirty percent of indecent material on the internet came from overseas and was beyond the reach of the law. Mr. Justice Kennedy responded from the bench: "That's a weak argument. If the United States has a public policy, it can lead the way, and maybe the rest of the world will follow."[16]

There is, of course, no reason why global leadership, whether for internet policy or for any other policy, has to come from the United States alone. Any country which develops a sensible internet public policy can lead the way and the rest of the world may follow.

Hate speech on the internet is not just an old threat in new clothes. It is a whole new monster. Radio and TV technology needed regulation to be viable. The regulatory schemes in place for technological reasons could be used to prohibit use of the airwaves for hate speech. The internet, in contrast, arose and can survive without regulation. Technology allows us to do nothing about the internet, and it will still flourish. But doing nothing here, like doing nothing elsewhere, is an abdication of responsibility.

Laws prohibiting hate speech, even in this brave new technological world, remain a solution to the problem of hate speech on the internet. However, laws, here as elsewhere, are not the only, or always the best solution. Even without new laws, there are many ways to combat hate speech on the internet.

The first and most obvious is to post a website. The Anti-Defamation League of B'nai Brith, for example, has a website about combatting antisemitism.[17] Posting a website to combat Holocaust denial is best exemplified by the Nizkor project led by Ken McVay.[18]

The Nizkor project website allows anyone to discover all the lies, the evasions, the distortions that permeate Holocaust denial on the internet. While Holocaust information is not the only answer to Holocaust denial, it is surely one answer. Holocaust denial on the internet can be answered by Holocaust information on the internet.

The "Golem Gazette," edited by Harry Abrams of Victoria, British Columbia, while it was in operation, was an on-line news service sent by e-mail to subscribers, without charge. It provided information and analyses to those interested in combatting hatred. Sending out e-mail newsletters to lists of subscribers, like posting informational websites, are initiatives anyone on the internet can undertake.

The Golem Gazette service was confidential, in the sense that the subscriber list was blind copied. Those receiving the news service did not know who the other subscribers were.

The service drew attention to news stories from around the world on the battle to combat hate, including reports from correspondents. The service, as well, monitored hate sites and hate list-serves, providing information and updates on these sites and list-serves. This sort of initiative is easily replicated. Any one can set up a list-serve, sending out information to recipients who are interested.

One of the most useful activities hate speech combatants can do is maintain and provide lists of offending sites. The lists can be maintained on a website; they can be sent to list-serve subscribers; they can be included in blocking programmes; they can be sent to indexed search engines so that hate sites can be properly labelled; they can be sent to access providers as part of a campaign to have the sites shut down. Like anti-virus software, hate-speech website listings can themselves be provided over the internet, and constantly updated. Providing listings of hate sites is just another form of hate watch activity that should be part of the agenda of hate watch groups.

This form of activism is crucial, given the sheer volume of material on the internet. It is unrealistic to expect search engines and access providers to identify and weed out hate speech on their own. Content monitoring is beyond the capacity of access providers and even the best-intentioned must rely on complaints. Internet vigilance, like human rights vigilance every-where, falls on us all, but it is the particular purview of human rights organizations.

The internet is as powerful a tool for combatting hatred as it is for spreading hatred. The primary internet effort of hate opponents should be to use the communication potential of the internet to advance the cause of tolerance, knowledge, and understanding.

Another non-legal answer to hate in cyberspace available to individuals is software blocking programs, programs that block access to hate sites or delete objectionable language. There are blocking programs in existence with such names as Net Nanny, SurfWatch, Cyberpatrol, and Cybersitter. SurfWatch blocks sites and categories its researchers consider undesirable for children. Net Nanny provides a master list of sites and categories to block, but gives parents the ability to specify what is blocked. Net Nanny also has a monitoring function, to allow parents to see where children have been on the internet.[19]

Parental supervision is more relevant to pornography than hate speech; the harm of incitement to hatred is not age specific. Nonetheless, because children may be more susceptible to hate speech than adults, it makes sense to ask parents to restrict their children's access to it. Parental supervision can be as simple as plain old-fashioned keeping an eye on what children do and preventing them from doing anything to harm themselves, including visiting hate speech sites on the internet. That sort of parental supervision is time consuming, and for teenagers, unrealistic. Blocking programs provide another alternative.

Many people have access to the internet through institutions, whether it be their work place, a place of study, or a place of recreation. These institutions can supervise the use of the internet access they provide.

Institutional supervision often relies on blocking. The University of Manitoba, in Winnipeg, as far back as 1992, blocked access to pornographic sites for anyone using its computer network. University Vice President Terry Falconer said he would make the sites available for researchers doing serious work.[20] The public libraries in Austin, Texas and Oklahoma City have used filter programs to block access to sex sites. The Boston public library has installed filters on computers in its children's rooms but not on computers in its adult areas.[21]

Even though institutional blocking of hate sites does not make them inaccessible to anyone who leaves the institution and uses an outside computer, it does serve an important purpose, the purpose of marginalization and delegitimization. Just as it is inappropriate for schools to have hate books in their libraries, even though the books may be obtainable elsewhere, it is inappropriate for schools to allow their children to have access to hate speech on the internet using school computers. Any institution that denies the use of its computers for accessing hate is making a statement against hate, one that it should be making, and denying a platform to hate that it should not be giving.

Employers often insist that employees not access pornographic sites or send pornographic e-mails during work and on occasion have terminated those who ignored employer warnings. For instance, the *New York Times*, in February 2000, sacked twenty-three employees for sending bawdy e-mails.

Employers and schools should take a similar stance on access to hate sites and the sending of hate e-mail. Because any computer can keep track of where on the web it has been, and because any computer can require user identification before it is used, keeping track of user access to any site is, technically, eminently feasible.

Governments at all levels in market economy states employ between 30% and 60% of the work force. Public schools attract an even higher percentage of the school-age population. It should be a matter of government policy that all government employees should not access hate websites, unless the access is related to their work. It should be an education policy that students, at least students at public schools, should not access hate sites unless it is directly related to their studies. Employees and students should never send hate e-mails, harassing others with their hatred.

An insistence by employers and schools that employees and students not access hate sites during work and school would have a dramatic impact on the penetration of these sites. As well, the mere statement of a hate site no access to hate sites policy and no hate e-mail policy would be a stance against the promotion of hatred.

Access providers do not have to provide access to everything on the internet. They can provide access to only part of what is on the internet. For instance, iStar, an Ottawa-based internet access provider, in July 1996 cut off its customers' connections to thirty-five child pornography news groups.[22]

Access providers can use blocking programs the same way that parents or institutions can.

Blocking programs are, however, clumsy devices. If they block only sites with specific addresses, they have to be updated almost daily as new sites proliferate. If they block sites or language by using keywords or categories, they have unforeseen consequences, blocking all sorts of material that would not be considered hate speech by anyone.

For example, I worked on this book using various computers, including computers in airport lounges while travelling. The computer lounges all had Net Nanny installed on them and whenever I opened various chapters of this book from a floppy disc, Net Nanny crossed out whole swathes of the text, including significant portions of this chapter.

As well, blocking programs cannot block audio or video, only text. Yet, much of the hate on the internet today is both audio and visual.

Automatic blocking based on identifying words and text can never be sufficient to combat hate propagandists since it may be necessary to repeat hate speech in order to refute it. For hate speech, the only form of blocking that makes sense is informed blocking by site.

A milder form of control is labelling. Hate books not banned from a library can be catalogued as hate speech and shelved in a hate speech section of the library. While one can debate whether or not libraries should have, for instance, Holocaust denial books, it is unquestionably wrong for Holocaust denial books to be labelled as history and shelved in the history section.

Right now browsers or search engines do not label sites. When a search engine identifies a site discussing, say, Treblinka, only an informed user can determine whether the site is giving historical information or is attempting to perpetrate a hate speech fraud. Search engines should be developed or modified so that hate speech sites are labelled as such when they pop up on the screen. Listings of hate speech sites will have to be programmed into the search engines to allow for this labelling.

While the typical search engine works by search for user-identified words, there are some search engines that work by way of index. Index-based search engines categorize websites by subject matter. These search engines should label hate sites as hate sites. Right now, for instance, the search engine Yahoo! labels Holocaust denial as revisionism. A Holocaust denial site should be labelled as such.

The most effective method of removing hate speech from the internet, by far, is withdrawal of services to hate-mongers. A website, to be accessible to internet users at all times, has to be hosted on a computer that is itself active and connected to the internet at all times. Hosting a website can be a substantial expense. Many internet access providers, for a fee, offer their own computers as hosts for websites for customers.

Internet sites can be either interactive, where anyone with access to the internet can post materials to the site for all to see, or they are controlled by the host, who determines what will be on the site for others to see. Interactive sites, news groups, and chat rooms, are less problematic than host-controlled websites. Hate-speech news groups tend to be overwhelmed by those condemning hate speech or disputing its malicious claims.[23]

Access providers should not, in any circumstances, host hate-speech websites. Any such websites currently hosted should be removed from access provider computers. Denying of hosting will not remove hate-speech websites from the internet. Nonetheless, it will create a disincentive to using the internet for hate speech by making it more expensive, requiring hate promoters to set up and maintain their own hosting computers.

Hate promoters can also hide or disguise their websites by posting an anodyne site, but with a hidden or disguised link to a hate site. The first site is, to all appearances, not a hate site. Yet, the direct linkage to hate web pages is improper and should not be there.

We should be alert to camouflaged hate sites as well as to explicit sites. In addition, all users, networks, on-line services, and access providers should refrain as much from direct linkages to hate sites as from explicit hate speech.

Hate speech conveyed by e-mail is arguably more problematic than hate messages on websites, since e-mail is sent directly to a receiver and is, usually, not public. Basic access to the internet, however, for e-mail as well as for websites, requires an internet access provider. Internet access providers are commercial enterprises and are free to offer or decline their services to whomever they want, provided they are non-discriminatory. An internet access provider is under no obligation to provide internet access to any person who uses the internet to disseminate hatred.

While there is a fundamental human right to freedom of speech, there is no fundamental human right to an internet access account. Legally, the guarantee of freedom of speech in the Canadian Charter of Rights and Freedoms applies to governments and not private companies such as internet access providers. The same is true in other countries with constitutional free speech guarantees. Internet access providers can withdraw their services from those who are abusing the services to spread hatred, and cut off the access of hate promoters to the internet.

Indeed, it is common now for internet access accounts to be withdrawn, not for hate speech use, but for spamming. For instance, MCI, a global access provider at the pinnacle of the internet system, has a no tolerance policy for spamming. They state: "We will not tolerate the use of our network for spamming or other similar abusive behaviour." MCI also prohibits other forms of e-mail abuse, such as harassment and the posting of illegal materials. MCI considers all these practices abusive of recipients. Engaging in any one of them may result in the termination of the offender's account.

If service providers can cut off accounts for spamming, there is no reason why they cannot also do it for hate speech. In some instances they have done so. America Online in September 1997 shut off the internet access that it had provided to the British extreme right-wing group United Charlemagne Hammer Skinheads in advance of charges laid against that group. In the United States, the site <WhitePower.com> was booted off its Las Vegas internet service provider, even though in the United States there are no hate-speech criminal laws.

There is a tendency for internet hate promoters to gravitate to amenable providers. For instance, the internet access provider Fairview Technology Centre in the Okanagan Valley town of Oliver, British Columbia had at one time at least twelve different hate groups using its services.[24] These included the U.S. Nazi Party, the National Socialist Movement, the European Nationalist Party, the Heritage Front, Skin-Net, the Euro-Christian Defence League, and Charlemagne Hammer Skinheads.

The National Socialist Movement has been subject to police action in Britain. The Charlemagne Hammer Skinheads have been subject to police action in both France and Britain. There have been charges against members of the group in France. After the termination of its access to the internet by America Online in September 1997, Charlemagne Hammer Skinheads re-established access to the internet in November through Fairview and maintained that access for four months, using it to spread hate, including advocating the murder of British playwright Julia Pascal and Swiss journalist Ludwin Fischer. Only in the week of March 9th, 1998 did Fairview end the internet access it gave to Charlemagne Hammer Skinheads.

A unique aspect of the internet is that not only can anyone get an e-mail account or post a website, but also anyone with internet access can be an internet service provider. Nonetheless, access to the internet exists in a technological hierarchy. Theoretically it is not necessary to pass up and down through every level of this hierarchy to make use of the internet. For instance, it is possible to communicate on the internet just locally or nationally. For international communication, everyone on the internet passes through the hierarchy, including the few major internet service providers at the apex, such as MCI and Sprint, who interconnect with each other to create the global network.

A local internet service provider who caters to hate groups is usually at the base of this hierarchy and can maintain a connection to the internet only if the internet service provider up the chain allows the local provider to do so. Just as local service providers can and should cut off access by hate propagandists, so should national or global internet service providers cut off the access of local internet service providers if those local providers allow hate propagandists access to the internet.

On behalf of B'nai Brith Canada, I wrote to Michel Belec, Senior Counsel to BC Tel in March 1998 regarding Fairview Technology Centre. I asked BC Tel to notify Fairview that BC Tel would terminate Fairview's access, and all its customers', unless Fairview terminated access for those of its customers who were propagating hatred over the internet. B'nai Brith noted that BC Tel's standard internet service agreement with customers provides that the agreement may be terminated upon notice.[25] Furthermore, access may be terminated at any time there has been or is any breach of any term or condition of the service agreement.[26]

One of the terms of BC Tel's service agreement is that every customer agrees to comply with BC Tel's polices respecting use of the internet as provided from time to time.[27] Presumably BC Tel's contract with Fairview contained similar terms. B'nai Brith asked BC Tel to inform Fairview that it is the policy of BC Tel not to allow the internet to be used to promote hatred.

Telus, the Alberta counterpart of BC Tel, at one point was the internet connectivity provider to an internet service provider who hosted a customer spammer. Telus gave the internet service provider forty-eight-hours notice, telling them they had to pull the plug on the spammer or Telus would shut down the internet service provider and put all its customers out of business. With one hour to go, the internet service provider pulled the connection on the spammer. Telus did not require a criminal conviction in order to act. Indeed, it is not even clear that spamming is a criminal offence.

Promoting hate speech is a far more harmful activity than spamming. Spamming, at its worst, leads to failure of the internet. Hate speech has led to the murder of millions.

Bernard Klatt, the President of Fairview, had previously asserted that he had no obligation to terminate internet access for those of his customers using that access to promote hatred unless there was a criminal conviction against them. Despite what Klatt said, it was also true that he had no legal obligation to maintain access. Nor had BC Tel. While, of course, any material that is illegal should not be posted on the internet, BC Tel was under no legal obligation to allow the posting of everything that can withstand legal scrutiny.

B'nai Brith reminded BC Tel that it does not have for the internet the same obligations it has for telephone service. For the telephone, there is a legal obligation to provide services, subject to exceptions. One exception is that BC Tel may deny telephone service to a customer who has used or permitted others to use the telephone to make annoying or offensive calls. For the telephone there is no independent requirement of illegality. The standard service contract with customers allows for telephone service to be cut off when the phone is used in an abusive or offensive manner, whether that use is illegal or not.

If telephone service, which there is a legal obligation to provide, can be cut off even when the telephone is used legally, then surely an internet service account can also be cut off, in a situation where internet access is used in an offensive or abusive manner. Since there is no obligation to provide internet access and there is an obligation to provide telephone access, it would be perverse for BC Tel to use a higher standard for cutting off internet access than for the telephone. Legally, the BC Tel standard for internet access cut-off could be lower than its standard for telephone cut off.

The BC Tel response was to insist, on expiry of their then existing contract with Fairview, that the new contract contain a term indemnifying BC Tel for any damages for which BC Tel might be liable as the result of the material hosted by Fairview. Fairview, rather than sign the contract proposed by BC Tel for renewal, gave up on providing internet service.

One common technique for combatting hate speech is approaching those who would provide a platform for hate-mongers and asking them to withdraw the platform. If a university student organization invites a Holocaust denier to speak on campus, the League for Human Rights of B'nai Brith Canada might ask the organization to withdraw the invitation, explaining to them who the speaker is, and why the invitation is inappropriate. If a hotel rents a meeting room to a neo-Nazi extremist group, the League might ask the hotel management to cancel the room rental arrangement, so that the meeting cannot take place.

There is no reason why a similar technique can not be employed with phone companies and internet access providers. Hate speech combatants can approach internet access providers to ask them to withdraw their services from hate-mongers abusing those services to spread hatred. Anti-hate-speech advocates can point out the nature of the hate speech contested, the damages of hate speech, why corporate responsibility to the community means that the services should be withdrawn.

Something like that happened with Fairview Technology Centre. Sol Littman of the Simon Wiesenthal Centre asked Fairview to stop providing internet access to hate-mongers. Bernard Klatt, the owner of Fairview, stone-walled, but the local cable TV company where Fairview had its offices told Fairview to get out.[28]

Internet access providers can and should have codes of conduct stating up front that they will deny their services to hate promoters. The prohibition of internet use for promoting hatred should also be in all internet access contracts. That way, not only could internet access be denied at the start or end of a contract to an abusive user. It could stop during the term of the contract. Access providers should make it clear to every one of their customers that he or she is liable to be cut off if the service provided is abused to propagate hatred.

Access to the internet requires two elements, an electronic connection and an address. Normally they go together; the provider who gives connectivity also gives the address. However, there are some situations where they are separate, the address coming from one source and the connectivity from another. Either internet connectivity or an internet address, or both, can and should be refused to hate propagandists. Address allocators, as much as access providers, should insist, as a condition for the provision of their service, that the service not be used for the purpose of promoting hate.

The distribution of internet addresses is controlled globally by a cooperative named InterNIC consisting of three members, Network Solutions Inc., the National Science Foundation, a United States government agency, and AT&T. InterNIC could insist that every access provider insert into its subscription contract a requirement that the internet not be used for hate speech.

Internet access providers have grouped themselves in various countries, as well as internationally, into voluntary associations. In North America, there are the Canadian Association of Internet Providers[29] and several U.S. state associations, including associations in Texas, Florida, Mississippi, Ohio, and Washington. These associations often have codes of conduct. Whatever else these codes contain, they should contain a prohibition on the hosting of hate-speech websites and a denial of access to hate propagandists.

The associations also need complaint response mechanisms, perhaps modelled on press council complaint systems. A person who sees objectionable material on the internet should, first of all, complain to the internet service provider of the hate promoter. If the hate promoter's internet service provider refuses to do anything, the complainant should address the internet service provider's connectivity provider. If the connectivity provider refuses to do anything, the next step should be the association of internet service providers to which the connectivity provider belongs. The association should adjudicate the complaint after considering submissions from the complainant and the target of the complaint.

How do we decide whether something on the internet is hate speech? One solution is to rely on information provided by hate speech combatants such as the Anti-Defamation League of B'nai Brith. Another is arbitration. Internet users in their access agreements could agree not to post hate speech on the internet and agree to accept the rulings of an arbitrator, should anyone complain that a posting is hate speech. Complaints could be made through the internet and virtual magistrates, themselves operating on the internet, would rule on whether the system operator should delete the challenged postings. The Cyberspace Law Institute of Washington D.C. has proposed such an on-line arbitration mechanism, for all internet contract disputes though not specifically for hate-speech disputes.[30]

There could be a provision in every internet access contract that users agree not to post hate speech and agree further to abide by the arbitrator's decision on whether a contested posting is hate speech. Anyone who refuses to sign on to such a provision could be denied internet access.

Just as users have internet access contracts with access providers, so too do local access providers have internet access contracts with national and global access providers. These contracts too should have anti-hate-speech stipulations. Access providers up the electronic chain should be entitled, during the term of a contract, to withdraw or refuse to provide services to lower-level access providers who in turn refuse to insist that their customers sign a contract forbidding the use of the internet for hate speech.

The insertion, by access providers, of anti-hate-speech stipulations in subscriber contracts can be accomplished through a model global, uniform contract. The notion of a global contract for the provision of a service has many precedents. It exists, for example, for airline passenger service. Global airline ticket terms were agreed internationally and are to be found in the Convention for the Unification of certain Rules Relating to International Carriage by Air signed at Warsaw October 12, 1929 and amended at the Hague on September 28, 1955.

It is unlikely that global address allocators or global access providers would use their powers over who connects to the internet to do anything related to internet content without international support. It would be arguably presumptuous for global address allocators or global access providers, who are essentially American, to impose content controls on the internet without that international support.

International support could come from an international convention; however, international support for banning hate on the internet does not require an international convention. An international convention is, after all, inter-governmental, and the solutions being proposed here are all non-governmental. It is perfectly possible, even desirable, for the global internet access providers to come to a common accord on the need to ban hate from the internet, and the means to do it, without any government involvement at all.

A consensus by global access providers could be developed with global human-rights non-governmental organizations. There is really not much difference, at least at the conceptual level, between a corner grocery store's refusing to carry pornographic magazines, or stocking them in places outside the reach and view of children, in response to customer demand, and global access providers' kicking hate speech off the internet, because that is what their customers want. In the global village, human-rights organizations are entitled to voice internet customer hate speech concerns.

As desirable as all these private remedies are, many of them may be ineffective and others will remain unavailable without the cooperation of the internet infrastructure. We may have to turn to prohibitory laws. There are essentially three types of laws, laws directed to software, laws directed to senders, and laws directed to conveyers.

Laws affecting software are perhaps the least technically problematic. Hate propaganda on a floppy disk or a CD-ROM is little different from hate propaganda in a book or a video. Floppy disks and CD-ROMs can be seized the same way that books or videos can be, and their distributors can be prosecuted the same way book or video distributors can be.

Internet technology is not an obstacle to prohibitions against senders of hate, as long as the sender is physically within the jurisdiction of the law. A hate promoter in France operating through the internet is as much within the reach of French law as a hate promoter putting pamphlets on windshields of cars. Traditional French anti-hate law would be applied in the traditional way against such senders.

There is a case in progress now before a Canadian Human Rights Tribunal against Ernst Zundel for sending hate through the internet. The complaint was lodged by the City of Toronto's race relations committee and by Sabina Citron, a Holocaust survivor. The website for the contested material is in California. Zundel, however, is in Canada and is allegedly supplying the material that is being distributed through the internet. The Canadian Human Rights Commission referred the complaint to a Human Rights Tribunal. The tribunal began its hearing in May, 1997.[31]

Zundel went to court asking that the referral of the complaint to a tribunal to be set aside on the ground that the tribunal had no jurisdiction to hear the complaint. His counsel argued that there was no jurisdiction, because the Canadian Human Rights Act gives a tribunal jurisdiction over hatred communicated telephonically, and what he was accused of having sent over the internet was not sent by telephone.

In court, Mr. Justice Evans ruled that the position of the Human Rights Commission that internet transmission was transmission by telephone had a rational basis. So the tribunal could proceed. Whether the position of the commission was ultimately correct would be for the tribunal to decide, subject to review by the courts.[32]

While today the internet uses telephone wires, at least for some part of the transmission, tomorrow internet communication may be completely on cable, or even on air. The Canadian Human Rights Act needs to be amended to provide for that possibility, as well as to remove any doubt there might now be whether the present law applies to the internet.

The United States Supreme Court, when striking down the 1996 Communications Decency Act as unconstitutional because of its overbreadth, suggested more narrowly tailored legislation that might survive constitutional challenge. One suggestion was regulating some portions of the internet such as commercial websites differently from others, such as chat rooms.[33]

Ken McVay, for example, has argued that interactive websites should not be banned because the discussion carried on in them allows the naive to see how the claims of hate-mongers can be refuted, how the fraud is perpetrated.[34] Hate-speech host-controlled sites are a different matter.

Where the host computer is outside a country, and the persons providing the material to the host are also outside the country, then the law is severely limited in its reach. Germany has legislated against foreign internet material by penalizing those in Germany who knowingly provide a connection overseas to content that is illegal in Germany, where it is "technically possible and reasonable" to prevent it.[35] The big question is whether prevention is technically possible and reasonable.

Some forms of prevention are technically possible and reasonable. For instance, someone with an internet site in Canada can link their Canadian site with a hate speech site abroad. The link is made knowingly. Removing the link is both technically possible and reasonable. A law directed to preventing connection with foreign, internet hate-speech material can easily get at that sort of link.

On-line services such as America On-Line, Compuserve, or Prodigy combine information services on their own controlled network with access to the internet. These on-line services can control the information they themselves provide. However, the only way they or internet access providers can cut off access to objectionable material on the internet is to use blocking devices with all the limitations described earlier. If specific sites are blocked, new sites can spring up to take their place. Free speech absolutists make a point of doing just that, producing mirror sites to replicate blocked sites.

Penalizing global on-line services has had an anti-competitive effect. In order to comply with German law, CompuServe in December 1995 cut off access to about two hundred sites. Most CompuServe content going to customers everywhere came from computers in the United States in Ohio. At the time, CompuServe had no way of cutting off the material to Germany alone. CompuServe's four million customers around the world fell under the sway of the German ban. Customers of other on-line services had no such limitations.[36]

Judge Jean-Jacques Gomez of France ordered the search engine Yahoo! to block French web surfers from Nazi hate sites posted in the United States. Yahoo! claims that the blocking the judge ordered is technically impossible.

In August 2000, the judge appointed an independent panel of experts to work out the technical hurdles for the black out.[37]

The United States Congress has passed the Digital Millennium Copyright Act to protect copyright on the internet. For the purposes of this discussion, what is significant is the imposition of a complaint and take down mechanism. Internet service providers are subject to liability for allowing any material that infringes copyright to pass through their networks. Potential liability is triggered by a written notification claiming copyright infringement. Once notification is received, liability can be avoided by expeditiously removing or disabling access to the infringing material.[38] Although this law is about prohibiting copyright infringement and not banning hate speech, it demonstrates that banning is eminently possible when the internet service provider is located within the jurisdiction that enacts such a law.

The most effective ban on internet hate speech would be a global ban. There are already international standards obligating states to prohibit hate speech, in the International Covenant on Civil and Political Rights[39] and the International Convention on the Elimination of All Forms of Racial Discrimination.[40] The United States, from which over sixty percent of the internet sites originate, has signed and ratified the International Covenant on Civil and Political Rights, albeit with a reservation. The reservation states that the obligation to prohibit hate speech in the covenant "does not authorize or require legislation or other action by the United States that would restrict the right of free speech and association protected by the constitution and laws of the United States."

An international convention requiring states to ban hate speech on the internet should not be too hard to achieve, since it would be only a specific application of an already accepted international standard. The Government of Canada has suggested such a convention. The Honourable Herb Gray, when he was Solicitor General, said: "One solution [to hate speech on the internet] might involve some type of international convention or agreement where countries would come together to control the use of the internet."[41]

Because hate speech on the internet is a global problem, it is not only necessary but fitting that the solution be global in scope. Because propagation of hatred is a violation of human rights, promotion of respect for human rights should be the work of all humanity. Lest we forget, the internet reminds us that human rights are universal. The internet makes us undertake the work of human rights at the level we *should* be undertaking it, on the scale of the planet.

Notes

1. Anti-Defamation League. "Hate Group Recruitment on the Internet" *Research Report* (1995); David Sitman, "Propagating Anti-Semitism on the Internet," *Justice, The International Association of Jewish Lawyers and Jurists* (March 1997), No. 12.
2. *Understanding Media: The Extensions of Man.* MIT Press, 1994, p. 5.
3. Bob Schmitt. "The Internet and International Politics," *International Herald Tribune,* April 2, 1997.
4. Matthew McAllester. "Net freedom at risk," *Ottawa Citizen,* November 25, 1996 (reprinted from *Newsday*).
5. *Understanding Media: The Extensions of Man.* MIT Press, 1994, p. 68.
6. Pages 22, 23.
7. Pages 30, 31, 300–302.
8. At page 310.
9. Jared Sandberg. "Net Results: Some nasty creatures in Cyberspace," *Globe and Mail,* December 13, 1994 (reprinted from the *Wall Street Journal*).
10. Hans H. Chen. "Online Hate Sites Target Teenagers: Were Harris & Klebold Typical of Disturbing Trend?" New York (APBnews.com), April 25, 1999.
11. "Internet game fights hatred," *Winnipeg Free Press,* March 25, 1997.
12. *Understanding Media: The Extensions of Man.* MIT Press, 1994, p. 17.
13. At page 64.
14. Matthew McAllester. "Net freedom at risk," *Ottawa Citizen,* November 25, 1996 (reprinted from *Newsday*).
15. Chris Wattie. "Rights groups urge Internet crackdown," *Winnipeg Free Press,* June 3, 1997.
16. Linda Greenhouse. "Justices Weigh Decency Rules For the Internet," *New York Times,* March 20, 1997, p. A11.
17. At <http://www.adl.org>.
18. The internet address is <http://nizkor.almanac.bc.ca>.
19. Mel Duvall. "Censoring the 'Net: Software helps parents control kids' access," *Calgary Herald,* July 27, 1995, p. D7.
20. Alexandra Paul. "U of M taking byte out of offensive software," *Winnipeg Free Press,* May 9, 1992; "Ban denounced," *Winnipeg Free Press,* May 15, 1992.
21. Amy Harmon. "To Screen or Not to Screen: Libraries Confront Internet Access," *New York Times,* June 23, 1997.
22. "Pornography cutoff 'common sense'," *Globe and Mail,* July 13, 1997.
23. David Sitman. "Propagating Anti-Semitism on the Internet," *Justice, The International Association of Jewish Lawyers and Jurists* (March 1997), No. 12, p. 9.
24. "Internet server home to racist sites," *Globe and Mail,* July 13, 1996.

25. Clause 11.

26. Clause 11(iii).

27. Clause 2.

28. "Internet server home to racist sites," *Globe and Mail*, July 13, 1996; "Hate literature incidents cited," *Winnipeg Free Press*, July 27, 1996.

29. Its address is 750 Hurondale Drive, Mississauga, Ontario, L5C 4N8; the phone number is 905-279-6417 and the fax is 905-279-9418; the e-mail address is <kawchuk@io.org> and the website address is <http://www.caip.ca>. The executive director is Ron Kawchuk.

30. Gerry Blackwell. "A Jurisdiction Called Cyberspace?" *Canadian Lawyer*, March 1997, p. 21. See also websites <http://vmag.law.vill.edu.8080> and <http://www.cybertribunal.org>.

31. "Internet case against Zundel will go ahead," *Winnipeg Free Press*, May 28, 1997.

32. *Zundel v. Attorney General of Canada*, T–2765–96, June 15, 1999, Federal Court Trial Division.

33. "Free speech and the Internet," an excerpt from the judgment reprinted in the *Globe and Mail*, June 30, 1997.

34. Quoted in Gareth Sansom, "Illegal and Offensive Content on the Information Highway," Industry Canada, March 23, 1995, p. 41.

35. Tony Czuska. "Germany does its bit to curb 'Net," *Winnipeg Free Press*, July 5, 1997.

36. "Lowest-common-denominator censorship," *The Economist* (reprinted in the *Globe and Mail*, January 6, 1996); "Cyberspace censored," *Winnipeg Free Press*, December 30, 1995.

37. Brian Love. "Judge extends date for French Yahoo blackout," *National Post*, August 12, 2000.

38. Title 17 United States Code Chapter 5, section 512(c)(1)(C).

39. Article 20.

40. Article 4.

41. Jim Bronskill. "Canada urges world pact to cut Internet hate," *Winnipeg Free Press*, March 28, 1995.

Chapter Thirteen

Remedies

PROHIBITING HATE PROPAGANDA is a matter of human rights. It means preserving and promoting the human rights of those groups vilified by the hate propagandist.

Protecting freedom of speech is a matter of civil liberties. It means allowing people to express themselves on the full range of ideas and topics. In the area of hate propaganda, human rights conflict with civil liberties. In the conflict we have to do what we can to preserve both values.

In order to prohibit hate propaganda, there have to be restrictions on civil liberties. However, we should impose restrictions reluctantly rather than enthusiastically. We should do it in as limited and precise a way as possible. We should keep our eyes on the danger we are trying to avoid, and direct our measures to that danger alone. We should use techniques that serve the purpose we seek and no broader ones. We should be wary of the chilling effect of hate propaganda laws on legitimate speech and seek to limit that effect.

When confronted by intolerance there is a sequence of steps we can take, each more serious than the last. The simplest most direct step is contacting the person making the intolerant remarks and asking him or her to stop. When intolerance comes from ignorance, we can inform. When intolerance comes from insensitivity, we can sensitize.

Against the hate propagandist, however, the direct approach is unlikely to work. The hate propagandist proceeds by design, not by accident. A propagandist is someone engaged in a continual pattern of activity over time. Propaganda is not propaganda if it is just an off-the-cuff remark, if it is an isolated incident. As we have seen, the typical hate propagandist is caught up in a world view of his own making. The propagandist not only believes the propaganda, but the propaganda is so imbedded in his own view of

173

himself and others that he has no independent perspective from which to judge the propaganda he disseminates.

In the *Terry Long–Aryan Nations* case, each taped telephone message ended with "The Aryan Nations are not afraid of the truth." The Aryan Nations were not afraid of the truth, because they are impervious to the truth. Hate propagandists develop a paranoic all-encompassing vision into which the truth cannot penetrate. Attempting to inform and sensitize, to persuade and convince quickly becomes a waste of time.

After persuasion, the next step on the escalator of remedies is quarantine. The hate propagandist should not be given a platform to broadcast his hatred. He should not be invited to speak or debate. Others should not participate in debates with him. Radio and TV programs should not invite him on their shows. Schools should not hire him as a school teacher where he can use the schoolroom to poison the minds of children, where he would serve as a perverse role model.

Editors of newspapers should not print letters that contain hate propaganda messages. Libraries, schools, and universities should not offer hate propagandists meeting rooms and speaking halls. Publishers should not print hate propaganda messages. On a voluntary basis, without the law, it is possible to do a good deal to cut off avenues of communication, to prevent the hate propagandist from getting out his message. Clear internal policies, effectively enforced, with mechanisms for dispute resolution and appeal, would avoid the need to invoke the law.

Following upon quarantine, the next step up the escalator is legal remedies. In attacking hate propaganda, as we have seen, there can and should be a range of remedies. For the more serious, the more intransigent cases, criminal remedies are necessary. As a first step, however, before criminal remedies, we should try civil remedies. If civil remedies are effective, criminal remedies become unnecessary.

Civil remedies for hate propaganda approximate more closely the remedies for other, unacceptable, abuses of free speech such as libel and slander. Civil remedies are, for that reason, easier to justify as exceptions to free speech than are criminal remedies. In Canada and other countries, civil proceedings for libel and slander are common, are accepted. While Canada's criminal code does allow for prosecutions for defamatory libel, prosecutions for this offence are extremely rare.

Civil remedies are more direct than criminal remedies. While criminal remedies prosecute the propagandist after the propaganda has been disseminated, civil remedies can prohibit the propaganda before it has been distributed. Civil remedies can work to cut off the avenue of distribution.

Because criminal remedies lead to punishment of the propagandist, criminal trials quickly become a forum for the propagandist. The propagandist claims persecution, victimization. It is more difficult for the propagandist to portray himself as a martyr in a civil case when he faces no risk of punishment, when the risk he runs is only that he must cease propagandizing.

Let me present an analogy. Those who argue against gun control say that guns do not kill, people do. There is an obvious fallacy to that argument, because killing is a good deal easier with guns than without, and the argument has had little effect, at least, in Canada.

Yet, even if we accept that argument, it is not one that can apply to hate propaganda. It is ludicrous to say newspapers do not propagandize, people do; radio does not propagandize, people do, and so on. If we take away from a propagandist his means of communication, we have effectively stifled the propaganda. If the propagandist cannot use radio or television, if he cannot import or export, if he cannot print or publish, if he cannot phone or mail, then the propaganda is stopped. He may, nonetheless, be able to communicate his hatred to his neighbours, the people he meets in the streets. However, for all effective purposes, he is stopped.

Civil remedies have this advantage well: the standard of proof is less stringent. The standard of proof in criminal cases is proof beyond a reasonable doubt. The standard of proof in civil cases is proof on the balance of probabilities. In a civil case, if a court believes it is more likely than not that the material will incite hatred, then the remedy is available. In a criminal case, if there is a 49% chance that the material will not incite hatred, then there is a reasonable doubt. The jury will have to acquit. If eleven jurors think, beyond a reasonable doubt, that the material will incite hatred, but one does not, the jury cannot convict.

Proof is easier with a civil remedy for a second reason. A criminal remedy requires proof of intent. A civil remedy does not. All that has to be proved is that hate propaganda was disseminated. It need not be proved that the hate propaganda was distributed for the purpose of promoting hatred. The disseminator may claim some other motive. In a civil case it will not matter. In a criminal case, unless the prosecution can prove that the distribution was done with the intention of promoting hatred, the court must acquit.

Yet another advantage of civil remedies is the fact that they may be initiated by individuals. They do not need the concurrence of the state for initiation. In several countries, including Canada, a hate propaganda criminal offence requires the consent of the state prosecutor before a prosecution can be launched. Private prosecutions are an impossibility.

Civil remedies of prohibition, as well, lessen the chilling effect on freedom of speech. When civil libertarians criticize hate propaganda laws, the point of criticism most often made is that the offence of hate propaganda is too vague. Alan Borovoy, in *When Freedoms Collide*, writes "in order to avoid the possibility of prosecution, people might be impelled to ensure that their speech steered as far as possible from the prohibited zone."

Under the civil remedy of a prohibition or an injunction, a person is not punished later for disseminating something which he thought was legal at the time. A court order of prohibition is a warning. A person is told in advance what is punishable and what is hate propaganda. If he wants to avoid prosecution for violation of the prohibition order, he knows very specifically what not to do.

Of course, for prohibition orders, as well as for prosecutions, there are court proceedings. However, in a civil proceeding, as opposed to a criminal proceeding, the person concerned does not have to be present. An accused is required to be present at his own criminal trial. If he fails to show up, he will be arrested and brought forcibly to court. If he wants to avoid punishment, he has to defend himself.

In civil prohibition proceedings, the person concerned need not appear. Indeed, in the Aryan Nations proceedings in which I participated, the Aryan Nations did not appear. The Aryan Nations, Terry Long, and the Church of Jesus Christ Christian, against whom the complaints had been made, were not compellable. If they did not want to spend the time and effort involved in going to court, they did not have to do so.

Even the possibility of legal proceeding where you do not have to appear, where you do not have to incur any legal costs, where you run no risk of punishment may have some chilling effect. However, the chilling effect is obviously a good deal less.

Civil remedies have disadvantages as well. Group libel statutes, which in Canada exist in the provinces of Manitoba and British Columbia, require individual direction. It is not just that the individual must complain. The individual must carry the total burden of the legal action. The person who is a member of the vilified group must bear responsibility for the action from start to finish for the remedy to work.

Yet, hate propaganda is not just an attack on the vilified group. It is an attack on the whole community and its values. If we leave responsibility for addressing the wrong to the vilified group, we absolve society from its duty to redress the wrong. We send a false message to members of the vilified group, that the community as a whole does not care about their victimization. We isolate the victim and leave him to his own recourses.

Hate propagandists often operate out of paranoia, fantasizing attacks by the group they vilify. They portray their propaganda as a defence against this fantasized attack. Victims may be reluctant to invoke civil remedies on their own, because it feeds the paranoia of the propagandist.

As well, any legal action is an expensive and time-consuming activity. Where a whole group is vilified, it becomes onerous to expect one member of the group to assume the burden of the litigation alone. Volunteer organizations are chronically underfinanced. It is asking too much to expect organizations to which the victims belong to assume the burden of the litigation.

For a civil remedy to be effective, it must be state directed. An individual should be able to initiate the remedy with a complaint. He or she should have to do no more.

A state-directed remedy is a public comment that the community at large cares about the propaganda, that it rejects the propaganda. A state-directed remedy avoids the vagaries of individual direction. It does not require finding someone willing and able to undertake the burden of carrying forward a court proceeding to its conclusion.

Human rights acts, establishing human rights commissions, provide an example of state-directed civil remedies. Human rights commission are professional specialized bodies. The individual complains to the commission and the commission decides whether to proceed with the complaint. If the commission goes ahead, it does so in the name of both the commission and the individual.

However, typically, commissions are mandated to seek conciliation before other remedies. Where conciliation is not possible, a remedy is sought from a human rights tribunal, independent from the commission. Often the primary remedy sought is an end to the human rights violating practice.

Yet, conciliation is a feeble remedy against hate propaganda. In Canada, the Human Rights Acts of British Columbia and Saskatchewan include hate messages as prohibited discriminatory acts and mandate the human rights commissions established under those acts to mediate a settlement between the person complaining and the target of the complaint. However, to suggest that we approach hate propaganda from the perspective of persuasion and conciliation is insensitive to the nature of what hate propaganda is.

An attempt at conciliation suggests that there is a group conflict, a dispute between the victim group and the group the propagandist purports to represent. The whole notion of conciliation of a dispute gives some credit to the paranoic view of the propagandist that he is under attack from the victim group. Hate propaganda is not a disagreement with the victim group, but a premeditated attack on an innocent bystander. The problem cannot be resolved by some form of accommodation with the victim.

So, my initial position is that we should invoke civil remedies before criminal remedies. However, they must be the right sort of civil remedies. They should be state-directed, like the remedies provided under human rights legislation by human rights commissions and tribunals, rather than relying solely on the individual, and they should focus on prohibition rather than on conciliation.

With that position I want to turn to two Canadian cases, the case of *John Ross Taylor* and the use of the telephone for hate propaganda; and the case of *Ernst Zundel* and the use of the mail for hate propaganda. These cases illustrate why state-directed civil remedies are preferable to both privately initiated civil remedies and criminal remedies.

Canada has had a range of legal options to deal with hate propaganda. They take a variety of forms but they have had one feature in common. For years, they have sat on the statute books unused.

The hate propaganda offence in Canada's criminal code has been on the books since 1970. By 1978, there had not been one reported prosecution. The offence requires the consent of the attorney general of the province. Attorneys general were simply not consenting. It was not as if there was no hate propaganda, no complaints. There were both. However, the answer was always no.

The present Canadian Human Rights Act became law in March 1978. One of its provisions prohibits spreading hate propaganda by telephone. Use of the telephone for hate propaganda is defined as a discriminatory practice. The act allows everyone who believes that another person has engaged in a discriminatory practice to file a complaint with the Human Rights Commission established under the Human Rights Act.

The commission has to investigate the complaint. It can refer the complaint to a Human Rights Tribunal, which has the power to order a discriminatory practice to stop. A tribunal order can be made an order of the Federal Court of Canada and enforced in the same manner as a federal court order. If the person disobeys, he can be prosecuted for contempt of court.

The Western Guard Party was founded in Canada in 1972. John Ross Taylor became its leader in 1976. He used the telephone to recruit members and convey his message. He distributed cards with his number on it. Callers heard a pre-recorded hate propaganda message.

In late 1978 and early 1979, months after the new Human Rights Act came into effect, the Canadian Human Rights Commission received a number of complaints about Taylor. The complaints came from David S. Smith, the Toronto Zionist Council, Ajalon Lodge, and the Canadian Holocaust Remembrance Association. Sabina Citron, a Holocaust survivor, is the leading figure in the Canadian Holocaust Remembrance Association.

The commission duly investigated the complaints. It decided the complaints had substance and presented them to a Human Rights Tribunal. The tribunal hearing on John Ross Taylor was the very first hearing on any matter under the new Human Rights Act. The tribunal gave a lengthy and learned judgment. It issued an order requiring Taylor to cease his propaganda. He did not. He was prosecuted for contempt of court and convicted. His sentence was a year in jail, which he served.

Taylor complained about his conviction to the Human Rights Committee established under the United Nations International Covenant on Civil and Political Rights. His complaint was dismissed as inadmissible. The Human Rights Committee ruled that the opinions which Taylor sought to disseminate "clearly constitute the advocacy of racial or religious hatred which Canada has an obligation under article 20(2) of the Covenant to prohibit."

When Taylor got out of jail, he began his propagandizing again. He was convicted again. By this time, the Canadian Charter of Rights and Freedoms was in effect. It went into effect April 17, 1982. Taylor was again sentenced to one year in jail, in April, 1984 . He argued this time against his conviction on the grounds of the Charter guarantee of freedom of expression. He lost the argument at the Federal Court Trial Division, the Federal Court of Appeal, and the Supreme Court of Canada.

Ernst Zundel was using the mail for hate propaganda. The Canada Post Corporations Act allows the minister responsible for the post office to prohibit the delivery of mail addressed to or received by a person who is committing an offence by means of the mail. The order is an interim order. The person concerned may ask for a review of the order. If he does, the minister must appoint a Board of Review. The board holds a hearing and advises the minister. The minister, after receiving the advice of the board, may make the order final, or lift the order.

Sabina Citron complained about Zundel to the minister responsible for the post office. The minister issued an interim prohibitory order on the grounds that Zundel was using the mail to commit the offence of hate propaganda. Zundel asked for a review. A Board of Review held a hearing in February and March of 1982. Ian Scott for the Canadian Civil Liberties Association intervened to argue that the order against Zundel should be lifted. (Scott later became the Attorney General for Ontario responsible for the prosecution of Zundel.) The board, in October, 1982, did recommend the lifting of the interim order. The minister followed the advice of the board and lifted the order.

As I wrote above, the *John Ross Taylor* judgment was long and learned. The judgement of the *Zundel* Board of Review was, by contrast, short and ignorant. The board said, for instance, "The board believes that before it is a much larger problem or struggle between two peoples; i.e. the Germans and the Jews."

That, of course, was the position of Zundel. He claimed the Holocaust was a sham, a Jewish hoax, an attack on German honour. He has made a career of denying the Holocaust to defend, so he says, the German people against this Jewish attack.

One hardly expects a tribunal examining hate propaganda to swallow the propaganda whole and accept it as fact. That is what happened in the *Zundel* postal case.

Another reason the Board of Review gave for its recommendation is one, as we have seen in earlier chapters, that universities and libraries also use, the absence of criminal proceedings. The board noted that Zundel had not been convicted under the criminal code. The board adopted the argument of the Canadian Civil Liberties Association that if an offence had been committed Zundel should be prosecuted.

During the period of the interim prohibition order, Zundel's hate propaganda operation was shut down. In an interview he gave in 1985 to the *Globe and Mail,* Zundel said that the Holocaust Remembrance Association, through its complaint to the minister responsible for the post office, had crippled his operation. His publishing outfit, Samisdat, in 1985, had, so he said, still not fully recovered, although his mail privileges had, by then, been restored for about three years.

By 1982, when Zundel got his interim postal order lifted, the criminal code situation had gone from bad to worse. After years of inaction, the Attorney General of Ontario had launched a criminal code, hate propaganda prosecution of the most bizarre sort.

Buzzanga and Durocher were two francophone activists from the Windsor area who felt the francophone community was not doing enough to defend its rights. The two printed and distributed some anti-francophone literature with the intent of stirring the community up, of awakening it from its apathy, in the hope that it would become more vigorous in asserting francophone rights.

Buzzanga and Durocher were prosecuted for hate propaganda and convicted. On appeal in September 1979 their conviction was set aside and a new trial ordered. The criminal code says that the offence of hate propaganda must be committed wilfully. The trial judge, J. P. McMahon, in his instruction to the jury, said that "wilfully" meant intentionally as opposed to accidentally. However, the court of appeal held, in the judgment of Mr. Justice Martin, that this was a misdirection.

In the opinion of the judges of the court of appeal, Justice McMahon did not distinguish between the intention to disseminate material, which may promote hatred, in order to achieve some other purpose, and the intention to disseminate material for the conscious purpose of promoting hatred. According to the court of appeal, only the second type of intention is covered by the word "wilfully." Because the trial judge did not properly define "wilfully" a new trial was ordered.

That judgment made the crime of hate propaganda a good deal harder to prove. The court had ordered new trials for Buzzanga and Durocher; however, the Crown never prosecuted them. The judgment temporarily stopped prosecutions for hate propaganda across Canada. Because of the Board of Review decision for Zundel in the post office case, Citron needed a criminal conviction against Zundel. As a result of the *Buzzanga and Durocher* decision, no attorney general would launch a prosecution for hate propaganda. Yet consent of an attorney general was essential.

Faced with this obstacle, Citron tried another route. In order to have his mailing privileges stopped, Zundel did not need to be convicted of hate propaganda. He just had to be convicted. As long as the offence was an offence that related to what he was mailing, his mailing privileges could be stopped.

Citron hit upon the offence of false news. The false news provision of the criminal code was a little used, antiquated offence, carried over from the nineteenth century. Whatever disadvantages it had, it had this saving grace: unlike hate propaganda, it did not require the consent of the attorney general. A private prosecution could be launched.

Citron did just that. Bowing to the inevitable, once she started, the attorney general took over the prosecution. The attorney general got a conviction, though the conviction was overturned on appeal.

After Zundel's conviction and before the decision on his appeal, I approached the minister responsible for the post office. On behalf of the League for Human Rights of B'nai Brith Canada, I asked the minister to reinstate the postal suspension against Zundel. The obstacle to suspension on which the Board of Review had focused, the lack of conviction, had now disappeared.

The minister refused. Part of the sentence against Zundel was that he not speak or write publicly about the Holocaust for three years. Michel Côté, the then minister, wrote me in 1986, that he had no evidence Zundel was disobeying the order. The minister was not prepared to impose a prohibitory order on mere suspicion alone.

Paralleling the *Zundel* case in Ontario was the *Keegstra* case in Alberta. The *Keegstra* prosecution was also, in its own way, attributable to the failure of civil remedies. Keegstra was a school teacher in Eckville, Alberta forcing his students to learn the Jewish conspiracy theory by rote, failing them if they did not regurgitate it as he dictated it to them. He continued in his position twelve years before he was finally terminated.

If he had lost his teaching job when he began these corrupt teaching practices, little harm would have been done. His medium of communication was teaching. If that medium had been cut off, his propaganda would have been silenced.

The evidence was incontrovertible. The students had verbatim notes of their lessons. More than that, behaviour of such dimensions needed the strongest possible statement of societal disapproval. After twelve years, he had done so much harm to so many students that a criminal prosecution became imperative. Failure to prosecute would have been a tacit acquiescence in his views.

Following upon the *Keegstra* and *Zundel* prosecutions were the prosecutions and convictions in Ontario of Andrews and Smith. Citron had shown that a refusal by attorneys general to prosecute under the hate propaganda section of the criminal code could be circumvented by a private prosecution for publishing false news. That realization made it easier for attorneys general to consent to prosecutions for hate propaganda.

Civil and criminal remedies, in Canadian law, have been inextricably linked. It is impossible to tell the civil story without reference to criminal law. Indeed, the very existence of criminal litigation in Canada was caused by the failure of civil remedies.

The first lesson I believe we have learned from these cases is the need for a specialized tribunal. The Human Rights Tribunal in *Taylor* gave a better judgment than the Board of Review in *Zundel* partly because the *Taylor* tribunal was a human rights tribunal. The Canadian House of Commons Committee on the Participation of Visible Minorities in Canadian Society, in its report of March 1984 titled "Equality Now," recommended that the jurisdiction over hate propaganda of the post office, customs, and the Canadian Radio and Television Commission all go to the Canadian Human Rights Commission. The report justified the proposed transfer by saying the commission "is already sensitive to and experienced with issues of racism and racial discrimination."

A human rights remedy is better than other remedies, civil as well as criminal. Criminal prosecution is either too easy or too hard. If the consent of the attorney general is required, consent can be difficult to get. If consent of the attorney general is not required, then private prosecutions can be launched, which may be frivolous or abusive. A human rights commission, criminal remedy avoids both these extremes. A complainant can start the process without any prior governmental consent. Bureaucratic screening prevents the matter from going to a tribunal if it is frivolous, designed to harass the very people the legislation was supposed to protect, or otherwise abusive.

A human rights remedy shifts the emphasis of the case from the civil liberties of the perpetrator to the human rights of the victim group. In human rights cases, although the complainant has standing as a party to the case, it is the human rights commission that assumes the burden of presenting the case to the human rights tribunal. The human rights commission acts, not in the name of the complainant, but in the name of human rights.

Human rights tribunals not only produce better judgments, but also are more sensitive to the nature of the problem of hate propaganda and more likely to take action against it. In the *Terry Long–Aryan Nations* case, B'nai Brith attempted to invoke all possible remedies. It approached the Attorney General of Alberta for a prosecution. It asked the *Red Deer Advocate* not to run the ads containing the Aryan Nations' phone number. It complained to the Alberta Press Council about the ads in the *Red Deer Advocate*. It approached the Alberta Telephone Company to take action against the use of its phones for hate propaganda. None of these avenues was effective. The only administration that showed an interest was the human rights administration. Only the Human Rights Commission was prepared to act.

The same can be said about the case of Malcolm Ross, the New Brunswick school teacher and hate propagandist. No one seemed to be willing to do anything about Malcolm Ross. The attorney general did not want to prosecute. The school board where he taught did not want to fire him. Newspapers published his propaganda as letters to the editor. Only the New Brunswick Human Rights Commission was prepared to take action.

The *John Ross Taylor* case produced a good judgment. However, it did not produce a good result. Except for the period when he was in jail, Taylor persisted in his activity. Neither the prohibition order, the conviction, nor the sentence dissuaded him. Recidivism, of course, is a danger with any criminal offence. With hardcore hate propagandists, it appears endemic.

The postal remedy, for all its faults, had at least this advantage. While the prohibitory order was on against Zundel it was effective. The order was directed not to Zundel, but to those who delivered the mail. They complied with that order whether or not Zundel would have complied with any order. Taylor would have been far more hampered if his telephone privileges had been suspended. Telling him not to use his phone for hate propaganda, but then making it possible for him to use it in defiance of the order, gave him the opportunity to play the role of a martyr in both his eyes and the eyes of his followers.

I have argued previously that the link must be broken between the criminal law and the civil law in institutions like libraries and universities, and their policies. It must also be broken in the Canada Post Corporation Act. The requirement that there must be reason to believe an offence is being committed before postal privileges are suspended inevitably brings criminal considerations to bear in the invocation of a civil remedy.

The criminal law is hedged with safeguards because it is criminal law. Whether or not, for instance, the word "wilfully" should remain in the criminal law, there is no need for it to exist in the civil law. Indeed, in civil remedies that do not incorporate the criminal law, there is no such requirement. Incorporating the criminal law means incorporating criminal law defences that have no place in civil law.

Much of the civil liberties debate about hate propaganda has focused on the use of the criminal law. An effective operating civil law remedy will, no doubt, fail to please every civil libertarian. However, at least the magnitude of the concerns will be lessened.

How does one prohibit hate propaganda? The answer, I suggest, is carefully. An effective first recourse using civil remedies is, I believe, the careful way to proceed.

Chapter Fourteen

Truth

SHOULD TRUTH BE ALLOWED as a permissible defence to a charge of propagating hatred? One of the primary arguments for freedom of speech is that it helps us arrive at the truth. Lee Bollinger, in *The Tolerant Society*, has called getting at the truth the dominant value associated with free speech.[1] When we do not allow truth as a defence to hate propaganda, we are restricting speech in a particularly dramatic way.

Truth is not a permitted defence for the offence of hate promotion in several countries where hate propaganda is prohibited. For instance, in England, the Race Relations Act, which penalizes publication of material likely to stir up hatred, does not have truth as a defence. In France, a law which penalizes incitement to hatred also does not allow truth as a defence.

Canadian law has grappled with the question whether truth should be a defence and answered it in different ways in different laws. For hate propaganda by telephone, prohibited by the Canadian Human Rights Act, truth is not a defence.[2]

For the old offence of spreading false news, truth was more than a defence. Knowledge of falsity was an essential element of the offence and the burden was on the Crown to prove, beyond a reasonable doubt, that the news was false.[3] Ernst Zundel was charged with spreading false news, that the Holocaust did not happen. After two trials, and two convictions, the Supreme Court of Canada found unconstitutional the provision under which he was charged. In consequence, Parliament removed the offence from the statute books.

For the offence of hate propaganda in Canada's current criminal code, truth is a defence, with the burden on the accused. Falsity is not an essential element of the offence. However, where the Crown does establish the offence of promoting hatred has been committed, the accused can, nonethe-

186

less, be acquitted if he or she establishes that the statements communicated were true.[4]

While the burden on the Crown is to establish the state's case beyond a reasonable doubt, any defence the accused may raise must succeed if it is established on the balance of probabilities. The standard of proof is less when the accused has to establish truth than when the Crown has to establish falsity.

Canadians have had some experience with these laws in recent years. John Ross Taylor of the Western Guard had an order of the Canadian Human Rights Commission lodged against him, prohibiting him from using the telephone for hate propaganda.[5] The Human Rights Act survived the constitutional challenge made in the *Taylor* case by passing the proportionality test. The courts said the challenged provision of the Human Rights Act was reasonably drawn, and tailored precisely to the practices it was designed to attack. The Federal Court of Appeal considered that the legislative scheme showed restraint rather than severity. All this was said in spite of the fact that truth is not a defence.

Counsel for Taylor tried to smuggle in the defence of truth. His counsel argued that because his purpose was to tell the truth he could not be convicted of contempt. The courts held that even if Taylor were to have established that his only purpose was to tell the truth, he would be no less guilty of contempt. The offence of contempt of court consists of the intentional doing of an act which is prohibited by the order. It is not necessary to prove that there was an intent to be contemptuous of the court.

Jim Keegstra in Alberta and Andrews and Smith in Toronto were both convicted under the hate propaganda provision of the criminal code. Keegstra was convicted after a jury trial. Andrews and Smith were convicted after a joint trial before a judge alone, without a jury. Keegstra, on appeal to the Alberta Court of Appeal, had his conviction set aside as unconstitutional. Andrews and Smith lost their appeals to the Ontario Court of Appeal. The Crown appealed the *Keegstra* decision and Andrews and Smith appealed their cases to the Supreme Court of Canada. These cases were heard at the same time as the *John Ross Taylor* case. The appeal of the Crown in the *Keegstra* case was allowed.[6] The appeals of Andrews and Smith were dismissed.[7]

The Supreme Court of Canada held that the offence of hate propaganda in the criminal code was constitutional and that the defence of truth was not necessary for the offence to remain constitutional. Mr. Justice Dickson said:

I find it difficult to accept that circumstances exist where factually accurate statements can be used for no other purpose than to stir up hatred against a social or religious group. It would seem to follow that there is no reason why the individual who intentionally employs such statements to achieve harmful ends must, under the Charter, be protected from criminal censure.

From a practical point of view, the most troubling of these cases was the first *Zundel* case, where the Crown had the burden of proving falsity, and no judicial notice of the Holocaust was taken. The trial became a forum for Zundel's Holocaust denial hate propaganda. The obvious was put in artificial doubt by the nature of the trial.

The *Keegstra* trial was also troubling, but less so. Keegstra attempted to establish the truth of his theories. However, because the prosecutor was not put in the absurd position of trying to prove the obvious, the part of the trial where truth was an issue did not cause the same problems as it did in the *Zundel* case.

In the second *Zundel* trial, truth was less of an issue because judicial notice was taken of the mass murder of Jews by Nazis during World War II. In the *John Ross Taylor* case truth was not an issue because the accused could not raise it as a defence.

There are a number of different reasons why truth should not be a defence to a hate propaganda charge. One is that where truth is a defence, the trial becomes a forum for the propagandists. What sort of forum it is depends very much on what sort of media coverage the proceedings are given. It is unpredictable whether any trial will be reported or not reported, reported well or reported badly; reported in a prominent fashion, or given cursory treatment.

Certainly propagandists themselves will use hate trials to publicize their ideologies. The first *Zundel* case was a classic from this point of view. If Zundel wanted to try for acquittal on the charge of knowingly spreading false news, all he had to do was show that he did not know that the news he was spreading, that the Holocaust did not happen, was false. Instead he went about trying to show that the news was true, that the Holocaust did not in fact happen. This was a strategy that was almost certain to lead to a conviction. When a jury is asked to convict or acquit on the basis of whether the Holocaust did happen or did not happen, there is little doubt what the verdict will be. Yet, because Zundel was able, by the nature of the case, to put the Holocaust in issue, he was able to publicize his propaganda in a way that would not have been possible otherwise.

That sort of publicity is not inevitable for hate propaganda cases. It is not even possible where truth is not a defence. Even where truth is a defence, that sort of publicity will not occur in every case, depending on the happenstance of media coverage.

We should not create defences or abolish defences based on the possibility whether the media will cover a trial or not. Yet, we must bear in mind that every trial is and should be accessible to the public. Moreover, we must be aware that hate propagandists will try to use trials for their own ends.

Zundel behaved not far differently from the way Joseph Goebbels and Julius Streicher did in pre-Nazi Germany during the Weimar Republic. What that Weimar history shows, as the *Zundel* prosecution itself shows, is problems with the way the law was working. The Goebbels, Streicher, and *Zundel* prosecutions do not undermine the value of the laws as such. They do put into question allowing truth as a defence.

The existence of truth as a defence creates a perverse effect. Instead of the law serving as a deterrent, an incentive develops to violate the law and use the courtroom as a platform.

The dynamics of publicity for a hate propaganda trial are different from the dynamics of publicity in the ordinary criminal case. In the ordinary criminal case, the accused does not normally want publicity. He or she is embarrassed by the charge. In spite of the presumption of innocence, there is a cloud that hangs over the accused simply because of the charge. Evidence in the case, even when it leads to an acquittal, may be of a highly compromising nature. In criminal law, there is a long history of accused and witnesses seeking exclusion of the public and the press.

In an ordinary criminal case, the interest in publicity comes from the Crown's desire for the prosecution to serve as a deterrent. More generally, the desire for publicity is an expression of the public interest. It is important not only that justice is done; but, as well, that it is seen to be done. The public gaze deters the courts from behaving in an aberrant and arbitrary manner.

These values remain in a hate propaganda case. Publicity is needed here too if convictions are to serve as a deterrent. Publicity or at least public access is needed as well to ensure that justice is seen to be done.

Nonetheless, the fact that the accused may want to use the court as a forum, the fact that other accused in the past have used hate propaganda trials as forums, must be taken into account. To a certain extent, any hate propaganda trial is a forum, whether truth is a defence or not. The trial will give the accused publicity. The charge will give the accused an occasion to seek publicity. The very possibility in hate propaganda cases has led some to argue that there should be no hate propaganda laws on the books at all.

It is my own belief that we need hate propaganda laws and that the reality of publicity about these cases, even where truth is an allowed defence, is not a reason for refraining from enacting the laws. The publicity the hate propagandist receives in the context of a trial is negative publicity. The propagandist acquires notoriety rather than fame. His ideas reach a wider audience, but in a context where they are refuted. The publicity a hate propaganda trial receives is not just publicity for the propaganda. It is publicity for the refutation as well.

Mr. Justice Dickson, for the Supreme Court of Canada, said the publicity around hate propaganda trials "serves to illustrate to the public the severe reprobation with which society holds messages of hate directed towards racial and religious groups." He added "the message sent is that hate propaganda is harmful to the target group members and threatening to a harmonious society."

The questions of truth or falsity that are posed are not just questions where the hate propagandist's answer is offensive. The very question gives offence.

Are blacks dirty? Do Jews control the world? Are Serbians bloodthirsty? Are Tutsis genocidal? The very attempt to answer these questions demeans the administration of justice. The degradation is particularly acute where the burden of proof is on the Crown. It would make a mockery of justice to have the Crown go about attempting to prove such things as blacks are clean, or Jews do not control the world, or Serbians do not enjoy killing. In reality, for many offences this would not happen. Though the offence of hate propaganda may be clearly committed, the absurdity of proving falsity would prevent the Crown from ever launching a case. Indeed the more obvious the hate propaganda, the more absurd the propaganda assertions being made, the less likely the Crown will prosecute because of the absurdity of proof.

The evil of hate propaganda is not only in the conclusions reached. It is in the questions being asked. Hate propagandists approach the world with a frame of reference that is skewed to conform to their own world view. Hate propagandists live in a self-contained world of delusive paranoia where the vilified group is the enemy and they are the defenders of virtue.

A prosecution where truth is a defence adopts the frame of reference of the propagandist. The trial asks the question the propagandist asks, adopts the approach to the world the propagandist has. A hate propaganda trial where truth is a defence may reject the answers of the propagandist. Yet, it accepts the question of the propagandist as valid ones, and gives credence to them.

When an event happens in court, it has a different status than when it happens out of court. One reason we press for the prosecution of Nazi war criminals, as I have done, is that it is an official recognition, a statement by the state that these crimes have happened, that what was done was wrong, that the perpetrators should be punished. All of that could be said outside of court. However, statements in court are more than statements of individuals expressing opinions. They are pronouncements of society acting as a whole.

What happens in court, as well, is more than just declaratory. It is constitutive. Court procedures are not just statements of what has happened. Court procedures are themselves events that happen. When a person is convicted of a crime, what has occurred is more than just the uttering of a statement that the person is guilty. What has occurred is the conviction itself. The person is liable to punishment. He has a criminal record. The situation has changed, for the accused, and for society.

We must not lose sight of these consequences of court proceedings when we launch a hate propaganda case. When a court case asks a question that a hate promoter would ask, it gives a status to the question it would not otherwise have. The trial may not make the answer of the hate promoter legitimate. However, it makes the question of the hate promoter legitimate. That is something no hate propaganda trial should do. It is not just that the assertions the hate propagandist makes are awkward and demeaning to disprove. The very asking of these questions in court gives the questions a status in society they should not have.

The media coverage of the first *Zundel* trial illustrates this point. While attitudinal surveying after the trial showed no resulting increase in antisemitism, the Zundel message was nonetheless highly publicized and unremittingly antisemitic.[8]

The harm it caused in the anguish it inflicted on survivors of the Holocaust and the Jewish community in general was real. It was an affront to the community to have their suffering ridiculed in this public way.

What, after all, is the whole point of human rights and fundamental freedoms, of which freedom of speech is a part? The underlying value is promotion of human dignity and individual worth. Hate propaganda is an attack on the human dignity of the vilified group. In the words of Mr. Justice Quigley, the trial division judge in the *Keegstra* case, the wilful promotion of hatred "contradicts the recognition of spiritual and moral values which impel us to assert and protect the dignity of each member of society."

The reasons that lead us to legislate against hate propaganda in the first place should impel us to want to legislate against truth as a defence. Otherwise the goal we have sought, of protecting vilified groups from hate propaganda, is undercut by the very means we have used.

The truth will out. It is both wrong and futile to suppress truth. However, a hate propaganda trial where truth is not a defence is not an attempt to suppress the truth. What is at issue is not whether the truth will be told or hidden. Rather the issue is whether the trial will be used to publicize an investigation that no one concerned with the search for truth would undertake.

It is important to keep in mind who are being convicted in hate promotion cases. If the search for human dignity is the foundation for all rights and freedoms, this foundation supports, at its next level, a commitment to democracy. Free speech is important to society both because it allows the self-realization of individual human beings, and because of its contribution to democracy.

Yet, those who promote hatred against identifiable groups are enemies of democracy and free speech. They use the opportunities free speech gives to attempt to undermine the truth-seeking process.

It is hard to credit the neo-Nazi movement, the current targets of hate propaganda prosecutions in Canada, as defenders of Canadian democracy. On the contrary, they are committed to destroying it. Their aim ultimately is a suppression of all but their truth.

We cannot pretend the danger of neo-Nazism is not there. Part and parcel of that danger is the goal of neo-Nazis to end forever the search for truth, to impose only their official truth.

If we are interested in seeking truth, if we are interested in protecting democracy, these interests argue against protecting expressions aimed at subverting the truth-seeking process itself. When we protect expression that is attempting to subvert our very efforts to protect expression, then we undermine our own efforts to seek truth, to promote democracy.

Yet another reason why truth should not be admitted as a defence is that it makes prosecution a high risk game. When an accused is acquitted it can be for any number of reasons, some of which may be highly technical or specific in nature. Yet, if truth is a defence, there is the risk that an acquittal will be seen as a court affirmation of the truth of the hate propaganda.

When an accused denies the Nazi policy of genocide, the murder of six million Jews, the existence of the gas chambers, as Zundel did, when these facts are put in issue, as they were in both *Zundel* trials, there is a risk that an acquittal, on no matter what grounds will be seen as a determination that there was no Nazi policy of genocide, that there were no six million killed, that there were no gas chambers. Zundel, himself, would no doubt have asserted that an acquittal meant exactly that. The risk of interpreting a verdict in that way is almost reason enough for not having truth as a defence.

Moveover, allowing truth as a defence leads to a mischaracterization of the issue before the courts. The harm of hate propaganda is not the harm of saying something that is false. Making a false statement is not, and should not be a crime. Allowing a defence of truth gives a mistaken impression that what the accused has done wrong is to say something false. Yet that is not the harm against which the offence of hate propaganda is directed.

The focus of a hate propaganda trial should be whether the accused promoted hatred. Even true statements can be parleyed in such a way as to foment hatred against a group identifiable by race, religion, or ethnic origin. Allowing truth as a defence suggests there is a right way to promote hatred, by plastering together a string of true statements in such a way that hatred is the likely result, and a wrong way to promote hatred, by using false statements. If hate propaganda is to be curtailed by law, as I believe it should be, then it should be curtailed no matter how hatred is promoted.

Alan Borovoy of the Canadian Civil Liberties Association has said we have to feel uncomfortable when we put someone behind bars for telling the truth. Yet, that is not what we are doing when a court convicts a propagandist of promoting hatred. The propagandist is convicted for his promotion of hatred, not for his use of the truth to do it.

Is a person without truth as a defence left defenceless? I would say no. The Canadian Human Rights Act, which does not allow truth as a defence, has dealt with real and substantial issues in the orders it has made. In particular, tribunals under the Human Rights Act have had to examine whether the messages communicated were likely to expose the victims to hatred on the grounds of race, colour, national or ethnic origin, or religion.

In the Criminal Code of Canada there are two hate propaganda offences, public incitement of hatred, and wilful promotion of hatred. Public incitement of hatred likely to lead to a breach of the peace is an offence, whether the statements communicated are true or not. Truth is not a defence and the absence of truth as a defence for this offence has not raised the concern of commentators.

Indeed, none of the defences legislated for the other offence of wilful promotion of hatred—truth, religion, reasonable belief in truth, and removal—are defences for the offence of public incitement of hatred. Yet the offence of public incitement of hatred meets with no criticism. That is also true of the offences of sedition and obscenity. Truth is not a defence to either of these offences. Nor is it commonly suggested that it should be.

The notion of excluding the truth in court is an everyday occurrence in other legal contexts. It should not seem strange or abhorrent in this context. In the ordinary criminal case, where evidence is prejudicial to the accused, or confusing or misleading to the jury, the evidence will be excluded, even though it is true. For instance, evidence of other crimes committed by an accused is inadmissible in his trial, even though there is no doubt as to the truth of the criminal record of the accused, because admission of that evidence would be prejudicial to the accused.

The Law Reform Commission of Canada says that truth should be a defence because otherwise we put at risk legitimate scholars who insert themselves into areas of controversy by publishing factually accurate material critical of socially important groups. Yet scholars would be at risk only if, in addition to injecting themselves into controversy, they promoted hatred.

Mark MacGuigan, a member of the Special Committee on Hate Propaganda, chaired by Maxwell Cohen, whose report was published 1965, said in the House of Commons in 1970, that it would be unseemly for someone who is taking a position which could be demonstrably shown to be true to be convicted because of the circumstances in which he uttered the word. I suggest promotion of hatred is itself unseemly, in its totality, and it is equally unseemly for a court to be subjected to an inquiry whether hate propaganda is true or not.

The Cohen Committee said that there will almost always, if not always, be a public benefit derived from true statements about groups, because generalizations about groups play a vital role in public discussion. Again, here it is hard to see the public benefit in promotion of hatred. It is hard to accept that hate propaganda plays a vital role in any public discussion. It is also worth noting that this conclusion was not unanimous; Samuel Hayes, one of the committee members dissented, and would have wished truth to be excluded as a defence.

Mr. Justice Dickson, who gave the majority judgment of the Supreme Court of Canada in the *Keegstra* case, said that there is very little chance that the views of society inherent in statements intended to promote hatred against an identifiable group will lead to a better world. To portray such statements as crucial to the betterment of the political and social milieu is, he ruled, misguided.

Allowing truth as a defence is more than just adding an unnecessary restriction to prosecutions. Allowing truth as a defence to the offence of hate propaganda is self-contradictory. It means accepting the notion that some forms of hate propaganda may have a constructive role to play in public discussion.

For the offence of hate propaganda, if the defence of truth is removed, will it not arise in some other fashion? Will not all of the other defences— religion, reasonable belief in truth, and removal—have to be taken away in order to keep truth out of court? If we take away all the defences, have we not gone too far?

Assuming the other defences besides truth remain, I would argue that the defence of truth would not creep in some other way. The most obvious way it would enter indirectly is through the defence of reasonable belief in truth. However, this defence is limited. It is restricted, according to the criminal code, to statements "relevant to any subject of public interest, the discussion of which was for the public benefit, and if on reasonable ground [the accused] believed them to be true." The problem with hate propaganda is not just the conclusions it reaches, but the subjects it discusses. Allowing a discussion of the subject matter of hate propaganda, if raised in the guise of a reasonable belief in truth, forces us into inquiries which are decidedly not for the public benefit. The defence of reasonable belief of truth, once an accused arrives in court, can be circumscribed to prevent a trial on truth or falsity.

The criminal code has the defence of truth for defamatory libel as well as for hate propaganda.[9] Does it make sense to remove the defence of truth for hate propaganda and yet retain it for defamatory libel? Or, to put the question another way, if I believe, as I do, that the defence of truth should be retained for defamatory libel, how can I justify removing this defence for hate propaganda. Hate propaganda laws are sometimes called group libel laws. Does it make sense to draft the two sets of laws differently?

The law of defamatory libel, although it allows truth in defence, does not allow it as a complete defence. In order for truth to be a defence, not only must the accused prove that the defamatory matter was true. The accused must in addition prove that the manner in which the publication was published was for the public benefit at the time it was published.

In other words, if the defamatory libel was true, but the accused cannot establish that the manner in which the publication was published was for the public benefit, then the accused must be convicted.

If we intend to have the hate propaganda law parallel the defamatory libel law we would not have truth as a defence on its own, but would add, as an additional requirement, that the manner in which the propaganda was published was for the public benefit. However, publishing hate propaganda is never in the public interest, except, of course, if the publication is to point out hate propaganda for the purpose of its removal. This is already a defence regardless whether the hate propaganda is true or not.

Similarly, in the law of defamatory libel, there is the defence of fair comment.[10] When a person makes a comment that is fair, reasonable, and true, there is no libel. However, when a person makes a comment that is unfair and malicious, then the comment is still libellous, even though it may be based on a set of true facts. A person cannot defend a libel charge with fair comment, if, at same time, the defendant was malicious and unfair.

Yet the wilful promotion of hatred is, by definition, malicious. Removing the defence of truth in hate propaganda laws actually gets us closer to defamatory libel law than keeping in the defence of truth does.

What is at stake in a libel case is an individual's reputation. Libel is not restricted to promoting hatred against an individual. It means any statement that will lower a person in general esteem. However, hate propaganda is a good deal more damaging than lowering someone in esteem. So even if malice represented a different and higher legal standard than wilful promotion of hatred, it is justifiable to maintain the defence of truth for libel and not for hate propaganda.

This argument is all written on the assumption that the laws will be used properly. Let us make the opposite assumption, that the laws will be abused. Do we not need truth as a defence to protect the innocent from unwarranted prosecution from a vindictive attorney general? Will not the fact that an accused can use truth as a defence make a vindictive attorney general hesitate before prosecuting?

I have several responses to this argument. One is that it is inappropriate to look at laws in this negative light. If laws are going to be abused, why have any laws at all? This sort of argument against a hate propaganda law is equally an argument against a murder law. It is not an argument that is specific to the issue of truth as a defence to hate propaganda.

Second, if an attorney general is truly vindictive and determined, no possible defence will stop him or her. The harassment from prosecution will be its own end, regardless of the defences that can or cannot be raised.

Third, if we are to assume the worst, we have to assume the worst both ways. The worst that can happen without hate propaganda laws is, as we have seen, genocide, the mass murder of innocents, a Holocaust. The worst that can happen without effective hate propaganda laws is far worse than the worst that can happen with hate propaganda laws carried too far. If we are to balance off evils, having hate propaganda laws on the books that are abused is a lesser evil than giving hate propaganda free rein.

Whether we should control hate propaganda and how we should control hate propaganda is a difficult issue for any society committed to democratic values and freedom of expression. All the same, I suggest, the bedrock of democracy is not freedom of expression alone, as an absolute, but tolerance as well. If we lose the tolerance that makes democracy work, the possibility of uninhibited free speech will not save it. On the contrary, uninhibited speech, without tolerance, may indeed accelerate the demise of democracy. In order to encourage and further the tolerance of diverse and varied groups in our society, it is necessary to have hate propaganda laws. It is equally necessary, I suggest, to remove truth as a defence in these laws.

Notes

1. Oxford University Press, 1986.
2. *Statutes of Canada* (1976–77), Chapter 33, Section 13.
3. The former criminal code section 181.
4. *Criminal Code* section 319(3)(a).
5. (1991) 75 D.L.R. (4th) 577.
6. (1991) 61 C.C.C. (3d) 1.
7. (1991) 61 C.C.C. (3d) 490.
8. Mosaic Press, 1986, p. 73.
9. *Criminal Code* sections 311, 611, 612.
10. *Criminal Code* section 310.

Chapter Fifteen

Effective Laws

TO HAVE EFFECTIVE LAWS to combat hate speech means more than removing the defence of truth from a ban on hate speech. For one, Holocaust denial should be specifically prohibited by legislation.

Equating Holocaust denial with hate speech is, of course, necessary to justify a specific prohibition of Holocaust denial, but this alone is not sufficient. Why is it necessary to have a specific prohibition of Holocaust denial?

One reason is certainty in the law. Statutes often combine the general and the specific. A standard drafting technique is to state a general principle, and then add specific examples. The specific examples are there, partly to illustrate the meaning of the general principle, partly to avoid litigation about whether the general principle applies to the specific examples, and partly because of the importance of the specific examples. General legislation is almost always passed with specific situations in mind. It makes eminent sense actually to refer to those specific situations. The specific examples headline the purpose of legislating the general principle and the insertion of the specific examples removes all doubt that the general principle applies to those examples.

Adding Holocaust denial to a hate prohibition law would illustrate the meaning of hate speech. It would avoid litigation about whether Holocaust denial is hate speech. It would headline the importance of Holocaust denial as a form of hate speech. It would be a warning to the gullible and a proclamation by society of its abhorrence of this form of hate speech.

Despite the fact that in the cases of *Ross*, *Zundel*, and *Keegstra*, four juries and one human rights commission have found Holocaust denial to be hate speech, specific legislation would serve a point. These cases, *Ross*, *Zundel*, and *Keegstra*, do not serve as legal precedents binding other courts in other cases. The decisions in these cases were findings of fact, not rulings of law. Without specific legislation, in every case where the issue whether Holocaust denial is hate speech arises, it would have to be relitigated. The attorney general or the complainant would have to be prove all over again that Holocaust denial is hate speech. Specific legislation would obviate the necessity of reproving this fact case after case.

If Holocaust denial is hate speech, what about other forms of historical denial, other forms of genocide denial? For instance the Armenian genocide in the early years of this century is formally denied by the Turkish government. Is this denial hate speech? Should this, or others, too be stated explicitly as a specific example in legislation?

I have for years advocated bringing to justice war criminals and criminals against humanity by speaking, debating, participating in radio call-in shows, answering correspondence, and making submissions to Parliament and the Commission of Inquiry on War Criminals. One question I am constantly asked is, Is A or B a war crime? Should X or Y be prosecuted? The answer I have given is that the whole point of advocating justice for war criminals is to have a system that would answer those questions carefully, fairly and dispassionately. Instant judgements based on common knowledge do not constitute a fair judicial process.

My answer to questions about specific forms of historical denial is the same. I do not claim to judge whether all forms of alleged hate speech are hate speech or not. It seems pretty clear to me that Holocaust denial is hate speech. However, saying Holocaust denial is hate speech is like saying Hitler was a war criminal. Saying so does not mean I can state with confidence, for every single person against whom allegations are made, who is and who is not a war criminal.

Other forms of historical denial could possibly be specifically prohibited as examples of hate speech. An examination would have to be done, as I have attempted in chapter five with Holocaust denial, to show that these other forms of denial are also hate speech, and hate speech of such significance to justify their being singled out for specific mention. Any other form of historical denial that passes this examination should indeed be included as a specific example of the prohibition.

Another reason why a specific prohibition of Holocaust denial is necessary, even where truth is removed as a defence, is this. While generally it makes sense to say hate speech is wrong, whether components of the speech are true or not, it makes no sense at all to say that Holocaust denial is hate speech whether the Holocaust happened or not. Yet, unless Holocaust denial is specifically prohibited, that, in effect, is what we could be saying when the offence of hate speech has no defence of truth. The foundation for saying that Holocaust denial is hate speech is the fact that the Holocaust incontestably happened. In order to avoid the absurdity of suggesting that the existence of the Holocaust is a matter of indifference to a Holocaust denial hate speech prosecution, Holocaust denial should be specifically prohibited.

Apart from the specific prohibition of Holocaust denial, a legal agenda remains: the need to avoid technical distinctions in the legislation and its enforcement that would make a hate speech law unworkable. The failures of Weimar Germany show that hate speech laws can be sabotaged by these distinctions.

Out of free speech concerns, Britain has been more hesitant than continental European countries such as France and Germany to develop and use its hate speech laws. In Britain, there are such laws, but they suffer from a number of weaknesses. The British Parliament enacted the offence of incitement to racial hatred in 1965. The law was strengthened in 1986 but, despite the changes, the law has been ineffective. There have been few prosecutions under the law even though a high volume of virulent hate propaganda circulates in the U.K.

An inquiry into matters arising from the death of Stephen Lawrence prompted the United Kingdom government to revisit its anti-hate laws. Stephen Lawrence was an eighteen-year-old student killed in April 1993 at a bus stop in an unprovoked knife attack. The only reason for the murder was that Stephen was black. The British government announced a judicial inquiry into his death on July 1997. The report of Sir William Macpherson was released in February 1999.

The Board of Deputies of British Jews, in its submission to the 1997 inquiry, stated:

> The existing law to combat incitement to racial hatred has proved less effective than expected. The law is technically complex, and imposes so many barriers that prosecutions are rare. We have submitted to the government proposals for a more effective law; we have also urged the government to introduce specific legislation to outlaw Holocaust denial as occurs in most other European countries.[1]

As one might expect in a country without fully effective hate laws, in the United Kingdom there are a disturbing number of hate crimes. One technique the far right uses, both for publicity and for recruiting, is racist chants at football matches. Monkey chants are shouted and bananas are thrown from the stands whenever a black player gets possession of the ball. Paper crosses, symbolic of the Ku Klux Klan, are burned. Far-right newspapers are sold outside the stadiums. There are attacks on blacks after the matches. The far-right instigators encourage others join in with them and recruit those who seem willing to go along.

The Stephen Lawrence killing was at the most serious end of a whole spectrum of racist incidents. These incidents are significant in number and increasing in recent years. From 1991–92 reported antisemitic incidents rose 9%.[2] From 1992–1993, reported antisemitic incidents increased by 18%.[3]

In 1988, the police recorded 4,383 racially motivated incidents in England and Wales against both ethnic minorities and whites. The figure for 1989 is 5,044; for 1990, 6,359; for 1991, 7,882; and for 1992, 7,793.[4]

The Board of Deputies of British Jews recommended that the Public Order Act of 1986, which criminalizes incitement of racial hatred, be amended in numerous respects to improve its effectiveness. The board recommended the offence be expanded from just hatred to hatred, hostility, or contempt. The offence of "stirring up" racial hatred should be expanded to cover encouragement or advocacy of racial hatred. Instead of requiring that racial hatred "is likely" to be stirred up, it should be enough if it is reasonably foreseeable that racial hatred may be stirred up. The court should have the power to order that no future copies of offending material be distributed. The consent of the attorney general for prosecution should no longer be required, but private prosecution should remain prohibited.[5]

The board recommended the offence in the Malicious Communications Act of sending also include delivery and that the act should be amended to make it clear that the words "indecent or grossly offensive" are not intended to relate to pornographic material only. The board also proposed a totally new offence of vilification of a member of an ethnic group.

The Public Order Act of 1986 as well creates an offence of threatening, abusive, or insulting words, or behaviour likely to cause harassment, alarm, and distress.[6] The government concluded on review that the powers under this provision were not sufficient to reflect the more serious forms of racial harassment. It accordingly took steps to strengthen the legislation and a new offence of causing intentional harassment has been created. In general, the main recommendations of the Board of Deputies of British Jews have been supported by the Select Committee on Home Affairs Report on Racial Violence of 1994, the Labour Party, the Liberal Democratic Party, the Commission for Racial Equality, the Bar Council, the Law Society, and to a lesser extent, the Commissioner for the Metropolitan Police.

Regrettably, technical distinctions continue to exist in enforcement of Canadian hate speech laws that hinder their effectiveness. For example, one of the defences that the criminal code provides to the offence of propagating hatred is the good faith expression of an opinion on a religious subject. Various attorneys general in Canada have refused to consent to prosecute apparent hate promoters, giving as a reason the fear that the accused could raise successfully the defence of religious expression.

The promotion of hatred is not an intrinsic part of any organized religion. Rather, for promoters of hate, religious opinion is a mask for prejudices which intrinsically have nothing to do with religion. Hate promoters twist religious teachings and conceptions to condone prejudice.[7] That is how the law should be interpreted and, I would hope, would be interpreted. Yet, because of a technical interpretation attorneys general have given, criminal cases against some apparent hate promoters in Canada have never got to court.

Even after we have cleared the legal underbrush of all technical distinctions, we are still not there. As Weimar Germany has also shown, prohibitions alone cannot bear the entire legal load of combatting hatred. In addition, penalties must not be derisory.

In deciding an appropriate penalty for hate speech, we must be aware of one significant difference between hate speech and other crimes. For most offences, the perpetrators do not want to be caught and do no want to be tried. If they are tried, they do not want their trials to be heavily publicized.

For the hate propagandist, none of this is true. Being caught and being tried is part and parcel of the propaganda effort. A trial becomes a public platform for the hate speech itself. If punishment is not real, it is a platform won without penalty. For other crimes, detection and conviction will themselves be deterrents to the crime, but for hate speech the only real deterrent is the punishment. If the punishment is not meaningful, the perpetrators win a public platform for their hate speech at no real cost to themselves.

For anti-hate laws to be effective, imprisonment must be possible. For clear and flagrant violations of the law, imprisonment should be imposed as a penalty. Furthermore, the term of imprisonment must be of more than token length. Nonetheless, in some cases, imprisonment may be disproportionate for the crime that is prosecuted.

Danilo Turk and Louis Joinet, as United Nations Special Rapporteurs on the Right to Freedom of Opinion and Expression, conclude and recommend that restrictions on freedom of expression be interpreted and applied restrictively.[8] In particular, the restrictions must be in conformity with the principles of legitimacy, legality, proportionality, and democratic necessity.

The principle of legality means that the restriction must be prescribed by law. The principle of legitimacy means that the restriction must have in view an object set out in international human rights instruments as a justifiable limitation on freedom of expression. The principle of democratic necessity includes both the principle of proportionality and respect for the rule of law.

Turk and Joinet are uneasy with sending someone to jail for hate speech. They say that, in fact, deprivation of liberty is clearly disproportionate in ensuring respect for public order and morality.[9] They say that there should be no provision for deprivation of liberty as a sanction save in wholly exceptional cases in which there is a clear and present danger of violence.

There are two points that must be made about this concern of Turk and Joinet. One is that it is not directed specifically against imprisonment for hate speech, rather more generally against imprisonment for speech that threatens public order and morality. When they turn to the more specific subject of hate speech, Turk and Joinet are less categorical. Rather than making assertions, they only raise questions. They ask: "Can the abuse of expression really justify deprivation of liberty?"[10]

Second, their reason for objection to imprisonment is bizarre. They fear that imprisonment will lead to torture, disappearance, or detention without trial. They ask: "in light of the abuses associated with imprisonment, should not this penalty be called seriously into question?"[11]

It is an exaggeration to say that detention without trial, torture, and disappearances are inherent in imprisonment. In many countries, there is no real risk that imprisonment will lead to any of these abuses. Even in those countries where the abuses exist, the proper objection is opposition to the abuses themselves, not imprisonment.

Clearly torture is a disproportionate penalty for hate speech. Equally clearly, it is a disproportionate penalty for any crime. Nonetheless, the general point that Turk and Joinet make is a valid one, that the penalty for hate speech may be disproportionate to the offence and it should not be.

Government opposition to hate speech is a problem of both too little and too much. Hate speech directed against minorities or those not part of a country's ruling elite often goes unchecked. In some countries, it is all too common for criticism of the government and its supporters to lead to imprisonment for propagating hatred.

For instance, Abd al-Rahman bin 'Amir al-Na'imi was arrested in June 1998 by the Government of Qatar and held without charge. Amnesty International believed that the sole reason for his detention was his involvement in a petition opposing the government's plan to give women the right to vote and to stand for elections. Amnesty International understood that the petition did not advocate violence or hatred. In a letter to the Ministry of Foreign Affairs of Qatar, the human rights organization stated that, if its understanding were correct, this person was a prisoner of conscience and should be released.

Activists should be prepared to call for the release of a person who is imprisoned for hate speech where hate speech is being used as a pretext for imprisonment on other grounds. Where a hate speech law is applied unequally, unfairly, or perversely, imprisonment should be opposed. Hate laws are, on occasion, used with speed and harshness to punish the intemperate criticism of those in power. Yet those same laws are ignored when hate speech comes from the established.

For non-governmental organizations to call for the prohibition of hate speech places new and different demands on their skills and resources. Amnesty International, for instance, in a 1995 publication on Burundi, called for the government of Burundi to "to take action against those inciting human rights violations by prohibiting the broadcast of inflammatory messages."[12] So, it can be done and it has been done. All the same, this sort of effort is new and unsystematic.

Vigilance means not just looking at the alleged violations of hate speech laws in isolation, but also looking at the context in which they occur. Is the punishment an attempt to punish propagation of hatred or is the law being used to punish criticism of the powerful? In some cases, answering that question may be difficult. In those case, where the answer is easy, activists should intervene.

The international community has to develop the will and the capacity to promote respect for the obligation to prohibit hate propaganda. At the inter-governmental level, this means developing new mechanisms or using existing mechanisms to promote respect for this duty. At the governmental level, it means developing effective laws so that governments can be credible in promoting respect for this duty. At the non-governmental level, it means developing language skills, and understanding, and then monitoring, and reporting.

The criterion of "clear and present danger of violence" that Turk and Joinet invoke to justify imprisonment for hate speech is used in the United States to determine the constitutionality of hate speech laws. Experience with that test shows it to be a major impediment to effective hate speech laws. It is a criterion to be avoided.

There is a debate within the U.S. about how its Bill of Rights should be interpreted to give it contemporary relevance. There are strict constructionists who argue that the original intent of the framers should be respected. There are modernists who argue that the Bill of Rights should be interpreted to apply to twentieth-century reality. Even the most extreme modernists, however, still do not argue that the duty to ban hate speech should be equal to the right to free expression.

The American free speech culture does allow for exceptions, including the exception of incitement to violence, and hate speech, after all, is the most extreme incitement to violence known to humanity. The trouble is that the American test for incitement to violence is overly strict, the test of "clear and present danger." While hate speech is an incitement to violence, the danger it represents, when it is clear, is not present, and when it is present, is not clear.

The clear incitements to violence embedded in hate speech are incitements to genocide, ethnic cleansing. Yet, these incitements take a long time to bear their poisoned fruits. There was some sixty years between the spread of antisemitic eliminationist discourse in Germany and the Holocaust. The time when hate speech should have been banned in Germany, for the ban to be effective, was in the 1880s. By the time of the Weimar Republic, eliminationist antisemitism had already become widespread; it was already too late. Yet, in the 1880s in Germany, the danger that hate speech directed against Jews represented, while at least in retrospect we can say it was clear, was hardly present or immediate.

What was true in Germany is generally true. Hate speech works by permeation, by acculturation, by slow persuasion. It is most effective with a generation that has grown up knowing nothing else. By the time the genocidal killing machines have been mobilized, banning hate speech is pointless, because it has become internalized by the killers, the ethnic cleansers. The only time when banning will be effective is the time when it is the property of a lunatic fringe, when it is not taken seriously by the public at large. Yet, for Americans, banning at that time is far too soon, far too great an intrusion on freedom of speech.

To be sure, hate-motivated violence is not restricted to genocide. Racially motivated crimes happen all the time, in every country. They range from the most serious crimes of murder, rape, and violent assaults to crimes that may seem superficially trivial: painting graffiti, toppling tombstones, breaking windows. What many of these crimes have in common, despite their immediacy, is their opacity. It is often not immediately clear that a murder or a beating is a hate-motivated crime. States with weak protective systems do not keep statistics of hate-motivated crimes and have a tendency to minimize all crimes they cannot prevent or solve. Hate crimes are often dismissed as mere hooliganism, crimes of passion, the work of the mafia, or teenage pranks.

Non-governmental organizations, which have a stellar record for compiling and publicizing human rights abuses, are ill-placed to expose hate-motivated crimes. It becomes difficult to demonstrate the motivation of any crime when the crime is unsolved. It is especially difficult for international non-governmental organizations, which operate outside the borders of the country where the hate crimes are perpetrated.

Yet, it defies common sense to pretend that crimes are not hate-motivated in countries where the crime rate is high, where the state offers little protection, and where hate propaganda is spread without hindrance. It should surprise no one that hate speech, which is an incitement to violence, leads to violence.

One has only to look at refugee movements to see the connection between hate crimes and violence. Refugees expose human rights violations with their feet. When a minority flees a country that is flooded with hate speech against that minority, it is not just the hateful remarks that cause flight, but the hateful deeds directed against the minority.

However, for the U.S., the connection between hate speech and violence short of genocide, while it may be immediate, is not clear. The result is that no hate speech is banned.

American free speech absolutists use the metaphor of a slippery slope. They argue that the distinction between impermissible hate speech and permissible speech is impossible to make. Once a government bans hate speech, it steps onto a slippery slope and it will slide from the banning of one form of speech to another to the point where legitimate public discourse will be banned and democracy threatened.

This argument assumes that the slope is tilted only one way. However, every hill has slopes on either side. The slope of free speech limitations, leading to a pit of speech control and the police state is not the only slope. The other is the slope of untrammelled hate speech leading to the pit of unbridled hatred and genocide. It is incumbent on us to put grit to stop sliding on both slopes.

American free speech absolutism feeds into the American culture of violence. The American acceptance of incitement to violence, including hate speech, absence of weapons control, and the death penalty form an integrated whole.

An example of this integration was the case of Timothy McVeigh. McVeigh was convicted for the bombing in April 1995 of a federal building in Oklahoma City that left almost two hundred people dead. McVeigh was to all appearances motivated by *The Turner Diaries,* a novel by William Pierce. McVeigh kept the book with him at all times and sold it at gun shows.[13] *The Turner Diaries* is banned in Canada as hate propaganda. The explosives McVeigh used were legally in his possession.

The response to McVeigh's conviction amongst many Americans was not that *The Turner Diaries* should be banned, but that McVeigh should be executed. The death penalty was sought by prosecutors, and obtained.

Similarly, Buford Furrow opened fire on a Jewish Community Centre in North Valley California in August 1999 wounding several children. He is also charged with killing a Filipino postal employee one hour later. Furrow was an active member of a white supremacist group, the Aryan Nations. He had been a guard at their northern Idaho compound. When Buford turned himself in to the FBI, he reportedly said that he wanted his action to serve as "a wake-up call to America to kill Jews."

A munitions-laden van apparently abandoned by Furrow after the shooting contained a book written by Richard Kelly Hoskins, *War Cycles–Peace Cycles.* According to Rabbi Marvin Heir of the Wiesenthal Centre of Los Angeles, "Hoskins believes that Jews are a satanic threat to civilization and that people of colour are sub-human."[14]

Again, here the American response was not to seek the banning of the writings of Richard Hoskins. The prosecutor, instead, indicated that he would seek the death penalty against Buford Furrow.

In the movie *Sudden Impact,* faced with a thief about to draw a gun on him, Dirty Harry says "Go ahead, make my day." Americans allow incitement to violence to flourish, weaponry to proliferate, and taunt would-be perpetrators with the death penalty. Go ahead, Americans say to would-be criminals, succumb to the incitement to violence around you, use the weapons we provide, make our day.

However, the American emphasis on freedom of expression amongst all human rights is far from global. In many countries, there is no significant free speech debate of the sort revolving around the First Amendment in the U.S. The Canadian debate about the banning of hate speech is influenced, like so many other debates, by Canada's proximity to the United States. This is not generally true in continental Europe. Anti-hate laws are generally accepted as part and parcel of a normal democratic society.

For laws to work, the people who run the legal system must want them to work. Hate speech laws will never be effective unless police, prosecutors, and judges are sensitive to the dangers of hate speech. I have already given the sorry histories of the *Keegstra* case in the Alberta Court of Appeal, the *Zundel* case at the Supreme Court of Canada, and the *Ross* case at the New Brunswick Court of Appeal.

There is, as well, the case of *French,*[15] which highlights the need for a sensitized judiciary. The *French* case was a contempt of court prosecution. The Canadian Human Rights Commission had obtained an order that Wolfgang Droege and the Heritage Front cease communicating by telephone matters of the type attached to the order, or any other substantially similar messages which were likely to expose persons to hatred or contempt. The commission sought a contempt conviction against Droege, the Heritage Front, and June Louise French because of a telephonic message that French and Droege taped using French's voice. The commission alleged the message was substantially similar to the matters prohibited by the original order and was likely to promote hatred or contempt of the Jewish community.

Mr. Justice Cullen of the Federal Court Trial Division held first that the subject message was not similar to the baseline message. He held second that he was not satisfied beyond a reasonable doubt (the relevant standard in contempt proceedings) that the evidence before him demonstrated that the message was likely to promote hatred or contempt of the Jewish community.

What is most cause for concern, even beyond these holdings, is his statement: "I am also troubled that neither the CHRC nor Dr. Ehrlich took the time to examine whether there was even a grain of truth in some of the allegations in the subject message." The allegations which Mr. Justice Cullen suggested might contain a grain of truth were these: "Four men living in Metro will be deported from Canada for allegedly hiding their Nazi past. We will advise these men of attorneys who are more than willing to stymie Jewish lobbyists from harassing elderly citizens." "We feel the Jewish community is prepared to pull elderly men out of nursing homes and off life-support systems; not to seek justice but rather vengeance. Who are the real victims here, and how much of the tax payer's money is being fleeced to pursue the elderly?" "When will the government be finished seeking justice for the Jewish community?" "Never forget never forgive . . . Christ['s] answer to this mentality [of] rights [is], if you do not forgive neither will your Father who is in Heaven forgive you a transgression."

It is apparent from a reading of the transcript of the messages that they contained traditional antisemitic slurs, imbued with the stereotype that Jews are vengeful and Christians are merciful. For Mr. Justice Cullen to suggest that there may be a grain of truth in the allegations of this message is to suggest that there may be a grain of truth in antisemitism. This is a classic form of blaming the victims for their victimization.

It is obvious that judgments like this severely impede headway against hate speech. Mr. Justice Cullen's judgment shows insensitivity to the nature of antisemitism and a failure to appreciate the serious damage hate speech can inflict.

Canada is a country very different in its ethos and culture from the Weimar Republic. The eliminationist antisemitic fervour that pervaded Weimar Germany and allowed the Nazis to come to power is marginal in Canada. However, as the Weimar Republic has shown, to be effective in the battle against hate speech, some remedies, the non-legal remedies, are not enough. We need all the remedies, including effective hate speech laws.

Notes

1. "Board responses to public consultations: Matters arising from the death of Stephen Lawrence" posted at <www.bod.org.uk>.
2. "Anti-Semitism World Report 1993," Institute of Jewish Affairs, p. 61.

3. "Anti-Semitic incidents breakdown by category 1990–1993," Community Service Organization of the Board of Deputies of British Jews.

4. "Racial Harassment: Country Action, Legal Remedies," Anti-Racist Alliance, June 1983, p. 47; "Racially-motivated crime: British crime survey analysis" by Natalie Angemurraya and Catarina Mirles, *Research and Planning Unit Paper 82*, Home Office, Government of the UK.

5. See "Group Defamation Report of a Working Party of the Law Parliamentary and General Purposes Committee," Chair Eldred Tabachnik, Board of Deputies of British Jews, February 1992.

6. Section 5.

7. See Gordon Allport, *The Nature of Prejudice* (Cambridge, MA: Addison-Wesley, 1954); Elisabeth Odio Benito, "Elimination of all forms of intolerance and discrimination based on religion or belief," United Nations Centre for Human Rights, Study series 2, 1989, p. 40, paragraph 163.

8. "Report to the U.N. Subcommission on Prevention of Discrimination and Protection of Minorities on The Right to Freedom of Opinion and Expression," E/CN.4/Sub.2/1992/9, 14 July 1992; E/CN.4/Sub.2/1992/9/Add 1; E/CN.4/Sub.2/1990/11, 18 July, 1990.

9. 1990 Report, paragraph 152; 1992 Report, paragraph 83.

10. 1992 Report, paragraph 144.

11. 1992 Report, paragraph 144.

12. "Burundi: Struggle for Survival," AI Index: AFR 16/07/95, June 1995.

13. John Kifner. "Oklahoma Bombing Evidence Cites 2 Books," *New York Times*, August 21, 1995.

14. Tom Tugend. "JCC rampage suspected wanted America to kill Jews," *Canadian Jewish News*, August 19, 1999, p. 31.

15. *C.H.R.C. v. French*, F.C.T.D., T–619–95, March 25, 1996.

Conclusion

MORE THAN FIFTY YEARS after the Universal Declaration of Human Rights, there still remains a right whose very existence is contested, not only outside, but inside the rights advocacy community. For virtually every other right, the battle to assert its value has been won, even though the battle for compliance continues. For one right, however, the battle is more basic, more fundamental. Even fifty years after the Universal Declaration of Human Rights, we still have to convince the human rights community of the importance of this right.

I am referring, of course, to the right to be free from incitement to hatred. This right, with variations in wording, is in the Universal Declaration of Human Rights,[1] the International Covenant on Civil and Political Rights,[2] and the United Nations Convention on the Elimination of All Forms of Discrimination.[3] Yet, it is hotly contested.

Ask a person whether freedom of religion should be protected, whether the right to vote should be respected, whether the right to liberty should be honoured. The question would seem strange. The answer would be, "of course." There might even be surprise at the very question. An argument that these fundamental human rights should not be respected would be met with universal derision, not just from civil libertarians or human rights advocates, but from the public at large. Respect for fundamental human rights has become part of the accepted wisdom of democratic societies.

This general rule, however, suffers the glaring exception of the right to be protected from incitement to hatred. Ask several people whether hate speech should be banned. There will be hesitancy, uncertainty. Some will say yes; some will say no. Civil libertarians will oppose the banning of hate speech. Newspaper editorials almost uniformly argue that this one human right not be protected. In isolation from the general acceptance of human rights, this human right, the right to be protected from incitement to hatred, stands almost alone, neglected and scorned.

The full articulation of human rights has developed over time. Historically and conceptually, humanity has moved outward from a few rights to
the full range of human rights. Freedom of expression was one of the first
human rights to be articulated, ensconced in the Declaration of Rights of
Man at the time of the French Revolution and enshrined in the American Bill
of Rights, both in the eighteenth century. The obligation to prohibit hate
speech is to be found in instruments dating from after World War II.

For some, earlier in time means higher in status. The main opposition to
the banning of hate speech comes from free speech absolutists, who argue
that the right to freedom of speech is at the base of other human rights.

William Thorsell, a former editor of the *Globe and Mail,* has said:

> I hold that freedom of expression is not equal in weight with other
> fundamental human rights. Freedom of expression is the superior or
> core human right among the many others that are listed in its pres-
> ence ... Freedom of expression is a seminal, germinal, essential,
> necessary, prior right in the pantheon of rights.[4]

Now, it may seem churlish to argue with anyone about their favourite
right. In some ways it is like arguing with people about their favourite food
or favourite colour. One can expect a newspaper editor to have a special
liking for freedom of expression; I assume teachers are inclined towards the
right to education; doctors probably favour the right to medical care.[5] As a
lawyer, I have a weakness for the right to counsel.[6]

If a mere indication of favouritism were all that was at stake, I would be
happy to pass over without comment anyone's choice of a favourite right.
However, those who advocate freedom of expression often go on to deny the
equal right in the Universal Declaration of Human Rights to be protected
from advocacy of hatred. William Thorsell, elaborating his support for freedom of expression, stated "I do not support all the legal limits on free speech
that exist in Canada—our criminal hate laws, for example."

It is my view that all human rights have to be read together as a coherent
whole. Each human right is part of a package. Each contributes to the overall
goal of enhancing the worth and dignity of the individual. Each needs to be
nurtured, protected, and developed. No one human right trumps other human rights.

If one human right is considered absolute, or given priority, then other
human rights, necessarily, take second place. One facet of human development is thwarted so that another facet can be given free rein. Or, what often

happens, the rights of some are given lavish attention; and the rights of others are trampled.

The right to be free to say what you want and the right to be free from hate speech targeted against you are two fundamental human rights that must be kept in balance. Neither is absolute; neither must be given priority over the other. Both are essential for the preservation of humanity.

The Universal Declaration of Human Rights does not rank rights, and quite properly so. In a sense, the Universal Declaration does not assert many rights, but just one right with many facets, the right to dignity, self-realization, and self-worth of the individual. The Universal Declaration, in its preamble, refers to the inherent dignity of all members of the human family. For the inherent dignity of the individual to be respected, all rights must be respected.

Objectively, if we have to rank rights, which I am loathe to do, the right that stands head and shoulders above all others is the right to life. If you are dead, the right to freedom of expression is meaningless. The greatest crimes of this century are not crimes of censorship. They are genocide: the Holocaust, the Armenian massacre, the Bosnian ethnic cleansing, the Cambodian killing fields, and other mass killings.

If we go beyond this most basic right, the right to life, and ask which human rights violations led to these mass killings, surely the answer must be violations of the right to be free from advocacy of hatred. In the words of Mr. Justice Dickson in the *Keegstra* case in the Supreme Court of Canada, "The experience of Germany represents an awful nadir in the history of racism, and demonstrates the extent to which flawed and brutal ideas can capture the acceptance of a significant number of people."

We do not have to look hard to find a direct link between incitement to hatred and the worst violations of human rights. While the ranking of human rights violations, like the ranking of human rights, is invidious, the internment and deportation of Japanese Canadians and the steadfast Canadian refusal to grant asylum to Jews fleeing the Holocaust are amongst the most shameful episodes of recent Canadian history. Neither of these events can be traced to censorship. Both are the direct consequences of the then untrammelled incitement to hatred against ethnic Japanese and Jews.

The Holocaust did not begin with censorship. It began with hate speech. Auschwitz was built with words. The killing fields of Cambodia were sowed with slogans. The genocide of Rwanda was spread by radio. Bosnia was ethnically cleansed by television. It is a strange logic that leads human rights advocates to deny the very right whose violation led first to the Holocaust and then to the Universal Declaration of Human Rights.

Human rights are an interconnected whole, and it is therefore easy to link one right to another. Free expression is important to other rights, but other rights are equally important to respect for freedom of expression. Take any thread out of the quilt of rights and the quilt unravels. To choose only one thread and proclaim that this is the thread that counts is arbitrary.

In support of his position that every other human right is dependent on freedom of expression, Thorsell said: "it should be obvious that the very life blood of democratic politics is the right to free expression." It can just as easily be said that tolerance is the life blood of democracy. Without tolerance, neither democracy nor freedom of expression can survive. Incitement to hate speech is an assault on that very tolerance which is essential to the respect for so many other rights.

If there is one human rights lesson that has to be learned, and only one, from the grave violations of human rights of this century, it is the need to ban hate speech. Yet, it is a lesson that has not been learned. It is the lack of balance between rights that has been the prime culprit in inhibiting the development of laws against hate speech and their enforcement. For many who understand and respect every other human right, this right is misunderstood and ignored.

This misunderstanding does not just prevent laws from being enacted. It prevents laws, once enacted, from being enforced. It saps voluntary compliance on the part of book sellers, libraries, newspaper editors, internet service providers, and others. This basic human right is commonly flouted, with the result, that locally we continue to court disaster, and that globally we continue to inflict disaster.

Combatting hate speech requires action. For people to join the struggle against hate speech, they must be able to identify it, understand its seriousness, and be willing to stand up to those who claim their right to freedom of expression is violated. An imbalance against the right to freedom from incitement to hatred and in favour of respect for the right to freedom of expression is an everyday, practical reality. There is widespread understanding of the importance of freedom of expression, but general reluctance to act against hate speech. This book, by attempting show the importance of the right to be free from incitement to hatred, the problems with free speech absolutism, the possibility of defining hate speech, the need to work within institutions to confront it, and the potential for fair and effective legislation, tries to redress the balance.

More than fifty years after the Universal Declaration of Human Rights, its promise has yet to be kept. For at least one of its provisions, the right to be free from incitement to discrimination, the promise has yet to be whole-heartedly made. Incitement to hatred is the most acute form of incitement to discrimination. If we are to fulfil the promise of the Universal Declaration of Human Rights, we must respect not just some human rights, but all human rights, including the right to be free from incitement to hate.

Notes

1. Articles 7 and 14.
2. Article 20(2).
3. Article 4(c).
4. Speech to a conference in Edmonton commemorating the fiftieth anniversary of the Universal Declaration of Human Rights.
5. Article 25.
6. Article 11(1).

About the author

DAVID MATAS is one of Canada's leading human rights and refugee lawyers. He is the author of numerous books, including *Justice Delayed: Nazi War Criminals in Canada, Closing the Door: The Failure of Refugee Protection* and *No More: The Battle Against Human Rights Violations.*

David Matas travels widely speaking on human rights issues. He is coordinator of the legal network of Amnesty International (Canada) and senior honorary counsel to B'nai Brith (Canada).